For Maximina and John

with my affection

Isabel Schevill
April 28 / 87

RECOLLECTIONS OF A GOLDEN AGE

An Autobiography
by
RUDOLPH SCHEVILL
1874-1946

Latin American Literary Review Press
Yvette E. Miller
Editor

*In memory of Rudolph Schevill,
my beloved husband*
ISABEL MAGAÑA SCHEVILL

The Latin American Literary Review Press publishes Latin American creative writing under the series title *Discoveries*, and critical works under the series title *Explorations*.

Library of Congress Cataloging in Publication Data:

Schevill, Rudolph, 1874-1946
    Recollections of a Golden Age

    «A bibliography of Rudolph Schevill's publications, Karl Schevill»: p.
    1. Schevill, Rudolph, 1874-1946. 2. College teachers—United States—Biography. 3. Spanish literature—Study and teaching (Higher)—United States.
    I. Title.
PQ6020.S35A37   1985   460'.92'4   *[B]*   84-29985
ISBN 0-935480-19-6

ACKNOWLEDGMENTS

For their generous help and interest, we are deeply indebted to Fernando Alegría, Sadie Durnham Patek Professor of Humanities, Stanford University, to Herbert Lindenberger, Avalon Foundation Professor, Stanford University, to Kathleen Glenn, Professor of Spanish Literature at Wake University and to Dr. Sharon Swinyard.

* * *

Cover photo of Rudolph Schevill from a painting in 1898 by Rudolph's older brother, William Schevill. Black and white photo by Martin Herceg. Cover by John Patterson.

Rudolph Schevill in 1898

CONTENTS

PROLOGUE
by
Isabel Magaña Schevill

«Man's greatness depends not on his accumulated knowledge, but rather on the quality of his wisdom — a wisdom based on love, respect and understanding of one's fellow man.»
I recently found this quote among some notes of mine, taken many years ago in a seminar on Spanish literature, taught by Professor Rudolph Schevill, chairman of the Department of Spanish and Portuguese at the University of California in Berkeley. The impressive list of his works are proof of his distinguished career at Yale, his «Alma Mater,» and later at the University of California in Berkeley where he taught from 1910 until his retirement in 1942.

However, it is in this partial autobiography, *Recollections of a Golden Age,* which covers the years of his youth during the latter part of the nineteenth century and his initial experiences in his travels through Germany, France, Italy and Spain, that the scholar reveals himself more truly as the man I came to know: a delightful human being, who loved life and lived it fully.

What was special about Rudolph Schevill, who was my teacher and later my husband and beloved companion until his death in 1946, was the combination of two qualities: He was deeply sensitive to suffering — especially the suffering brought about by political upheavals, such as that of the Spanish Civil War of 1936-39, in which many of his close friends and colleagues died. At the same time, he possessed a youthful zest for life and a delightful, subtle humor, both of which he retained to the end of his life, and which are clearly evident in this partial autobiography of his youthful years.

He was a great scholar, but he never imposed upon his students futile tasks. He used to say that only those «poor devils» like himself, who had to do research, were condemned to look for insignificant details. For our youthful, eager minds, he chose only great works. His graduate courses on the Golden Age in Spain, and especially his courses on Cervantes' *Don Quixote,* were examples not only of his superb scholarship, but also of his humanity, his understanding of human weaknesses, his tolerance, his idealism, his wisdom.

Rudolph Schevill was en eminent scholar. I believe, however, that he was an even greater man. At ease with any intellectual, he was equally at home with the gardner, the carpenter, a student or a child. Children loved him because he was able to reach out to them and become a part of their young, unsophisticated world. I have never forgotten an episode in our early years of marriage that best describes this very special quality in him.

One Saturday afternoon, Rudolph was at his desk writing the «Presidential address» he was to deliver at the Modern Language Association of America meeting in New York. It was an important address and he was deep in concentration. Someone rang the door bell. I rushed to see who it was so that he wouldn't be disturbed. Standing there was little four-year old Tommy, the only child in our neighborhood. Tommy looked up at me and asked pleadingly: «Can Rudy come out and play with me?» My husband heard him. I saw him smile, obviously pleased and flattered by the child's request. Without saying a word, he pushed aside his writing, took the little boy by the hand and went outside to play with him for an hour or so. It was a simple, logical choice for Rudolph Schevill. The child's loneliness took precedence over his own work.

That touching episode, which I did not fully appreciate until much later, became for me a symbol of the man, of his life, his compassion, his philosophy, his spiritual greatness.

This partial autobiography ends with his return to Yale as Assistant Professor of Spanish and covers only the formative years of his brilliant academic career. But in it he recreates for us with insight and humor a vivid picture of the way of life in the latter part of the nineteenth century, both here and abroad.

* * *

RECOLLECTIONS OF A GOLDEN AGE

An Autobiography
by
Rudolph Schevill
1874-1946

CHAPTERS

* * *

Rudolph Schevill in 1938

A PREFATORY NOTE

In one of his prefaces, Cervantes laments the fact that he possessed no engraving of his face with which to adorn his book, before permitting it to sally forth into the market-place of the world. So he describes his own looks minutely in a pen portrait. He is singularly frank. All the defects attributable to that old enemy Time are there, regretfully placed side by side with a list of his departed attractions. A high forehead and laughing eyes are offset by a silver beard formerly golden; a few surviving teeth, ill-conditioned and most disadvantageously spaced, go fitly with a body formerly nimble but now bent. Once a brave soldier and heroic captive he is now only an author, a singularly depressing fall from ancient glory. And the chief lesson which he had learned from this melancholy course was enough patience to suffer adversity. I shall not seek to imitate a preface which merely reveals the fate of everyone of us — that we begin as a Beau Brummel, and rapidly decline into a Polonius with a plentiful lack of wit together with most weak hams. Cervantes had no dentist skilled in spanning chasms by a kind of Golden Gate Bridge, so he has reported only what was in his more stoic times a commonplace irremediable defection. In this matter silence is the wiser course for us all.

The life of any man begins much like a brook running through a simple traceable course. Each may get to be different from the others in its more capricious windings and in the changing prospects as it swells into a river and passes out into the sea. I began with a canoe small enough to paddle along the pleasant margins of my earliest years. Memories begin with open meadows in the suburbs of Cincinnati, Ohio, autumn woods and half-forgotten playmates, with those first falls and bruises inevitably repeated through later years. Then comes a securer boat worthy of the broadening stream, and there appear more significant aspects of the passing shores. The schoolhouse beckons; the customary bell rings out with its imposed cessation from play.

As the river widens, the art of navigation has to be learned. You must become a friend of wind and wave and learn to choose the most advantageous landing-places. Then follow years of exploration, the going ashore in strange realms, and meeting a variety of your fellows. This constitutes a kind of treasure-hunt in a world of adventure and blind chance; the result is the accumulation of much experience, hurtful or beneficial, and the discovery of much good and evil in the hearts of men. Storms and forced landings steel the soul; some may prove to be inhospitable shores where gates must be forced, «with dreadful faces thronged and fiery arms.» Having thereupon made a choice of occupation or profession, you either patch a shoe or build an empire, write a promissory note or an immortal work. You follow or you lead: you have a kind of Hobson's choice of being the anvil unless you roll up your sleeves and decide to wield the hammer.

To make the puzzle of life more perplexing Einstein, with his lucid theory of relativity, obscurely hints that the whole setup of this confused and dirty planet may be a futile and final game, that «once is enough.» It does not seem so to me. These pages may afford a hint why this earth can be a worthwhile place; not because of any incurable optimism on my part, but because I do not believe that wanton and irresponsible gods are making game of us helpless creatures. We happen to be irrational beings who still have to learn how to win and deserve life, and, in the interim, can thank whatever gods may be for our unconquerable soul. We all reflect, naturally, our own surroundings and our individual experiences, which add up to a purely personal equation. Therefore, I venture to suggest a more hopeful interpretation of all these apparent futilities, and proclaim as thoroughly acceptable the profound notion of Doctor Pangloss, that this is the best of all possible worlds.

With this brave conclusion, we can proceed and undertake a rambling voyage of the long ago.

* * *

The Schevill home in Cincinnati

SCHOOL LANE

My earliest years fell on amusing and clever times, when the great industrial age was likewise young. The Lambs of Capitalism were disporting themselves in relatively confined precincts, with a certain heed of the neighbor's landmark. If they presently acquired a voracious appetite for the pasturage of adjoining fields, it certainly was without my acquiescence or power to interfere. But my elders watched with concern their emboldened course in succeeding prosperous years, maliciously approving of the tax-collector when he applied his shears to the excessive wool on their backs. The successful intervention of that public functionary has always spelled the end of a happy stage in our industrial progress.

The heroic figures of my trusting youth were impressive personalities, among whom the names of Commodore Vanderbilt, Collis P. Huntington, Leland Stanford, J.J. Hill and similar giants may be vaguely recalled in some quarters. In reality they deserve to be classed with other conquistadores, such as Magellan and Cortés; they represented merely a later race of explorer and builder. But times are capricious and not sufficiently reverential, statures diminish and our vocabularies take on other meanings. Today a book entitled, «Pirates of Old» does not confine itself to the seven seas, but indiscriminately includes in its roster Knights of Industry and Robber-barons of the Mart.

Our own home was never on speaking terms with capitalism. The house, a big, three-story structure, was as foursquare and as prosaic to look on as a box of apples. Wide halls ran through the center from front to rear, ideally designed for our games which left indelible marks on floors and walls. There were rooms in the cellar and attic which I never succeeded in exploring to my entire satisfaction; those of the top story were generally kept locked, and small windows served rather more to keep out, than to admit, the light of day. Some of the closets and chests likewise retained inviolate their many secrets. A flat tin-roof, which resounded like the muffled rattle of a drum in every rainstorm, could be reached through a trap door. This was a strictly forbidden playground, not so much because of the danger of our rolling off into space, a contingency which would have gratified some neighbors, but because we continually ripped our trousers on projecting bits of rusty tin. In spite of this prohibition we used the house-top frequently as a hiding place, to the retrospective alarm of mother, and the retroactive anger of father when she told him of the exploit.

My family, which dwelt in this house almost thirty years, has managed to retain my unflagging interest, and I apparently showed excellent judgment when I chose my parents. We competed victoriously with Wordsworth's «Little Cottage Girl,» whose keynote «We are seven» was surpassed by us, as we were eight. Of our number, as in Wordsworth's, two died in their infancy; the remaining six, of whom I was the youngest, survived in contradiction of every law of probability. In an age when germs and microbes were unsuspected members of every household we defeated their wiles, and outlived all the commonplace accidents of youth.

My oldest brother, William, was about to turn into the best baseball player in the entire country, when father, mixed-metaphorically speaking, took that bull by the horns and nipped an earlier Babe Ruth in the bud by sending him to Munich. There he exchanged the bat for a painter's brush. When questioned about his occupation, I was inclined to elucidate any mention of his newly chosen career by proudly adding, «not house painter, but pictures». My second brother, Albert, was taken into the business; in this he was a mainstay during father's many years of invalidism and growing deafness. My third brother, Ferdinand, was very early seized by some inherited urge to become a teacher and elected to expound the erratic course of history to his uninformed fellowmen.

My sisters, Elizabeth and Marie, filled the house with what seemed to me an excessive amount of harmony, the one being a pianist and the other a singer. In due time, they attracted husbands by what those who had never been annoyed by their nagging, chose to call their infinite charm and numberless gifts. A younger brother is apt to be less blind. Elizabeth married Richard Durley, an Englishman and engineer and professor at McGill University. Marie chose as husband the Austrian-born sculptor Karl Bitter. These achievements made the family international, and relieved me of forming any ambitious program of my own. I was content to remain a youth to fortune and to fame unknown.

Any satisfactory testimony of the devotion shown by everyone to our mother would find the dictionary an inadequate help. We have

Johanna Hartmann Schevill

clung to her memory with undiminished piety, and unceasing wonder at the evenness of her nature, her understanding, simplicity and courage. There could only be among all a unanimity of opinion about one whose voice was ever soft, gentle and low, whose beauty never suffered the touch of inconsiderate time. When we were all scattered over the world, mother proved an ideal clearing-house of family news; the brothers and sisters, as is usual in large families, communicated with each other only at irregular intervals, but never failed to write to mother who, in turn, relayed to everyone the varied budget which she received from us. Her letters were a mixture of diary and family history, and constituted a record of the part she played in keeping us all together.

We have often wished that father had kept a diary: his early career was a composite of many ventures and adventures worthy of a detailed account. Only our imperfect recollections of his narratives and of those of his brothers, Albert and Otto, who experienced very similar vicissitudes, have served to revive essential details. In his early teens father had fled from Koenigsberg, his birthplace; it was not long after the Revolution of '48 which stirred so many rebellious, liberty-seeking youths to rise against oppression and the deadening lack of opportunities of a worthwhile career at home. Father managed to get aboard a sailing vessel which occupied untold weeks in crossing the storm-racked Atlantic, and finally landed him on the southern coast of the United States. He learned English early and well, although he never had any schooling, systematic or otherwise. Given the means and the opening, he might have chosen some career of an erudite or, at least, bookish nature. His interests in scientific subjects were always too distracting to permit him to become a practical business-man, so that, throughout his checkered course, he suffered ups (of small lasting benefit to the family), and downs (which I remember most clearly). Before his twenties he had wandered about the country engaged first by a florist in selling seeds, and, in the process, becoming everlastingly interested in botany. Then he was employed by a druggist in whose service he spent his evenings reading books on chemistry, medicine and related subjects.

Before my own advent father had managed, in connection with some Frenchman, to set up a prosperous tobacco factory which gathered and pressed the weed into some novel square shapes. Having thus greatly contributed to a growing national vice, he and his partner put their ill-gotten gains into a promising silver-mine in Colorado; this venture, like the tobacco investment, went up in smoke, and father found himself left with a growing family and the opportunity of

Ferdinand August Schevill

beginning some other highly unprofitable business venture. He frequently told us of recent discoveries in astronomy and instilled in us a habit of looking for the stars on clear nights. He read Shakespeare and Goethe to us, although I was often a listener only under duress. On Sunday mornings he could also be an entertaining companion in early outings with his sons and their friends, leading through Burnet Woods or Walnut Hills or to our well stocked zoological garden. Cincinnati finally became his last venture and definite abode, I assume, because the city had already attracted a group of cultured and musical Germans, and, not least, because he there met mother, recently arrived from Heidelberg, a slender, dark-eyed girl in her eighteenth year. We often teased father by telling him that he very much resembled U.S. Grant; this comparison, however, deserves qualification, for father was, according to mother's infallible judgment, a much-liked, handsome man, who never wore that puckered expression with which the great general was currently depicted.

A garden in front of the house was separated from the neighbor's by a hedge; in the rear, there was a spacious brick-paved yard, in the far corner of which I had contrived an enclosure for chickens, limited by paternal decree and lack of space to six hens and a generally short-lived rooster. Every one that I managed to rear became a bone of contention between myself and over-sensitive neighbors; they conveyed their opinions about untimely crowings to father, who in turn conveyed these protests to me. As there was no practical method of veiling the culprit's voice, each, in his turn, went the predestined way of his kind, simmering in a huge pot the number of hours commensurate with his years. I protested and mourned each demise, for they were prize birds, and take them for all in all, I have not looked upon their like again.

The windowless walls of a neighbor's house closed in the back of the rear yard and formed an ideal surface against which to bat or throw a ball. The patient residents would endure the incessant thump until threatened by lunacy, and at last a shriek of protestation would issue from somewhere, occasioned by cracking or dislodged plaster within. If the shriek persuaded us to desist from our batting practice, the respite which we magnanimously granted was generally brief.

A need of economy restricted the «help» afforded by servants; the repairs of the aging house, necessitated by the wear and tear of our large and active household, had to be limited to inescapable essentials. These circumstances gave me an opportunity to leap into the breach. Owing to the early departure from home of my brothers, and to the uselessness of girls in practical matters, many routine tasks devolved upon me. During too many seasons of the year there was the grass of the garden to be cut and the hedge to be trimmed, undertakings which mother stimulated now and then by the gift of a twenty-five cent admission to the bleachers at the ballpark. I mended panes broken by misdirected homeruns and learned to do odd carpenter's jobs, such as replacing worn floor-boards, or rusty door-hinges, deeds that remained unhonored and unsung.

In winter an archaic furnace was my sorest problem, for stoke as I would on cold days, the air which rose through the registers was more like the early breath of spring than heat generated by combustion. There was a singular disproportion between the heap of ashes that I carried out and the low temperature that rose into all of those chilly living quarters from the arctic cellar. Our sitting room, the windows of which rattled in every wind, was made livable only by an additional grate-fire. A worthy companion of the furnace was an equally ancient bricked-in kitchen range. The kitchen and a huge bathroom directly overhead occupied a separate building connected, like an afterthought, with the main house by a covered passage. Every Saturday afternoon the cook wrapped up her head and protected her ample frame with a kind of mother-hubbard, a militant preparation for the battle of extracting from the range's stomach endless buckets of debris amid clouds that looked like a volcanic eruption. Her tour de force in the culinary art was demonstrated on Sunday mornings, when the family recorded its fullest attendance. Hotcakes, served with plebeian Golden Syrup, were on that day a family tradition. For this ritual the skilled minion had ready a tubful of batter and brought to the dining room, through the passageway, her finished product in batches which resembled the leaning Tower of Pisa. When her batter and her feet had given out simultaneously, she snapped curtly: «That's the last,» and closed the door with a bang.

Since our elders had the habit of pressing small boys into the service of running errands to make good their indolent mental processes, we had to fetch an indispensable head of lettuce, or a dozen eggs in spite of the greater importance of the games which might occupy us at the moment. The nearest grocery seemed miles distant, halfway down Sycamore Hill; but I generally chose Mike Miller's, although it was even further away. This old friend had been an intimate when he was still the policeman on our beat. He was a short, roundish, good-natured person, capable at times of uproarious laughter which attracted us, or of a fierce professional glare that restrained and filled us with respect. Having resigned from the force he opened a small combination of grocery and butcher shop; its location seemed to me a judicious choice for the store was opposite a fire-engine house. There, too, I was at home with pals of long standing. The fireman's life was ideal. You sat on the sidewalk most of the day in shirt-sleeves, tilted back in a chair, with nothing to contemplate but the occasional prospect of a picayune conflagration always extinguished before you got there. Now and then we derived plenty of dramatic entertainment from the automatic opening of the stalls at the sound of the gong, and from the impressive and never-failing response of the horses trained to run under their suspended harnesses. The smoking monster of those days was greatly superior to the lifeless mechanized engines of today. I pity the boys who have never seen the real thing.

My circle of friends had older brothers whose various doings we tried hard to share or imitate, but we guessed from the treatment which we received at their hands that they regarded us as something of a pest. Neither mild cuffs nor the pretense of serious chastisement so as to be rid of us had much effect. One of their activities was putting on theatrical shows, and it was a red-letter day for us when they met more or less secretly to discuss the costumes and scenery for a play. The performances were given in an empty hay-loft over a large stable. Converted into docile errand boys, we were rewarded, by parental permission, with the privilege of staying up to see the show. One memorable occasion was the quarrel of Brutus and Cassius in which brother Ferd recited the part of Cassius, and I had to help mother in the conversion of an old bed-sheet into a toga worn by that Roman. Fortunately it did not occur to the audience which, in spite of the hard, make-shift seats, crowded the stable from pit to dome, to wonder how a commanding general came to wear a bed-sheet on the battlefield. After the quarrel another actor recited Antony's funeral oration over the body of Caesar, which was covered by another sheet stained with the blood drawn from an ink-bottle. The mighty Caesar fought his own demise so far as to fidget under the strain of Mark's ranting and to sneeze when caught by a blast of the usual stable draft.

Such an evening could not pass without imitation; our histrionic urge at the age of ten led us beyond our depth into an original dramatic composition. The plot that we devised had in it a vindictive burglar who while hiding in a barrel by the kitchen door is foiled by a stalwart cook. The latter, ignorant of the villain's presence pours a bucket of ashes on his head and makes him an easy captive. Our cellar, which was accessible from the street, furnished the stage, but we showed inadequate skill in contriving the properties and turning blankets into curtains to conceal the stage. The resistance of the barrel in which the culprit conceals himself before the curtain is drawn was much over-rated. At a critical moment the hoops gave way, and the whole thing disintegrated before the eyes of the public. The protagonist inside was taken wholly unaware; realizing that he was about to go down in hideous ruin, he clutched at the curtain and the whole contraption, back-drop and blankets, crashed to the floor with the barrel-staves. The kindly audience came to our rescue, and with a nail or two and some verbal encouragement the play was brought safely into port.

On propitious twilight evenings we indulged in the pastime of beaver-knocking; we tied our strings across the sidewalk at the most frequented spot and succeeded in removing the hat of many an unsuspecting passerby. Now and then, only our agility and a more detailed acquaintance with the neighborhood saved us from rough handling. Another scheme springing from the mind of idle devils was the trick of derailing the old horse-car at the curve. This could only be achieved in the gloaming, which permitted us unobserved to place a stone on the track at the effective spot. When the car came down the grade at a fair clip imposed by gravity, pushing the ancient and weary steed on ahead, the light box of the tram inevitably continued straight into the gutter beyond. We stayed long enough to hear the driver's oath, and then disappeared into a nearby wood. We were pursued only once by an irate Swede who never could remember the fatalities at the corner from one run to the next.

Beyond the garden was a vast world with paths wandering off into meadows or lanes fringed with scrawny woods. There we looked for buckeyes or the edible flat pods of the locust; we cut twigs for slingshots or hollowed them out into pistols; these, equipped with rubber bands, propelled paper wads at tempting bald heads. At the far end of Southern Avenue, known to us only as School Lane, which began opposite our house, there was a stone quarry. This yielded crushed rock to building contractors, and a by-product in the guise of a small petrified creature called trilobite, to naturalists. By exploiting the personal history of the trilobite of the Cincinnati hills a noted paleontologist, Professor Schuchart, gained much fame, but I could never see why. We often picked up specimens of this insignificant creature, which resembles both a spider and beetle, without suspecting its distinguished past.

Above the quarry hung what was left of the estate of Alexander H. McGuffy, that foremost name in the roster of school-readers.

27

Alexander was the brother of William McGuffy, the compiler of the noted texts. Tall, lean, with a square grey beard and a twinkle in his eye he had the appearance of a Biblical patriarch. He delighted in youthful friends, and we sought him frequently in his library, or we fell in with him as he passed through our noisy crowd on the lane in his long dark coat, carrying always what he himself called his «green lawyer's bag,» filled with books. He read to us amusing stories and regaled us with anecdotes in which all the adjectives were misplaced and the sense of the verbs was twisted, greatly enjoying our hilarity.

His brother, William, deserves a word as the begetter of the millions of school-books on which the education of American youth reposed for several generations. I myself am the product of the five or six grades of McGuffy Readers, but with a rather negative result, for these books are both noble and moral. On every other page of text, editor McGuffy lifted a warning finger against the unethical vagaries of youth. Already in his First Reader he indicated the dominant role of his teachings. «Be good, my boy», it said, «and let who will be clever. Does any one love a bad boy? Can his teacher love him? Certainly not. He loves to be idle, and talks and laughs in school. See how he hides his face with his hands, for it is red with shame. God loves those who are good». It is little wonder that these elevating principles have made us the superior people that we are. A recent Educational Review holds it a flagrant oversight that only two statues have been raised to William McGuffy, when there ought to be one in every town, «to keep alive the great truths taught in his Readers». These truths, unless I have misjudged my own generation, have proved rather that the resistance of youth to moral pabulum, passed out with a ladle, cannot be overestimated.

We learned endless pages of the McGuffy texts by heart. There was literature for you, good, bad and indifferent. The editor used a minimum of selective judgment, casting his hook into the stream of letters and keeping every fish he caught. Not even the veriest minnow was ever thrown back. Poetry of established repute could be found side by side with doggerel and mawkish Sunday-school effusions. The latter were generally anonymous, and the assumption was fair that the author was sitting in the editor's chair. Selections of this kind may still be read in copies which have survived by some caprice of time, to the discomfiture of those who cannot believe that such verse was ever taught to their fathers. Two are entitled «My Mother» and «My Mother's Hands». One voices the contrition of a bad boy whose unmentionable misdeeds have made his mother gray before her time. He calls her, «an autumn leaf decayed» and «he perhaps has made it fade.» It was probably the same boy who, in the second piece, apostrophized his mother's hands in the words:

«Such beautiful, beautiful hands,
They're neither white nor small.»

This disparaging start is rectified by the qualification that those aged wrinkled hands surpass «any sculptor's dream», that «beyond this shadow-land

Where all is bright and fair,
I know full well those dear old hands,
Will palms of victory bear».

This poem was more than even our spinster teacher could stomach, and we were crisply ordered to «omit this selection». But the extreme was reached in a tidbit which prompted us to blow a spitball at the one obliged to recite it before the class. It ran:

«I live for those who love me,
For those who know me true. . .
For the future in the distance,
And the good that I can do.»

The name of this inspired poet was not emblazoned on the page.

In the various editions of McGuffy Readers which succeeded each other, some of the saccharine selections were excised or modified, but no outward changes in civilization, or fancied progress of humanity could undermine the persistence of other masterpieces like «the Crazy Engineer», who drives a kidnapped train with its shrieking passengers at the ghastly speed of presumably thirty miles an hour; or «Meddlesome Matty», a pale ancestor of Hilaire Belloc's «Lying Mathilda», one of the delightful personalities of his Cautionary Rhymes. A noble piece called «Respect for the Sabbath Rewarded» was more likely to prompt every lad to detour on his way to Sunday-school and observe the Sabbath in the open spaces. To be fair, in these Readers the youth of our land could also become acquainted with choice bits taken from American and English poets. As the years went on, teachers with a more blunted moral sense or a weaker stomach suggested numerous eliminations, and discreet replacements increased the worthwhile selections.

It is entertaining to compare some types of Reader laid before the young in the schools of Victorian England. The contents of a series called The Manchester Readers were based on the well known pedagogic principle that all education rests on the three R's. The reading and writing consisted of selections in which ethics and patriotism had a more discreet share than on our side of the water. English history played a substantial part, and poetry included some humorous selections. If any laughing matter ever got into our Readers it was probably by an oversight. The dictum attributed to Napoleon that the English are a race of shopkeepers could have found some justification in one feature of their school-books. Immediately after a good historical selection the young Englishman suddenly found himself confronted with an exercise in arithmetic; this detail combined scholastic endeavor with practical finance, useful in later years. «Multiply», it said, «L3, 5s., 7 1/2d., by L6, 8 1/2s., 4d.» As a result of the complicated relations between pounds, shilling, and pence, the youth of Great Britain had to get an early start in this business of mastering all monetary intricacies. Subsequent schooling taught them likewise to master foreign monies, and thus acquire a goodly share of them for dear old England. Our own boys absorbed a noble morality in the classroom, but taught themselves unrelated principles of money-getting on the outside.

In our district school which dispensed this impressive education, everyone, from the principal down, firmly held as an article of faith that everything must be learned by heart. Even the janitor, who was probably appointed because of his flair for belles lettres, could have prompted us in our endless recitations of poetry and prose. It was thus no effort for us, long years afterwards, to recite Sheridan's Ride «with Winchester twenty miles away», or William Lytle's lines on Mark Anthony's death, «as the dark Plutonian shadows gather on the evening blast». We learned that the eagle is not only a bird given to rapine, but also the patriotic symbol of our Freedom which, «shrieked when Kosciuszko fell».

Hand in hand with this incessant memorizing of first-class third-class verse, we had to devote many hours to learning the principles of rhetorical stress. Where to place the chief accent? When must the voice dwindle to a whisper? This method was made clear by a scheme of large and small letters. Having been sent to the blackboard, we were supposed to give the correct reading of typical sentences in the following manner:

Lord Angus, thou hast LIED...

When Greece, her KNEES in SUPPLIANCE bent,
Should TREMBLE at his power.

In the sixth grade several boys would be sent to the board at the same time to indicate the proper emphasis of such idiotic lines as the following, on the immortal origin of which we were never enlightened: «This skull had a tongue in it, and could sing once». Some stressed «skull», others «tongue», or even magnified «once», on the assumption that the unknown singer sang only once and did not survive to perform a second time.

The McGuffy Reader gave the necessary directions as regards modulation, quality of the voice and the like, with fitting examples for young orators. «Come back, come back, the father cried», was accompanied by the marginal suggestion «to be read with passion». For «I have lived long enough», a plaintive note was indicated. «A very great portion of this globe is covered with water», required a tone of awe and calm; but the voice must rise to fierce anger in:

«Such hand as Marmion's had not spared
To cleave the Douglas head.»

Finally, the pupil was cautioned to read in a solemn tone; «Franklin is dead. The genius who freed America and poured a copious stream of knowledge throughout Europe is returned unto the bosom of the Divinity.» Franklin had been sleeping in that bosom many a decade and our indifference to his demise was not calculated to produce the proper lugubrious note. The sense of humor of some teachers in those days was so latent, that we were supposed to laugh only at a source of innocent merriment, such as the gauche efforts of a boy oratorically ambitious. Any mock-heroics intended to ridicule the solemn injunctions of book and teacher met with the severest reprimand.

Higher culture and better taste penetrated the frontiers of the McGuffy days slowly. Not only remote villages accepted these and similar textbooks, on the eastern seaboard they held equal sway. Their success may be attributed to the modest demands made on the culture of the teacher, not yet under the domination of slogans and schemes drawn up by Schools of Education. The naïveté and obvious patriotism of the material used met those demands which themselves struck a very genuine American note and voiced the moral sentiments characteristic of every American home.

My teachers were good representatives and purveyors in the

elements of American education distributed through the grade or grammar schools. They fitted into our old schoolhouse as does a picture into a frame. The building itself was peculiar in none of its aspects and could have been exchanged with any other Cincinnati school without a special effort of the imagination. Speaking of imagination, the less said the better, for no mental function was ever employed less in the construction of these edifices. They were by prescription ugly, devoid of all modern appointments, and looked like a brick pile set in the middle of a brick-paved yard. Barked knees, skinned arms and faces were the daily record of that unspeakable playground. A high grill separated the yard allotted to the boys from that of the girls; the untidiness of the former always made clear which was which. The nature of the out-houses with their unhygienic conditions arouses retrospective shudders and makes it evident that only by a gracious Providence were we spared the ravages of the Black Death or some other historic pestilence. Fate took better care of us than the school board. The heating system consisted of large, round, soft-coal stoves set in a corner of every classroom. These we took turns to stoke, intentionally raising the temperature until the furnace glowed with a white heat. The teacher who had left us to our own devices would not become aware of a temperature of ninety degrees until beads of perspiration stood out on her forehead, when she would order all the windows to be thrown up, always a welcome diversion.

The principal of the school was the bête-noir, literally and figuratively, of all the boys. He was tall, ungainly, ungracious, and swarthy, with a black, penetrating, and to us malevolent eye. His chief indoor exercise was the daily thrashing of the recalcitrants. He and his victim went through a routine performance in the upper hall, the floor of which was of iron, so that blows and shouts resounded through the hollow wells of the stairway with an impressiveness that might have filled Spanish Inquisitors with envy. When the fifteen minutes of recess were over, we formed in line at the main entrance, on which occasion the principal would unfailingly lean out from an upper window, bang the clapper of an immense hand-bell, and yell for attention. Then we were regaled with words of wisdom or reprimand. The former were few and the latter left us unscathed as they monotonously dealt with the eternal problems of untidiness and excessive noise.

Among the teachers at the district school were two spinster sisters, alike as peas in a pod; they were pale and fleshless, notably the older, (one would never have called either the younger): at least the one to whom I am referring was a wraith in appearance and must have lived on a daily minumum of nourishment. Both sisters were living ex-

32

amples of the ethical code of the McGuffy Reader. The parlous state of our young souls made their lives, dedicated to duty and discipline, a constant torment. Slang expressions and rowdyish words invited the thunderbolt of chastisement, and the culprit had to stay after school to write the offense on the blackboard, a hundred or more times, thus making him remember forever his vile deed or word. On the following morning the assembled class would be greatly edified. They could behold scrawled over the blackboard, «I shall never say damn again». This same teacher insisted meticulously on the difference between shall and will, cant and can't (which she pronounced caunt). The practical results of those kindly teachings have been manifest in the obvious fact that our profanity has acquired color and resourcefulness with the years, giving the lie to that promise written on the blackboard; and the grammatical principles so persistently dinned into our ears have had about the same following as the belief that the earth is flat.

Among other memories of my early teens the bleachers at the professional ball-games have a prominent place. My own active participation and repute in the national game were encompassed in a brief experience. Brother William's local fame as a ball-player was believed to indicate that there might be at least some latent talent in me likewise. I was consequently included in an important game between lower grades. I still think of that fatal June day when no one else could be found bold enough to play catcher and risk his life behind the bat. Of course we possessed no mask and it was written in the stars that the first foul tip should catch me on the nose, destroying once and for all every initiative to continue the game. Thus closed my baseball career before it had begun. Brother Will made up for it by helping me to enjoy the sport vicariously. On an occasional afternoon, he came for me to the school and through some excuse trumped up at the moment, which to any but a weak-kneed teacher would never have held water, extricated me from my educational toils. Off we then went through Bethlehem, a neighboring slum inhabited by the «micks» who were our traditional enemies and frequently sent us home with bloody noses or welts on our heads the size of a small egg. Then on through the whole of lower Cincinnati across numerous railroad tracks to the ball-park, where we monotonously saw the local «Red Stockings» licked. How much easier an occasional victory made the long trudge home!

A revered guardian spirit of our slighted and scorned generation was a budding lawyer of the town. He was a close neighbor called William Howard Taft, already familiarly known in those days as Big

Bill for his revealing smile, his large heart and the unfailing support on which the downtrodden among us could depend. We were always sadly in need of a shield against those old enough to be our seniors but not decent enough to be our betters and treat us with some trifling consideration. Such a shield was adequately supplied by the great personality and generous bulk of friendly Big Bill. He amply compensated us for the rough ways and the setbacks of life by the treat of taking us to a fair or a ball game, to which we set forth like small boats sailing under convoy of an imposing man-of-war. It would not have been an easy matter to describe our feelings, already sufficiently exalted, if we had realized that we were tagging after a future President of the United States.

My earliest political recollection is the assassination of James A. Garfield (1881), made indelible because it filled with profound sorrow a staunch Republican household. The news had been cried in the streets, and I had brought it home to a shocked family. Both President Garfield and his Secretary of State, James G. Blaine, had been exalted by father as nothing less than super-men. On one occasion I brought home a comic magazine called *Puck*, a sheet with blustering Democratic party coloring, and displayed to an angered parent some slanderous caricatures of those two idols of his. In those days political attacks in both words and pictorial illustration could be vulgar as well as immoderate, and generally implied the incredible unfitness of the objects of their contempt for the office which they held or sought. It was one of the few occasions on which I recall having stirred father's anger, for our memories of him are all gentle ones, and I never again ventured to pick up or bring into the house a copy of that outlawed magazine.

Many routine episodes of those days have left pleasant memories. There was the Saturday night bath, a ritual that had to be carried through in a room, the size of a hall, directly over the kitchen, and likewise separated from the rest of the house. Its conversion into a place of ablutions was one of those things that could never be explained; because of its unusual size it was like a piece of out-of-doors, especially when wintry blasts whistled through the thin walls. These gusts had to be met head-on in hasty sprints across an ice-coated porch open to the sky. The bathroom was warmed by a hot-air wood-stove that could be raised to a brilliant red glow by a few sticks generally gathered from the neighboring wood. If I had a friend spending Saturday night with me, we bathed simultaneously, since hot water, like opportunity knocking at the door, put in a brief appearance once and for all, and like intermittent geysers had a weekly cycle, which possibly accounted for the Saturday night bath the world over. During our rioting or wrestling we not only scorched our under-wear in our collisions with the glowing stove, but also retained an occasional blister on the sitting parts of our anatomy which had come too near the heated monster.

The water of the Ohio river which issued from the faucets retained in those days its historic dull brown color. Its turbid condition did not interfere with our needed purification, or there would have been no bath even on Saturdays. Henry Ford would have included our bathtub among his collection of domestic museum pieces. It was a glorified laundry tub made of wood and leaked perennially through the floor into the kitchen below, where the cook had to place a pan to catch the only showerbath in the house. To stop the seepage the tub had to be painted at intervals, but the paint which I myself applied many times came off in little hard flakes, so that you had to sit perfectly still during your bath, because sliding in that tub was equivalent to skinning yourself alive. The lovely ochre of the water and the icy temperature of the air would have been for the soft youth of today an obvious invitation to typhoid and pneumonia; but we all survived, healthy and fairly clean, and if others of that happy generation were taken away, it was by an act of God or other remote control.

Fortunately we could get our drinking water from a deep and cold well of excellent quality, although a bit over-fortified with a taste of iron. It was deep enough to keep mother in an apprehensive state over the risk we ran in playing near its brink. It was our only refrigerator for the butter and meat; they were precariously suspended in its black pit on an unsteady platform fastened by ropes that were always worn and near the breaking point. Now and then some of the family nourishment slipped off and vanished forever in the depths below. Those foregathered at luncheon might receive and stoically accept the cook's report that owing to no fault of hers the butter had just fallen into the well.

I cannot refrain from presenting our most unforgettable family doctor. He was roundly denounced in private as a bear, but invariably summoned again on the slighest pretext of some ailment. Although he and his horse and buggy may secretly have brought many a germ into the house, we were never afflicted by other than the routine diseases of youth. In fact he came more often just to look us over, and incidentally to catechise and tease us. He had a stubby square beard and walked with a decided limp; his fierce brown eyes made us speechless, until we discovered that they could also twinkle pleasantly. He would line us up in front of him, and then subject us to a confusing medico-educational quiz. His sentences were spoken in a rumbling German bass voice, without audible commas or periods or inflections, and he paused a moment only when he had done with one and turned to the next. A casual listener might have heard something like this: «Open your mouth are you studying arithmetic wider how much are 17 and 25 head back wrong stupid boy next — let me look into you ear so you are studying Roman history come closer how many Muses were there — six? Himmel —» and so on through the lot of us. I have a notion that he was a wise old bird in his way and really knew some things ignored by our doctors of today who specialize only in circumscribed nooks and corners of our anatomy.

My transfer from the district school to Woodward High School was the beginning of four very full years. If I tried to summarize the results of my earliest education, I would recall first its practical features. We had had endless spelling bees and were familiar with the lexicon from aberratin to xenophobia; we had to repeat the name and give the length of every river, important or unimportant, in the world. The exact height of mountain ranges was ready upon the tip of our tongues. Verse or prose flowed from our lips; much of it, especially the mushiest, such as the death of Little Nell and singsong poetry, like 'Tell me not in mournful numbers', is difficult to expunge from our memory to this day. Recitation of the names of the Presidents was as easy as those of the months, although today one is apt to forget where Polk or Pierce came in. We were taught Emerson's patriotic line «God said I am tired of kings,» but we had to know the dates of the four Georges and of Victoria none the less. Naturally most of these practical benefits were nullified or expunged in the High School years. There a wider and steeper track lay before me: not only did I have to undertake a long daily walk up and down Sycamore Hill, like the noble duke of York; I had also to get the measure of pleasant temptations and inviting ambitions which are astir in every lad, and to calculate the distance of horizons as yet of low visibility. There were new associations and opportunities the value and the goal of which I could not foresee.

SYCAMORE HILL

Admission into the high school meant promotion in several ways. The older boys were more inclined to let us hang around and even permitted us to take part in their games with increasing tolerance. Another adolescent generation had suddenly sprung up and come into its rights; we were now the naggers instead of the nagged. Thus we rose in the social scale. Well-meaning elders ceased to pat me on the head condescendingly, since they now considered me an acceptable specimen of the human race. There was, for example, the Ramsey family whose head was a lawyer of distinction and much learning; he had begotten several extremely elongated sons among whom Stanley was my particular intimate. We two were known as the long and the short of it. His father had had the habit of consoling me for my relatively diminutive size by assuring me that Napoleon was short, that Richard Wagner was short, with other similar irrelevant comparisons. This friendly assurance, intended to put me at my ease in the presence of six-footers, turned out to be highly inappropriate, for I was certainly not cut out to be either a conqueror or a composer. When I entered the High School this revered mentor looked upon me as if I had suddenly grown a foot, and occasionally unbent to discuss baseball, politics, or religion with me. My brothers no longer hinted that I was probably a foundling, and allowed me to consider myself a bona fide member of the family.

I have often maintained that the curriculum of Woodward High School was the best and most entertaining in the world. This was chiefly due to a number of highly competent as well as peculiar and amusing teachers. Although memory, left to itself, is bound to exaggerate the peculiarities more than the competence, the latter surely was unusual and seems more so retrospectively, when compared with what I have since experienced in school or college. The educational set-up handed out a little of everything and stimulated in the classes an interest in many fields. I am inclined to attribute to it not only the beginning of my habit of scattered reading, whether in literature or in science, biography or travel, history or language, but also my limited achievement in a specific field. In religion I went through the innocuous experience of many adolescents of wanting to enter the ministry, presumably to spread in a pagan world a new light of brotherly service. I was turned from that brief altruistic and sentimental mood by stronger influences. The chief one, no doubt, was father's scientific bent, and his frequent talks about a world of facts. The natural beauty of my early surroundings, and the freedom of making the acquaintance of the Cincinnati hills and woods in solitary wanderings accelerated the change. I soon realized that I had mistaken a fuzzy emotional idealism for a call or mission very dimly outlined in my mind. During this transition I was guilty of the reprehensible act of writing verse, aberrations today explained or condoned because they furnish «an outlet for self-expression», although I think my own were only the usual adolescent vaporings which accompany mental or spiritual growing pains. Some of my early concoctions have miraculously survived among baseball scores and clippings of current events. Re-read later they make the perpetrator look about furtively in the apprehension that someone may be looking over his shoulder and so become acquainted with such unblushing sins of his youth.

Some of the High School subjects did little more than continue the lower school studies, notably those in English grammar, now designated as elocution. The parsing of sentences went merrily on to the tune of new rules of expression and gesture. These we had to preserve for all time in notebooks. An unimpeachable record set down at the time contains remarkable verities telling us that, «the arms move upward, downward and around the body to express what is above, below or on a level with the speaker. Descending gestures belong to the sphere of the intellect and are employed in general thought, such as historical or 'geo', (which abbreviation makes equal sense as geographic or geodetic); ascending gestures belong to the imagination and express elevation of thought.» To this phase of my education I showed boundless resistance. Eloquence and public speaking have always been abhorrent to me; the doctrine of the ascending gesture seemed only one more of those elevating influences which has left no trace in (what a Chinese, speaking of himself, would call) my wholly despicable character.

In order to face the entrance examinations of Yale College I continued the study of arithmetic into algebra and geometry, with logarithms and some trigonometry. Having faith in the judgment of my elders who believed that mathematics were the best discipline of the mind because figures never lie, I later extended the benefits of that unprofitable discipline for two more years at college. The peculiarities of mathematics have made me ask many times what strange brains could take pleasure in those weird calculations in which we indulged during our many years of figuring. Our first efforts in these mental exercises were mild, and consisted in such fascinating problems as for example, if a cistern can be filled by 4 pipes in 3 hours, how long would it take 8 pipes to fill 1/3 of it: as if any sane man would add more pipes to bring in less water. Entirely irrelevantly the teacher of mathematics would suddenly say, «reduce an acre to square centimeters.» Disregarding the gleam of insanity in his eye, we set to work on a page of endless figures, instead of proclaiming with the freedom of opinion conferred on us by the Bill of Rights, that there could be no sense in seeing an acre so reduced.

Our teacher in the advanced courses was an unusually able mathematician who displayed a speed in difficult calculations which filled us with amazement. He taught us to make complicated multiplications and divisions without the aid of pencil or paper, and he instigated rivalries in the quickest solution of problems put on the blackboard. We did not entertain the warmest feeling for him personally as he was inclined to underhand doings, such as waiting behind doors or in obscure passageways to catch miscreants red-handed. His initials, G.W.S., and not we, were responsible for his secret nick-name, Great Western Sneak. He was, on the other hand, ready to grant extra privileges to the more assiduous pupils, making up for his severity with the plum of an early dismissal from school.

There were various subjects in which we undoubtedly did drink deep. During the four years of High School we had single terms only of physics, chemistry, physiology and botany. If «a little learning is a dangerous thing», we were never aware of it, and Pope, as usual was mistaken. And today, what student has any notion what or where the Pierian Spring was? So we enjoyed those modest draughts of varied information, and when called on today for any facts we can boldly assert that we knew them once. Our instructors were excellent in giving us those facts. The teacher of botany was a lean little lady with a pincenez through which she blinked with her small sharp eyes, and she always addressed the class in a snappy attention-please-and-sit-up-straight kind of voice. At the drop of a hat she could give the Latin names of a hundred blossoms. Her approval of dead pressed flowers was boundless, and I remember her generous praise of my herbarium, an album of faded wild specimens which I still preserve. She awakened in us the same response as a mechanical toy and, once started, she kept going evenly through the hour. Yet she stirred in us a real interest in the structure of flowers, and the veriest class moron ceased to yawn when she displayed the disjecta membra of each specimen under her magnifying glass. At such moments her cheek would flush just a trifle, suggesting a tinge of enthusiasm over her success in having made us reach for a bit of education.

Our assignments and experiments in physics and chemistry were of an elementary kind; they would today, in view of our fabulously equipped laboratories, be comparable only with the brewings of an alchemist of the Middle Ages. We shattered innumerable test-tubes and retorts by mixing wholly inimical substances, and we seared our hands over the invisible blue flame of a Bunsen burner. This diabolical invention was the teacher's delight, and we had to describe the principle of the wretched thing in every examination.

The chemistry instructor was an elderly man with long grey hair, an ill-kept beard and a moderately prominent stomach, in fact, belly. He wore a shabby suit of clothes always covered with chalk, for he spent his happiest hours at the blackboard, writing out formulae and solutions of problems without a semblance of fatigue. The legend was current among us that he had survived some catastrophic explosion which had left him with a stiff right hand. In consequence, he had learned the trick of using both hands at the board, beginning far on his left, then taking over the chalk with his right hand between his stiffened thumb and index, and continuing with incredible speed to the far right. This was so fascinating to watch that we sat motionless until the dexterous feat had been accomplished. He must have come from some spot in New England, for among other peculiarities of pronunciation he always called sharp «shap», and the «oo» in spoon he made short as in «crooked». When we mentioned a glass retórt, he would say for the twentieth time, «rétort; a retórt is a shap reply». He was powerfully built, for he once picked up an offending boy and heaved him bodily out of the window which fortunately was on the ground floor.

The teacher of physiology might have been beautiful in her youth; she was a fair blonde with large expressive very blue eyes and an unvaryingly tired smile. She described with extraordinary equanimity the terrible things that went on in the human stomach when replete with food and occupied in the complicated process of digestion. She related minutely, as though she had witnessed it, the case of some soldier whose stomach had been laid open by a knife-thrust, permitting an unobstructed observation of the process going on within. She painted the situation in such warm colors, that I can see to this day the inquisitive noses of the doctors inserted in the vitals of their victim, while they were at the same time recording the furious workings of hydrochloric acid, or what not. Her rehearsal closed triumphantly with the discovery that the stomach will digest everything except itself.

The most conspicuous example of the unconsciously comic type was our instructor in German. He was a native Teuton, and there could never be any doubt that he knew and spoke the language, and never, by any chance, in a whisper. For lack of room we were obliged to attend his classes in the auditorium, a vast space which re-echoed with his deep gutterals, *ach, ursache, aaber* and the like. He had a majestic brown beard, which he frequently clasped; thick glasses and a low forehead under a closely clipped head of hair. He never wore anything but a long Prince Albert coat, and he always walked slowly with his hands locked behind him. His chief English phrase used in correcting our sentences on the board was, «You cooldn't use dat», crooned or drawled at great length as he milked his beard. At the end of every week, those of us who had been assigned to the care of this Germanic vigilante were supposed to hand him a routine statement claiming the privilege of early dismissal from school, owing to good grades. This paper, generally some shapeless fragment, bore only our name and the word «privileged». The spelling of this word was always a stumbling block and almost wrecked our holiday, for it never escaped his watchful Prussian eye. The following Monday morning would find him erect before the class, waving our three or four scraps of paper, and notifying us that privileged (he called it «brifilitched») had been flagrantly mispelled. Thereupon he wrote on the board the incorrect forms and included a lesson in English. I hesitate over the spelling of the word to this day. In one of his classes I told a lie which I probably ought to have regretted, but never did. His long brown coat and his thick-soled shoes had been more irritating than usual. When he stopped abruptly at something, «urrsprünglich», or «Ungerrrechtigkeit», or some untranslatable idiom, and fixed me through his thick glasses with the question, had I talked to my neighbor, I answered «nein». But I realized from his gaze that he knew that I knew that he knew that I had lied. The matter was dropped as unimportant, but I never again felt at ease with him, and was presently transferred to another study-room.

The outstanding personality among my high school teachers was William Pabodie, instructor in Latin and Greek. Without being an exacting disciplinarian he won our deepest respect. He was a slight man with grey hair ending in upturned curls at his neck; his head resembled some of the busts of Homer that stand unheeded around schoolrooms. Although no humanist in any profound sense, he was a sincere devotee of the classics, and we believed that he knew the Iliad and the Aeneid by heart. A Greek inflection was to him the noblest work of God, and for those of us who had to pass college entrance examinations, the recitation of innumerable forms of verbs became a kind of indoor sport. He welcomed guests, chiefly parents or friends, whom he placed on the platform at his side. We were then supposed to give at random and with great speed endless inflections and declensions which must have sounded like gibberish to the visitor. No poodle ever performed more successfully, and the training which Pabodie gave redounded to his everlasting glory, for many of his pupils brought back commendable scholastic records in later life. He insisted on careful translations into English; like all teachers of the classics he had his pet passages, in connection with which he would, year after year, make the same commentary or tell the same story. Our copy books were now and then enlivened with such marginal notes as, 'joke and laughter'!

One advantage of those school days, as I see them retrospectively, lay in the fact that we had more men than women as instructors. This situation was attributable to the fact that women were not yet as adequately trained for the teachers' career as the men; they also made fewer demands for an equal education in the advanced fields. Some were exceedingly capable as teachers, but as a rule were most effective in the elementary subjects to which their preparation had been confined. Another advantage was that our classes were small, hardly ever exceeding fifteen or twenty in any subject. This was especially evident in the sections in mathematics, in the classics, and English literature. I still recall the caustic language and critical mind of our English instructor, A.M. Van Dyke; his biting remarks and even his bursts of rage were always followed by witty, intelligent and helpful commentaries that had punch and kept us thoroughly awake.

Outside of school, too, these years were among my most profitable. Cincinnati was a center of culture much of which could be ascribed to its German Colony. This included many choice spirits from the Fatherland. Music of all kinds was fostered; American families of wealth and prestige gave active support to an orchestra and to the Cincinnati May Festivals. These grew to be occasions of note and drew patrons from the entire nation. Theodore Thomas, a prominent conductor in American musical history, had established himself in Chicago. He was invited frequently to conduct in Cincinnati, and assured the festivals a high level of achievement. To those of us who had a seat among the select in the remotest part of the top-most gallery, he was an easily detected object, because of his bald and shining head. It was reported that Thomas on one occasion tired of this distinction, for he appeared at a rehearsal wearing a wig. Noting that he was the cause of some repressed merriment in the orchestra, he rapped for attention and said, «Gentlemen, laugh once and laugh loud, and that is all».

These May Festivals gave us an excellent opportunity of becoming acquainted with noted Oratorios sung by the world's foremost singers. A recital of their names may seem like ancient history indeed, but not many singers of today surpass them. We heard the English tenor, Edward Lloyd, the De Reszke brothers, David Bispham; and among the great women's voices, Ternina, Sembrich and Adelina Patti. Some I heard again later at the Metropolitan in New York, and in Europe, but those early impressions have remained my most profound musical experiences. Which leads me to add the common-place conclusion that as much excellent music as possible should be heard by boys and girls in their formative decade. All the experiences of later life taken together cannot match the results gained in the early susceptible years.

We had much music, good, bad and indifferent at home. I furnished the bad with my violin for about four years. A poet has said, heard melodies are sweet, but those unheard are sweeter; so I never received from the friends or neighbors obliged to listen to my harmonies, any encouragement that I adopt a musical career. Thereafter my violin issued from its case less and less, especially in later days in Yale. Thus another possible future for my unrecognized and discouraged talents came to naught. My two sisters, however, made up for my shortcomings, one vocally and the other with the piano. For a period of years sister Marie sang in the Unitarian church choir, and I, as her equerry-in-waiting, (with the stress on the waiting) took her to the Church on evenings of rehearsals, and waited to bring her «safely» home. There were no convenient street-cars nor busses in those halcyon days, and on many happy nights we plodded through rain or snow, cracking the ice in the gutters and sliding down appropriate steep places.

As regards the theatre Cincinnati afforded an opportunity of seeing Edwin Booth and Jo Jefferson; Sir Henry Irving and Ellen Terry arrived with their company almost every winter, and we walked a mile or two from our suburb, down Sycamore Hill, to the Grand Opera House and sat in the «nigger heaven». These were treats which we enjoyed as often as our allowances would permit. I well remember Booth in the parts of Macbeth, with Modjeska as Lady Macbeth, of Hamlet, Shylock and Brutus, on which occasion Barrett played the role of

Cassius. I do not mean to convert those distant boyish memories into critical opinions; nevertheless, many details of those nights are indelibly engraved on my mind. In those years I beheld the inside of a theatre for the first time and I was naturally much stirred by what I saw. Booth was a genius of supreme dignity and self-restraint, infinitely above the ranting and bombast of the school of Forrest and McCullough who had preceded him. His mellow and quiet reading of the lines, together with the musical richness of his voice, was bound to impress every youngster. In Macbeth, which is still for me the most gripping of Shakespeare's tragedies, he was at his best; the scenes of impending horror, such as the appearance of Banquo's ghost, made me hold on tight to my seat. Within a brief period both Edwin Booth and Henry Irving gave performances of the Merchant of Venice, and the great difference in their conceptions of the character of Shylock was instructive. Booth presented a more dignified, tragic member of a hated, unhappy race. Irving gave us an elemental, emotional Jew who snarled when he voiced his intention to be avenged and whetted his knife more excitedly than Booth's. Irving's Shylock was also more stricken and whipped at the close than Booth's impersonation. Neither actor showed any of the comic aspects given to the Jew's part in Shakespeare's time. But we youngsters were more engrossed in the love story of Portia and Bassanio, and the technicalities of the plot concerning the pound of flesh escaped us.

The conviction of those acquainted with the theatre was that Hamlet was Booth's most masterful effort. But four acts of sustained drama made the farcical attitude of the grave-diggers in the fifth a timely and welcome relief, and only the reappearance of Hamlet could have justified its interruption. Then the house listened enthralled to Booth's voice in which none has equalled him. «Has this fellow no feeling of his business that he sings at grave-making?», revealed not only how intimately allied comedy and tragedy are in Shakespeare, but gave poignancy to Hamlet's ignorance that the grave prepared was Ophelia's. The death of Hamlet himself was made unforgettable by Booth in Hamlet's last words:

> Oh good Horatio, what a wounded name,
> Things standing thus unknown, shall live behind me!
> If thou didst ever hold me in thy heart,
> Absent thee from felicity awhile,
> And in this harsh world draw thy breath in pain
> To tell my story.

The cast of actors in these great plays was always uneven; the casual hiring of mediocre talent by a travelling company was unavoidable, and the presentations even with Booth or Irving did not escape this blot. This was especially apparent in Julius Caesar, in which Booth and Barrett far outshone all others including the mighty Caesar himself. Among the last roles which the two popular actors played together, shortly before Barrett's death, were those of Brutus and Cassius. Barrett was already gravely stricken by illness, and the audience listened much moved to the scene in which the two Romans meet for the last time, each speaking the same poignant farewell. Booth's voice seemed to express deep personal feeling:

> Forever and forever farewell, Cassius;
> If we do meet again, why, we shall smile.
> If not, why then, this parting was well made.

Memory brightens with the privilege of having seen Jefferson in *Rip van Winkle,* and *The Rivals*; Irving as Mephistopheles in Goethe's *Faust* was a memorable pleasure, although *Faust* never was by any stretch of the imagination an acting play.

Through the heart of Cincinnati flowed an opaque canal, known as the Rhine, bearing sluggishly upon its surface much floatsam and jetsam. On its banks lived many born Germans and their American descendants. The oldest generation among them consisted of those who had fled from the tyranny of the Fatherland during the decade which followed the revolution of 1848. All of them were a profoundly liberal and liberty-loving group, and very politically minded. They at once identified themselves with the home of their adoption, and their enthusiasm for this country, to say nothing of their successful establishment in many varied careers, made the United States known proverbially in Germany as «the land of unlimited possibilites». Identification with the country of their adoption meant for them also identification with the Republican party, the party of Abraham Lincoln the Emancipator, their symbol of the loftiest principles of freedom and humanity. Father was logically every inch a Republican, and at every election he automatically voted the straight ticket of the Grand Old Party. A political disillusionment was in store for him when he learned with growing disquiet that there was a renegade among his sons. Brother Ferdinand was attending Yale College, and having come under the corrupting influence of free-traders like the great William Graham Sumner, he betrayed during his holidays at home the reprehensible bias of his mind. Worst of all, he expressed an unthinkable approval of Grover Cleveland, the Democratic candidate for the presidency, as well as actual commendation of the doctrine of laissez-faire and other theories. Their discussions in the garden still re-echo in my ears, and generally raged around the Republican tariff and Cleveland's criminal bent toward lowering the rates or something. Father would see himself beaten at last by the more recently acquired information of his recalcitrant son; then his last resort became good-natured vituperation, possibly not wholly free from malice, in allusions to the immense size of Cleveland's collar, an item he could have taken from the Republican comics, with the implication that no man with such a neck could have any brains. Not having any understanding of the merits of their argument, which was punctuated by father's repeated, «stop-a-bit-and-think», I was inclined to side with him on the questionable fitness for office of a man the girth of whose collar was represented as larger than the dimensions of his forehead.

I recall an unexpected and amusing feud which started in a corner of our world between a group of German Thespians and the German press. By chance I was present in the theatre when the feud received a public airing. The theatre was in the hands of a stock company that played every season, and salvaged its reputation and varied the monotony of always seeing the same performers by now and then inviting an actor of distinction from the outside. The company was always in the depths of impecuniousness, but it did its best with aged stage machinery which often miscued at critical moments. Once a noted tragedian, Von der Osten, appeared in a German version of Ohnet's *Maître de Forges* (der *Hüttenbesitzer*) played as *The Ironmaster* on the English stage also. I recall vaguely that a member of the cast, playing a part of some nobleman, appears in a box, and a dramatic dialogue ensues between him and the hero on the stage. At the end of the act, the curtain was lowered too soon, and the great tragedian pronounced his final words with only his boots visible. There was some consternation in the audience when a resounding «Donnerwetter» came through the curtain. Attached immediately to the final speech, it was in reality directed at the inept mechanic who had let down the curtain prematurely. It was after such performances that the press entered the picture. There were two newspapers in the German language in Cincinnati; the Volksblatt, Republican, and the Volksfreund, Democratic and, in consequence, never admitted into the house by our staunch Republican father. These two papers may have disagreed violently in their politics, but they were entirely harmonious in their published opinions of the merits of the stock company. The public now experienced an unexpected dramatic moment at the theatre, when the director, Heineman by name, appeared before the curtain and complained of certain malicious criticisms of the performers, printed in the German dailies. The unhappy situation, he explained, was brought about by the fact that the said newspapers had requested passes for all the staff, including their sisters, their cousins and their aunts, who turned out excessively numerous; the request had been refused. A few days later the eloquent protest of the director brought about a happy compromise; the staff and relatives received passes, the acting was praised, and the freedom of the press was triumphantly vindicated.

Those days brought to us our first family sorrow through the death in an accident of a much loved aunt, mother's sister and especially near to her. The ensuing days of grief together with domestic worries affected mother's health; her frailty increased during the year and the best medical advice was that she be relieved at once of the care of her large and impractical household. The many stairs which she had climbed incessantly in the daily routine had become too much of an effort; it was decided that she must have a surcease and take the waters of some appropriate springs in Germany. The house over which she had quietly ruled for thirty years must be given up, and a home commensurate with her strength was to be found. This was the close of a period of world history, more meaningful to me than the Fall of the Holy Roman Empire or any other relatively insignificant overthrow. To these poignant occurrences I owed my first trip to Europe. Mother, my two sisters and I were to leave in the spring and return in September. This was in 1891. The High School granted me leave of absence with the proviso that I make up the work missed before the beginning of the next school year. The dismantling of the house began at once; most of the furniture, including various priceless possessions of my own, disappeared for all time from the scene. It was not likely that any other family would muster the courage to inhabit that large shell of a house with its three floors and a score of rooms and hallways. So it stood empty intermittently for several years and presently was torn down. On our return from Europe in the fall mother's health was much improved, and we lived for a year in a diminutive house in the suburb of Walnut Hills. Having completed the last year of High School I passed the entrance examinations to Yale.

The world was now a wholly different one. I frequently walked over the intervening miles to the old house, wandering through the garden and the yard, gazing into the empty rooms and sitting in the old swing under the rear porch. The house had belonged to me more than to any other member of the family. I was most intimately acquainted with every part of the old structure, and with the long list of its idiosyncrasies and shortcomings, which I had tried to make good with my own hands. I recalled my attic room with its equipment for the complete carpenter. I had cut and sawed floorboards, repaired locks, and glued many a piece of rickety furniture up there under the eaves; the infinite buckets of coal that I had brought in and the ashes that I carried out had seemed memorable feats. Thus I had become identified with a corner of the world enclosed within sixteen vanished years. The garden was already overrun by weeds knee-high, the autumn leaves were blown about the porches and covered the walks. As I returned to the new home in the twilight I became aware for the first time of the capricious changes and insecurities which confront a boy trying to capture the drift of life in his teens.

A FIRST GLIMPSE OF EUROPE

Reliable sources tell us that the travel experiences of Socrates was limited to an occasional stroll down to the Piraeus, the harbor of Athens, or to a ramble over the Acropolis. In such small-town practice his life and mine are comparable: the travels of my early youth were entirely restricted to an «intramural» acquaintance with Cincinnati, to which I managed to add in the course of time portions of the city's immediate environment. These wanderings encompassed no more territory than could be reached by hiking, or by a minimum expenditure on the limited conveyances of those days.

Rare exceptions were inland voyages on Ohio River steamboats which plowed through its muddy waters in their round of visits up and down stream, calling at various towns, lazily discharging and taking on cargoes and passengers. The boats had a kind of protective discoloring owing to their mottled exterior that cried for a new coat of paint they were never destined to receive. On holidays or special-rate excursions they were filled with crowds intent on enjoying glimpses of the picturesque banks, notably on the Kentucky side, when they were not scrutinizing their lunch-baskets for a sandwich or a lost hard-boiled egg. The boats themselves were soft-coal monsters, whose soot, like the rains of heaven, was sent alike on the just and unjust. By their speed and unpredictable timetables they belonged to the same family as Lincoln's riverboat which never had enough steam to proceed and to whistle at the same time, so that every time it whistled it stopped.

Another grimy and happy experience was an excursion to Niagara Falls. These educational expeditions were peculiar manifestations of our mid-western civilization; they were inaugurated by profit-despising railroad magnates, who offered the public return-tickets to all the national wonders at phenomenally low rates, good for a few days, packing thousands of long-suffering hicks into scores of wooden sleepers and coaches which generally ran in several sections. Only divine providence prevented seemingly inevitable catastrophies. In length such a train competed with a freight, and we could count with pride the endless numbers of cars until they were lost around a curve. Every boy had his head out of the window all the way, tunnel or no tunnel, and impenetrable coal smoke filled the open cars with fumes as deadly as those of a lethal gas-chamber.

The excursionists lived in the midst of improvised lunch-rooms, sitting and sleeping in complete disregard of the scattered remnants of meals or of the rolling about of empty pop bottles. Of the journey I recall only the foolhardiness of a Captain Webb, who committed a widely advertised suicide by attempting to swim the Rapids. Since there were giants in those days, another distinguished personality went over the Falls in a barrel, not only to show his daring, but to spare his immediate relatives the expense of a common-place interrment by disappearing for good in a watery grave.

With such moderate experience of highway and byway, the prospect of crossing the seas to Europe filled me with a novel excitement, and a day in spring saw four of us, mother, my sisters and myself expedited on our way. Two of my brothers were already in Europe: William was brandishing the painter's brush in Munich, and Ferdinand was at the University of Freiburg, where he was studying history under Professor von Holst, who later taught for a brief time at the University of Chicago. For the first few hours of our journey I examined my pockets every fifteen minutes to be sure that I had not forgotten anything, or that I had not been robbed of tickets, or letter-of-credit, or cash, amounting to five dollars of my own. The great adventure was adding importance to my person as well as years to my life. I oozed responsibility as the only male of our company, on whom the welfare of three helpless women thenceforth would depend. A detail which hurt my pride was the undeniable fact that having neither the heft of a football tackle nor the height suitable for first base, my sisters frequently humiliated me by saying so that the general public could hear; «Never mind those bags, they are too heavy for you».

In New York City the dizzying speed of the elevated road was still new enough to make us crane our necks in wonder and excitement, and we played the part of gaping country cousins effectively enough to be ourselves a source of pleasure to blasé native New Yorkers. Occasionally I escaped from my sisters, and, in my own good company, looked over the Brooklyn Bridge and wandered about Castle Garden; there an aquarium had been installed in the old hall in which P.T. Barnum had introduced that nightingale, Jenny Lind, to the New York public. I also went to the Zoological Garden and began a record, which no doubt surpasses that of any traveller, of never having failed to call upon every collection of my fellows in cages, no matter where in the world.

Opportunities of absorbing culture could not be wholly evaded, so I was, under protest, dragged forth to inspect works of art by great masters at the Metropolitan Museum. The English language had not yet been enriched by the terms post-impressionism, cubism, and futurism; I could thus look at old paintings new to me, without having some scoffer at my elbow extol only ultra-modernists, and darken counsel by words without knowledge. At all events, those tiny seeds of culture were not scattered wholly in vain.

A small notebook has survived in which I daily set down in two or three sentences enough of a record to revive memories of a panorama of five months. In this earliest effort at a diary, the weather, which favored or hindered our plans, received unusually prominent mention. As a diary it is a skeleton wholly without flesh, but it suffices to bring back significant episodes and personalities. I noted in it that newly made acquaintances now and then seemed to look upon me as one more primitive specimen from the land of Chingachcook and Buffalo Bill. The indulgent smiles of occasional hosts implied that they did not consider me a likely person to appreciate all the aspects of their complicated and superior civilization. In fact it is probable that I reaped the fruit of those juvenile wanderings only after many additional years, necessary, as Kipling put it, to develop a' average kid, and make him end as a thinkin' man.

On a clear morning, the first day in May, we embarked on a small steamer of the Holland America Line. Presumably every feature of that boat would constitute a violation of the marine statutes today. A single propeller vessel, it averaged three hundred miles a day in fair weather; during storms we moved only up and down, obeying wind and wave. My diary states triumphantly: «All passengers are sea-sick except the captain and myself». I imagined every captain to be of a piece with the heroic pilot depicted in a McGuffy Reader, who, when his ship had struck the rocks, rushed below and heartened his passengers by shouting, «'we are lost', as he staggered down the stairs.»

A first glimpse of land made geographic realities out of the English Channel and the French coast. Our itinerary was to take us through Holland up the Rhine to the ancient city of Worms. We were to be the guests of a family that had been bound to mother's by the friendly ties of several generations.

The intricate process of becoming acquainted with European civilization gradually unfolded itself with all its sinister implications.

Unwittingly caught by a flood-tide of culture beyond my depth, I was carried through gloomy cathedrals and monotonous museums which looked much alike to me. For centuries Europe had been occupied chiefly with building great churches and painting innumerable pictures merely to hang them on walls by thousands in later ages, so they could be gawked at by ignorant foreigners, and, incidentally, to sustain an army of guides. On one occasion I slipped out from under the nose of a performing official in Amsterdam, and made my way to a pastry shop which I had discovered in passing. No such display of sweets had ever met the eye. That experience made of me an ardent patron of the European pâtisserie, and my lavish investment in pastry, in its many international varieties, has helped governments to balance their budgets.

Having acquired a year's culture in a few days we proceeded to the city of Cologne:

> The river Rhine it is well known
> Doth wash the city of Cologne;
> But tell me, nymph, what powers divine
> Can henceforth wash the river Rhine?

Whatever may have been the condition of that metropolis in the days of the poet Coleridge, it had become one of the neatest and busiest in Germany. It was already famous then for its *Eau de Cologne,* enough glory for any metropolis. My diary records nothing more than a visit to the zoo and to the cathedral. This zoo I introduced to my sons on later occasions, but when I displayed my gifts as guide through the cathedral, my efforts met only with an atavistic resistance to excessive culture.

From Cologne we continued up the Rhine on one of the river-boats to our destination. On the decks excellent meals were served, with superb views of the winding shores thrown in, at the sight of which the German tourists dropped their knives to utter, «grossartig» and «kolossal». They were no doubt merely emulating their Siegfried, much admired in his recent, very similar, Wagnerian Rhine-journey to Worms.

At midnight we reached the sleepy little city and received the cordial welcome of an unexpected assemblage consisting of grandparents, parents, children and retainers; they must have formed a goodly part of the population, foregathered to obtain a first glimpse of the strange inhabitants of the New World. I myself was conducted to a hotel by our host, there being no room for the family guide at his home. After considerable pounding and kicking at the huge portal of the inn, he succeeded in arousing the drowsy porter who, I later learned, spent his entire day polishing boots (the Germans call it *Stiefelwischen*) and his nights from twilight to twilight in profound slumber. The unhappy porter was greeted by a shower of abuse, a captivating national treatment of inferiors. An ordinary experience in your daily communication, notably with officials, was their habit of snarling a gruff response to an innocent question. Perhaps this upsetting manner was only an indication of the spiritual freedom still enjoyed by a great people, who in a highly competitive world found some release in shouting at each other when less than a foot apart. After such vociferous exhibitions the contenders always calmed down, the superiority of one of them in the social scale having been duly vindicated.

The porter, thoroughly awakened by the vituperation heaped upon him, led us to a room hermetically sealed since the Diet of Worms. I made an unconscious gesture to draw the heavy curtains and uncover a window, but both my host and the porter exclaimed that I was inviting a fatal pneumonia by such temerity. Finally, I was left unmolested in my unsanitary pursuits to get some contemporary oxygen into the room. I pried loose heavy wooden inner shutters, pushed out a loudly creaking casement that must have disturbed the dead and would have brought back the porter, had he not immediately retired to his interrupted slumber. In a whimsical essay on the charm of open sleeping porches and the benefits of fresh air, Charles Stephen Brooks convincingly exonerates Othello from the crime of smothering Desdemona; that innocent lady no doubt had the custom of sleeping in a four-poster enclosed by thick hangings, her windows being sealed likewise and heavily curtained, so that she was more than half suffocated before Othello could lay violent hands on her.

You have rightly guessed that on the next day we were taken for a walk to see the ancient sights which included the inescapable cathedral, now called *Dom*, and an ambitious monument dedicated to the actual presence in Worms, at the Imperial Diet of 1521, of Martin Luther. His is the most easily discoverable among several other figures, for he stands erect and defiant with one hand on a Bible; beneath him on his private pedestal is inscribed his famous utterance to the Diet: «Here I stand, I cannot do otherwise, so help me God». Modernist architects and sculptors, historically ignorant, interpret this statement as meaning that Luther, and his monumental associates, presented with flawless academic accuracy in bronze and stone, will in defiance of better taste stand there to the end of time.

Worms must be credited with the production of Liebfraumilch, the noblest of Rhenish wines, if you can get it; the legitimate vintage is limited to the environment of the Church of Our Lady from which the wine derives its name. Unfortunately I was not asked to sample the amply stocked cellar of our generous host; but I learned later that in the matter of choice beverages a complete European education supplies the willing learner with an endless variety. «Rosengarten», across the Rhine from Worms, enjoys honorable mention in the famous Nibelungen legend; it turned out a rather unpoetic spot, except for an inn, where on a fair night we sat around an enormous bowl of mulled spiced wine, the like of which the ancient heroes of the saga could not boast.

My brothers now arrived to make plans for the coming summer, without consulting me. Mother's health was the foremost consideration, so it was decided that she must take the waters of Bad-Schwalbach, near Frankfort. In that place my person was deemed a costly and superfluous addition, and my role of family-guide was transferred to the unsteady hands of my sisters. Brothers Will and Ferd showed no inclination to give up their ancient authority over my comings and goings, and decided that I would be least in the way with Ferd at Freiburg, where I could be restricted to my books and make up the work I was missing by my absence from school. On week-ends I could be released for an occasional outing, and be presented to my brother's academic friends with the proper apologies.

At Freiburg Ferd acquired a faint but visible halo, rising much in my esteem. From the worm which an older brother always is in the opinion of his browbeaten and belittled juniors, he developed into a tolerant companion and omniscient teacher; he was also my banker, gingerly handing out an occasional piece of fifty pfennings, about ten cents, with a spend-it-freely manner which seemed to imply that, according to my behavior, more might be forthcoming. We lived in an ancient dwelling in the Salzgasse erected in the middle ages in what was probably the narrowest street in the world. The small windows of my attic room opened on a tiled roof, the favorite promenade of the neighborhood cats with whom I tried to make friends in lonely hours. The maid servant of the house frequently inquired about my needs, hinting by her interruptions that I get out, so that she could make the bed and return the room to its former immaculate state. She appeared on Sunday mornings in her best form. Arrayed in her peasant costume with a gorgeous white hood and streaming black ribbons she looked not so much disposed to serve as to be served, and when she issued forth, her stately finery became the most prominent sight all the way up the street. A small table on which I set up my text books in Greek, Latin and mathematics gave the room a pretentious and studious air which I had not bargained for. It predicted days of forced labor, and a striped suit would fittingly have completed my cell. With predictable certainty I was, on my first liberation, hauled to see the town's glory, yes, another cathedral, this time disguised under the name *Münster*. A deep impression was left on my mind by the equally ancient university building, and by the behavior of the classes. My brother had offered to take me to a lecture, concealing me under his coat, but I proved a quiet listener and even remained awake, which was more than could have been said of the sham students. But my wakefulness was caused by the lecturer, Ferd's noted historian Von Holst. He had a long, agile figure, and before you could say Jack Robinson, he was in at the door and up on the platform beginning his lecture. A single tuft of rebellious hair stood erect on the top of his head and balanced the pointed beard on his chin. He had two piercing eyes which he naturally fixed on me: in the first place I had no business there, besides, I was almost under his nose and I was awake.

Freiburg, situated on the fringes of the Black Forest, occupies an unmatched site for a variety of outings. We climbed some of the more accessible hill tops, and wandered through woods and rolling meadows where I heard a distant hidden cuckoo for the first time. Ferd possessed an ancient bicycle which did very uneven duty for us both, I doing the pushing, and my considerate brother doing the pedaling, comfortably seated in the middle. On one occasion we had taken turns to get the bicycle up a long steep hill. Within a few hundred yards of the top I sat down by the road-side to catch my breath, only to see Ferd, who had continued to the summit with the old wheel, go whizzing by and be lost to sight at the foot of the grade. I have a recollection that he claimed afterwards he would have stopped halfway down to turn the wheel over to me, had not the speed at which he was traveling interfered with his generous intentions. When left to my own devices and there was no supervision of my doings, I spent my allowance on cups of chocolate and pastry. By costly experience I learned that an entire platter of miscellaneous cakes set before you was not to be devoured in its entirety, but cautiously, only a piece or two at a sitting, since the vigilant eye of the waiter hovering over you kept track of your appetite and permitted him to exact due payment for every cake consumed.

Thus pleasantly the days sped and with them the spring. No

doubt my brother was secretly gratified that my visit was drawing to a close. I had absorbed all the information he had to give, and could now be turned over for the next weeks to the tender mercies of Brother Will who had returned to Munich; this process, according to my newly acquired classical information, seemed like escaping from *Scylla* only to fall into the perils of *Charybdis*. The transition was made easier by a visit at a cousin's in Heidelberg, and a day or two at Schwalbach with the family.

In those days of freedom in Germany there could be no more engrossing and profitable occupation than study or idleness at a German University. Although I later chose Munich for my graduate work I was never wholly reconciled to that choice over Freiburg or Heidelberg. Nowhere in the world was there more inspiration to be captured, whether from their incomparably beautiful natural frame, or from the old-world character of their immediate urban setting, or from the intimate friendly life which bound together so closely students and teachers. In a sense, a visit to Heidelberg meant that I was going home, for mother was a native of the city, as I have already mentioned; her home, a comfortable old mansion, stood quite unchanged near the very banks of the Neckar, not far from the Karlsthor. Mother's cousin whom I called uncle to make a thin blood relationship thicker, had a son of my own age, and both he and his father immediately disclosed at the railroad station their fanatical love for long explorations of territory already well known to them. Their first questions were, had I a pair of stout boots, did I possess a Rucksack, did I easily lose my breath. All of this was bewildering until I learned that I was living among a people who are all quasi-professional mountain climbers, and love to drag the proof of their prowess into the conversation on the slightest provocation. A brother of my uncle, who had resided his entire life in Paris and therefore constitutionally despied the country and all unnecessary walking, came for a visit during my stay. We went to the station in the usual family concourse to meet him, and I saw that he, at least, was thoroughly aware of the situation into which he had got himself. After ten minutes of excessive display of affection all around, during which I was kissed by a bearded man for the first time in my life, the brother disclosed that he was prepared for the worst, saying, «You might as well tell me at once what mountain I am to be dragged today». When any expedition finally got under way, he, like Job, cursed the day he was born and ended by thoroughly enjoying it.

My aunt, being completely entangled in infinite domestic duties, never accompanied us. With the crack of dawn she arose to engage in a whirl of activity, tied a towel about her head, donned a most ample apron, and started in pursuit of her arch enemy dust. I never saw any, which she explained by the fact that men could only bring it in, but never see it. There was also a servant who, like all of her station, combined an unbelievable number of functions; these kept her in a kind of perpetual motion until late into the night. She was scandalized when I desired to polish my own shoes, a manifest degradation in her servant's eyes which had never beheld the like. If we happened to return from an outing in the late afternoon my aunt was completely transformed. She would be quietly seated, always in the same chair on the balcony when the day was fair, a small lace cap on her head, engaged in darning infinite woolen socks. This revolting footwear she also knitted for her males. Any innuendo which would be interpreted as a slur on her sense of order, instantly brought a flash into her eyes. When uncle, the most pacifistic of men, asked where the cork-screw was he received the peppery reply that everything in her household had its proper place. To which he would answer submissively, turning to me for moral support; «Too true, only no one knows where that place is».

Early on a clear morning of the newly-born summer I left for Schwalbach, the train winding through gracious forest and meadow land, where I saw deer grazing in the distance along the edge of a sheltering wood. Schwalbach itself had a benevolent and humanitarian atmosphere; there every bush and blade of grass had clearly been placed under medical care. It was a place of gentle walks, rolling lawns and well brushed and swept woods, intended strictly for valetudinarian uses, where every path was supplied with inviting benches placed at short intervals for the feeble and convalescent. Mother was greatly improved in health, and everybody was full of praises for the spotless environment and the regimented daily existence. My sisters welcomed me with some show of affection, presumably because I was to honor them for a brief stay only. Of course we started forth to see those unavoidable points of attraction which even a watering place could boast, and I drank from an infamously tasting spring which, the credulous asserted, had restored countless invalids to health. Having enjoyed for two days some excellent food, the only asset which the resort had for me, I continued my hegira to Munich. In Germany, no one ever missed an opportunity to go to the railroad station; if, on this occasion, the family's friends had not consisted of invalids only, they would all have come to the train to see me off.

At the mention of that unique city Munich, a shadow falls over my page. Any comparison of the Munich before the first World War, with the Munich of after years makes clear the poignant change which took place in that city's singularly privileged social group.

For the present I shall record only the radiance of my first acquaintance with the Bavarian capital, more than fifty years ago. My experience under the tutelage of brother Will was the opposite of an academic one. Late on a June evening I was met at the station by him and his intimate friend, the California painter Orrin Peck, at whose house I was to stay until the family's arrival from Schwalbach. We were then to move into one of the homelike Munich pensions typical of the long ago. After the kind of greeting which I expected, namely, «who let you out?», or something to that effect, I was seized by both men, swung into a droschke and borne away to deposit my baggage. Having complied with the order to wash up I was taken to the Löwenbraükeller, the largest of all possible beer-gardens; there you could see an unbelievable combination of infinite green tables and countless plump waitresses, you heard the incredible Bavarian dialect amid the din of the talk and the intermittent music of the band, you tasted the magic mixture of Liptauer cheese, garnished with chives, dill pickles, onions and whatnot, chopped fine and worked into a dainty mess; you made the acquaintance of dark rye bread cut into huge slices or wedges, of enormous white radishes cut into spirals, and finally came the climax in the shape of a stein of beer a foot high. This had been placed before me with that peculiar brotherly malice born of a desire to find out how much would put the kid brother to sleep. I was too excited and thirsty to show the desired effect, and if I could already take it then, I have continued to prove to my own satisfaction that the genuine Munich dark beer is the most satisfactory drink ever inspired by the unquenchable thirst of man.

Munich was at that time Germany's first Kunststadt, with a community dedicated entirely to art. It was my privilege, if not always to converse with, at least to appear in Will's extensive circle of friends, most of whom were artists, writers or actors. After years of separation, Will acted as if he almost approved of me; he did not present me to his friends with that resigned see-what-I-have-on-my-hands tone of voice. The home of the Pecks was presided over by Orrin's mother, a gentle woman with grey hair, of warm and kindly qualities, and by his sister Janet, a cultivated young woman, who formed the keystone of their hospitality. The name of Mrs. Margaret Peck will be familiar to many Californians, for she was one of the earliest and closest friends of Mrs. Phoebe Apperson Hearst, in the pioneer days of San Francisco. Through the home of the Pecks there constantly moved a kind of international procession of friends, typical of the manifold culture of the city. Among the guests of distinction were Lenbach, Carl Marr, Stuck, Messerschmitt, Blos, Rosenthal, Emil Keck; the latter's chief occupation seemed to be painting nothing but the Prince Regent in identical postures. All these men stood high on the roster of Munich painters. Their pictures constituted a cross-section of the canvasses which were created in the nineties. During that epoch a breach arose between the conservative group, more steeped in the traditions of the Academy of Fine Arts, and the Secessionists who presently exhibited their pictures in a separate hall; the latter justified their revolt by the use of more light and color and bold experimentation in a new craftsmanship. Their movement to the left continued its course later to all extremes of modernism. With the help of a friendly guidance I learned to appreciate these different points of view then under way. The customary yearly exhibition of paintings and sculpture at the Glass Palace provided for innumerable summer visitors a capital opportunity of becoming acquainted with much contemporary European art.

I was now seventeen and may have absorbed some of the *Kultur*, perhaps mostly through the pores. From the Blumensäale, a variety show called Tingel-Tangel, to Lohengrin and Tanhäuser, my first Wagner operas, and Mozart incomparably given at the diminutive Rococo *Residenz* Theatre, from band music of the beer halls to serious concerts, the range of opportunities constituted a liberal education. I saw Goethe's entire *Faust*, with its fantastic second part; afterwards, in the course of my student years, I met the actor Häusser, who was one of the best Mephistopheles of the German stage, and, through him, friends of the actor's circle. Plays by the foremost writers of the day, Hauptmann, Suderman, Max Halbe, also were given. Like a Strassburg goose I was stuffed with these rich tidbits by my new acquaintances who insisted on raising a manifest low culture level on this forced diet.

Munich was the center for a variety of outings; the nearby mountains and their many lakes were dotted with wayside restaurants which always rose to view at strategic places and filled the thirsty hikers with the prospective pleasure looming just ahead. The immediate surroundings are level and ideally designed for the bicycle which has flourished there, it appears, since its invention. Obviously I had not thoroughly mastered it in those one-sided experiences at Freiburg; nevertheless, I was persuaded to take it up again by the painter Messerschmitt, a great devotee of that vehicle. We discovered a seemingly adequate one in some second-hand shop, and proceeded to the most unfrequented countryside for practice. He chose a wide road at the side of a flourishing cemetery, making a rather fitting background for neck-breaking experiments. Messerschmitt was a hearty Bavarian, and at the same time a gruff, plain-spoken man, who had grown to be my highly revered mentor. Whenever I dismounted awkwardly and against my will from the somewhat oversized machine and went sprawling, he rasped in his dialect the choicest cuss words, appreciated only by South Germans and worthy of being recorded in the history of intimate terms of address.

The German war machine was in evidence at all times in those days. Awed tourists spent many hours watching the magnificent display of the soldiers trooping by on their way to the parade grounds, clicking instantly into a goose-step at the appearance of an officer, and whirling their faces at him with the mechanical reaction and grace of a Charlie McCarthy. Military bands played on fixed days under the Feldherrenhalle, beside the imposing yellow-gray royal palace; there I loafed to see the guard change, and waited hopefully to get a glimpse of an unprepossessing, smiling red-nosed old gentleman, called the Prince Regent of Bavaria.

On week-ends city crowds sought out the many picturesque spots along the shore of Lake Starnberg not far from Munich, where small steamboats called in their scheduled errands. The lake also held tragic memories for Bavarians, because of the violent death in its waters of the mad king Ludwig II, and of his personal physician and keeper, Dr. Gudden. Lake Starnberg became associated with an impressive personality, called by irreverent cynics a Grosses Thier (large animal) of society. This was Ernst Possart, famous tragedian and director of the theatrical and operatic world of Munich. An invitation extended to the Peck family to a Sunday dinner at the Possart's summer home on Lake Starnberg was stretched to include me also. Possart met us at the head of the lake, carefully arrayed in a white suit and white spats, presenting the grand front for which he was distinguished from the common herd, while we listened in silence to a pompous rehearsed welcome. All the world was to him a stage, and on or off the boards he lived up to the sublime role expected of his art. At the wharf, within a stone's throw of their cottage, we were met by his wife, a noted figure in the musical world, and by a young daughter of fifteen. «To see her was to love her», and in the following weeks, under the inspiration of that first meeting, I wrote better verse than Robert Burns. Once the Atlantic was between us, however, she, like all of her kind, permitted me to fade into oblivion with unwarranted celerity, an experience which, I have to admit, was not the only one of its kind in my life. «In a brief space, or ere her shoes were old», she married her doctor, presumably not for his superior qualities, but for his title.

Her father disappeared at once after our arrival, only to reappear for dinner dressed in a more formal, harmonious gray. The conversation at the table, conducted chiefly by our host, resembled a dramatic recital which lent solemnity to an allusion to the weather, or to a request made of the waiting servant. When we went out into the garden I overheard his voice giving orders to his valet, to lay out another suit of clothes. Some words of Faust's servant, that I had heard on the Munich stage only a few days previously, came to mind:

«Pardon, I heard your voice declaiming,
No doubt it was some tragedy in Greek.»

Frau Possart was a quiet subdued gentlewoman, entirely resigned to consorting with an intermittent Demosthenes. I suffered a humiliation at her hands which I have not forgotten. Having learned that I had within the week attended a performance of Tannhäuser, Frau Possart led me without a preliminary warning to the piano; having taken her seat she played a brilliant passage and then turned to me with the question, «Was war das?» If I had been given a problem in differential calculus, I could not have looked more sheepish, especially when she explained that it was the opera's best known theme, «Dich, theure Halle», adding, «How can one forget a thing like that?» So I took my departure having left the impression that I was probably a tone-deaf American savage. Although I was invited again, owing perhaps to the daughter's intervention, I was never given another opportunity to erase that stigma.

Mother's health having been restored, she and my sisters arrived at Munich and we could plan the last weeks of our stay. I took the occasion to resume my protection over the women to whom the sights of Munich had to be revealed by one who knew. My skillful introduction consisted of chocolate with whipped cream and plum tart at the Hofgarten. I lead them through museums and picture galleries with a convincing display of knowledge, and repeated the words of wisdom which had only recently dropped from the lips of friendly hosts or guides. My remarks did not get a very attentive ear, and I became convinced that girls are quite incapable of the real critical approach to the arts.

The impressions of those early days are related wholly to an external Germany, and not until my university years was I able to absorb something of the real inner Germany, so worthy to be recalled and lifted above the chaos of subsequent times. Enjoyable gatherings at restaurants and in the spacious beer-gardens, to which German families carried the atmosphere of their own dining rooms, were repeated with new acquaintances and varying hosts. The record of plays, of concerts and outings mounted, and with them experiences to be digested only in the course of time.

After a tiring program of sight-seeing mother was eager for a few weeks of quiet; brother Will, who knew the Bavarian mountains at first hand, suggested as suitable resorts Reichenhall and Berchtesgaden, near the Austrian border, both spots unsurpassed in their natural beauty. The villages themselves were not yet infested with energetic tourists filled and running over with love of nature, to which they would give vent by equipping themselves long before breakfast with hob-nail boots, an alpenstock, and the inescapable feather in the hat. At the inns quiet visitors were still to be found, who had come to enjoy the salt and mineral baths and to view, from a distance, the rugged mountain scenery. Notably at Reichenhall you were enclosed as in a secret valley where picturesque walks reflected the undisturbed peace of the surroundings. The green bastion of the forests that lay all around was veiled by intermittent rain-storms passing over the valley; unexpected brief showers sent us home drenched, until we learned to sally forth only with raincoats and armed, each one, with a Regenschirm, that hefty German brand of umbrella which had its counterpart nowhere in the world for weight and durability.

At Reichenhall I had my first experience in mountain climbing when a small group of us walked to the top of the Zwiesel peak. The German system which prepares these undertakings is a serious business. Every outing is always pre-arranged and admirably planned, its stages coinciding with an adequate sprinkling of half-way houses; so we set out on a late afternoon, slept at a small inn below the summit, and reached the top with its moderate altitude of some six thousand feet in time to see the sun rise and take in a grand panorama of the famous Salzkammergut.

Our brief stay at Berchtesgaden brings back a jumble of memories from which I can still disentangle an amusing descensus averni into a colorful salt mine which ran far under the earth. We were ferried by some Charon across a salt-saturated lake for which rite miners' suits had to be donned, and you were given a lantern to carry, as if about to be initiated into some secret society. Berchtesgaden was set down by the Creator during one of His happiest moods in the neighborhood of the Königsee, a lake framed by a magical setting of colorful, sheer mountain slopes. In gliding over its surface in a rowboat you managed to scrutinize its concealed nooks and capricious inlets, and get a glimpse of the light that never was on sea or land.

An outstanding personality of those days was to me that of Professor Peter Vogel, one of the unaccountable friendships which my unscientific brother Will managed to make, I never saw how. Vogel was a geologist, a traveler and a teacher and, besides, infinitely well read. He carried his broad information, his vast and varied experiences in an unobtrusive knapsack, but managed to let fall the tidbits of what he had to tell during our walks and climbs. He convinced me in later years, when he had accepted me as fallow ground capable of being tilled, of the benefits to be derived from ranging over the earth, through widely different countries and among strange people. I attribute to my association with him in later university years the craving of travel which has never left me, and which I was able to satisfy, as a boon of fate, in varied and fruitful ways.

1891 coincided with the hundredth anniversary of the death of Mozart, in consequence of which we attended a commemorative celebration held at nearby Salzburg, the city of his birth. The programs presented his chief compositions. Obviously much of so great a privilege passed over my ignorant head, but I can date from those days devotion to Mozart's music. I spent the days in and about the Hohen-Salzburg, as the city's citadel-castle is called. It has a superb setting for medieval tales of war and romance, with its high walls, its natural defense, to say nothing of endless stairs hewn in the rock, dark passages and lofty balconies opening on distant prospects.

The fall was now approaching, and the homeward journey at last loomed in the offing. We returned to Munich for a last farewell, and to gather our multiplied bags with their miscellaneous booty. The others decided to precede me in order to enjoy another gratuitous visit with kinsmen, an ordeal at which I violently and successfully balked. So I was left behind for another week's reprieve, with orders to join the family at the port of sailing. My last week was piled high with many doings, bicycle rides to nearby village taverns, with meals of cold meats, beer and cheese, of roast goose and cucumber salad and other unexcelled aristocratic combinations. It was amazing to see with what ease the people of Munich could pass from Fidelio and great singers on one evening, to beer gardens with band music on the next. Later it was brought home to me that the completeness of that easy culture was an aspect of the real greatness of Germany in the nineties. In that happy fusion of cultivated ideas about music, art, drama, sausages, beer, and all the stimulating human associations lived one of the most favored nations of Europe.

I was urged to make a stop-over on my way north at Nürnberg, not to mention two or three other places with which kindly people always insist on overloading your itinerary. Having taken in the great medieval city, I suddenly became aware of a repleteness of sightseeing, too oppressive to admit a single additional cathedral or monument. I did what honor I could to the glories of Nürnberg, and left imbued with the absurdity of the tourist notion that one must always see everything within reach, on the chance of not living to see anything afterwards. Indeed an early death seemed more pleasing than the prospect of beholding another famous work of art. Several days of uninterrupted sleep proved a better alternative, and gave the overfed Strassburg goose a much needed respite.

At my harbor destination which I reached ahead of schedule I spent the hours leisurely looking at steamers and dock activities and wondering to what port the many ships would go. Over the return voyage fell the shadow of impending school routine and the recognition that my holidays were over. The contrast between the world of which I had been a part, and the atmosphere of a mid-western city to which we were returning could not fail to leave a sense of rapid descent. Back to the C major of life, we were now in a strange and much diminished home, far removed from the old suburb of Mount Auburn. The necessary re-adjustments started a ferment of comparisons and memories and gave me an inkling of finer values. Perhaps in those days I attempted for the first time an unconscious follow-up of interests and lived more frequently in a world created by the imagination. My last recorded sentence in the diary was a brief, «the old school again». It was, however, quite new in another sense. I began to associate much that I was to learn with what I had read and seen and knew. Routine school work turned into something that related my own experiences with the contents of books, with the stories of men, with the creations and achievements of the mind, making an integrated and connected pattern. I was becoming conscious of certain attractions, even entertainment in lessons and study.

YALE COLLEGE:
ALMOST AN EDUCATION

How shall we recapture a flock of undisciplined memories long ago flown away with all the winds, or reestablish their proper sequence, even if recalled? Life has the trick of taking us into seemingly inconsequential byways more frequently than over a steadily travelled highway, yet in their ceaseless interchange, the byways are often the poetry and the highway the prose. Of which road did college form a part? I only know it was a happy and meaningful experience, but its peculiar significance was merged in later years and became fused with my education as a whole.

What induces a boy to go to college? Certainly not always an innate urge to become civilized. Of my classmates, some had drifted into college; others had had a Yale tradition behind them in the guise of an older brother (which was my case); still others believed in the «Yale spirit,» and desired to become acquainted with the fellowship for which Yale was famous, and, incidentally, to experiment with her capacity of injecting a harmless culture into passive youth.

How far apart schemes of education may grow in practice is apparent from any comparison of the curriculum of fifty years ago with that of today. Yale entrance examinations at that period listed twenty divisions of «subjects,» of which thirteen comprised phases of the Greek and Latin languages, literatures and history; four were mathematics, and the remaining three were the modern languages: English, French and German. The «classical course» of the Cincinnati high schools had kept this goal in mind for the benefit of prospective college students, with the addition, as I had shown, of very sketchy elements of American and of English literature.

Having successfully hurdled the barrier of the entrance examinations on three beautiful crowded June days, I could prepare my knapsack the following September for a memorable adventure. Any résumé of myself as I was at that auspicious moment would have disclosed that my miscellaneous information on a dozen subjects was slight, though shot through with much eagerness to learn more; that my ignorance of what the new life would be like or how collective friendships on so extensive a basis would have to be established was monumental. Three hundred classmates at eighteen would approach the thousand aspects of college activities and friendships from three hundred distinct angles and with three hundred different capabilities. Of these the most profitable or advantageous would be an easy ability to meet strangers, of which I had a thin veneer; similarity in experience and tastes, in which I was likely to differ widely from the majority and a happy unconcern about the scholastic or educational benefits to be derived from a college career, regarding which benefits I had a lot of idealistic notions.

The impedimenta required for a propitious setting forth had been carefully assembled by a solicitous mother. Among the various articles which she deemed indispensable was an umbrella intended to shield me against the New Haven rains. These she knew fell at all hours and seasons. Since mothers are always right, it poured when I reached my destination; but the umbrella which had got into everybody's way on the train and had been trodden on by fellow passengers was a sorry sight with its bent and protruding ribs. There were no taxis in those days nor any street-car to convey me anywhere near the lodging that I had spoken for. So I seized my bag, and clutching my useless umbrella by the waist, I plodded up Meadow Street to the center of town in search of the address somewhere on Crown Street. It was certainly a dreary fall day, with a solitary, already homesick youth entering an utterly unknown world. Most freshmen find classmates from the same preparatory school; in my case, the three or four others from Cincinnati had attended different schools, and were complete strangers. Brother Ferd had, with certain misgivings, provided me with the address of some classmates, Philip Wells and Herbert Smith, who lived in New Haven. They proved to be friendly advisers, but I myself was a very casual recipient of advice, and with the usual freshman imperviousness made too little use of their wisdom or experience.

The door of my destination on Crown Street was opened by a gentle grey-haired lady who seemed to require a moment or two to regain her composure and get used to — I could not tell whether it was my aspect or merely my rain-soaked apparel. But her experience with the many strange animals who in the past had come to lodge under her roof stood her in good stead; she soon made me feel at home in the room put at my disposal. The motherly care of this kindly soul extended itself to playing the part of Cerberus with her freshman protégés, shielding them especially against the assaults of designing sophomores. She thus unconsciously may have changed, if not ruined, the career of some budding prodigies residing under her wing, whom rough handling by ruthless sophomores might have turned from the mice that they were on their arrival into the men that they might have become by the time they graduated. I only discovered later that the good hostess had on several occasions ejected sophomores who had planned to drag me forth for a proper initiation into the real ways of a college world. Her justification was the one current in those days, that hazing resorted to «brutal» methods to try the fortitude of the victim, even jeopardized his health, and thus stirred the wrath of the town.

New Haven was in the nineties a city in which genuine beauty of street or garden was to be found as a rule only to the north of the city Green, on Hillhouse and Whitney Avenue, and in the outlying countryside, where the picturesque wildness of East and West Rock constituted one of the chief attractions. To the south and east of the Green lay the business sections and certain districts ugly enough to deserve the name of slums. You had to cross them to get to the waterfront, beyond which spread the great face of the Sound and across the Sound the Long Island shore.

In its buildings and grass plots the old Yale campus was far behind many other colleges, both as to architectural and horticultural charm. With the exception of the historical brick row which incorporated what was left of the ancient college, the majority of the recently erected buildings surrounding the main quadrangle were first-rate atrocities. Many have since been pulled down to the great relief and benefit of the architects engaged to replace them with endless blocks of sumptuous structures; of the brick row only South Middle, rebaptized as Connecticut Hall, is left as a monument and as an example of Yale's commendable, now forgotten, simplicity.

The building that remains most clearly in the memory of Yale men of my time is Battell Chapel, to which we were bound to resort, by the inexorable law of compulsory attendance, every morning in the week. No one ever questioned its unqualified right to be called an architectural platitude; the thought of it recalls to me a picture postcard of Notre Dame of Paris which a classmate sent to Billy Phelps with the laconic greeting: «This has Battell Chapel lashed to the mast.»

This meeting house was my immediate objective when for the first time I fared forth in quest of the college ground. In compliance with the regulations covering enrollment, all freshmen had to convene in Battell and learn their particular assignments to courses and sections. The prescribed curriculum imposed not only limits upon our subjects of study, but also upon the range of the earliest friendships formed. In our first academic setup we were grouped into sections alphabetically, and the list beginning with Sawyer and ending with Strong, so often called aloud, still resounds in my ear. For a long time, in this way, my acquaintances were drawn from small class sections. My circle of friends might have been enlarged if I had made the effort to participate in some field of athletics, for which Yale had a great name. But I was never attracted by organized exercise, and my diffidence was opportunely encouraged by my preference for the detached world of books. So my course became one of questionable merit, pursued by such as are apt to achieve the name of grind and, as a result, miss the chance of more intimate friendships. But it is unlikely that a more active college life would have radically changed my inclinations or my career. A fatalist might argue that our choice is written in the stars, and the cynic reply that it is more likely to be dictated by the easy life afforded by a soft armchair. When for two score years you have had before you youth of varying caliber, on whose lives neither stars nor a soft armchair have exerted any perceptible influence, you may be pardoned for setting down more obvious conclusions. Competition discards, at the outset, the drifters who never make a choice, but are blown as wind along the waste. The attention of teachers, in the course of four college years, is therefore centered on students who are going places. The probable career of these is determined when they are freshmen through some inherent spark fanned by opportunity or by their new associations. The intensity with which the new fire burns is dependent on some innate urge born of a combination of causes, among which are the broad obvious ones of endowment, inheritance, and physical condition. There are also the unpredictable imponderables of personal peculiarities or social gifts. Among them may be aggressiveness or diffidence, mental curiosity or physical inertia, either a quick response, or none at all, to environment or to people.

The old Yale curriculum stirred the inner world of only a minority. Some of the subjects from which we were permitted to make a choice would seem today singularly remote and impractical. On our first afternoon I was assigned to sections in Latin, Greek, Mathematics, and English, and given the choice of French or German. To a freshman taking his seat at today's banquet table with its Smörgasbord of an unlimited choice among the natural sciences, the social sciences, the languages, philosophy, the fine arts, and other dishes designed for a supplementary dessert, the pitiful list presented to us must seem more like a remnant of medievalism than an education.

Today students rate Greek and Latin as languages deservedly dead. But even fifty years ago the tide was rising against the classics, and as soon as compulsory courses could be dropped for free electives, the study of Greek and Latin was discontinued by the majority of my classmates. Advocates of the classics were powerless to stem the hostile tide and for decades fought a losing fight to prevent the advent of our present «Greekless» culture. Very recently the stimulating, up-to-date English writer, J.B. Priestley, stepped forward to defend the «Greekless» multitude which had been contemptuously referred to «in the prosy work of an elderly Oxford don.» Priestley uses the specious argument that we don't expect people to write Chinese or understand Egyptian hieroglyphics, so why Ancient Greek? This analogy, everyone will admit, is plain silly. I wish Mr. Priestley could teach some of our not only Greekless, but Latinless classes. Not long ago, in a class of mine, we stumbled on a reference to «the chaste Lucretia,» and I ventured timidly to ask to whom the passage referred. A bright-eyed, knowing young woman raised an enthusiastic hand and with conviction replied: «Lucretia Borgia.» «Almighty God,» I said, or words to that effect, «you are the first to apply to Pope Alexander and his Borgia family the adjective in question.» Thus, Mr. Priestley, the student stood forth in all her educational dishabille, exposing herself on two counts instead of one: abysmal misinformation in the content of modern Roman history and unqualified ignorance of the ancient story.

What was it that drew the average undergrad away from the useless classics? It may have been parental pressure, or the opportunity of a practical career beckoning from some offices with desk and comfortable chair waiting to receive the latest B.A. It may have been the fact that the classics meant work without immediate profits, and college life was intended for an agreeable fellowship only, postponing for four years the obligations imposed by a practical career. What perplexed me was the fact that study and good fellowship should have been by many considered mutually exclusive. Because I enjoyed Greek and Latin, I automatically fell into a very small group, driven into itself and forced to accentuate certain qualities that were in general disfavor. The average undergraduate was as prone to extol the popular qualities of the jolly good fellow as he was merciless in his censure of the unpopular traits of inconspicuous, retiring classmates.

Anyone visiting by chance the rooms of the usual happy undergraduate, might have found there four or five spirits congenial to one another, drawn together by their common dread of being left alone with nothing to do. As subjects of conversation, the favorite college activities alternated with an awed analysis of a budding popular leader of the freshman class, with equally awed discussions of the occult brotherhoods. At such moments, anyone who was not among the chosen was soon left in the dark. These stretches of unoccupied time and the generous means to buy entertainment enjoyed by many men, also caused a logical cleavage. When I saw my classmates lying on window seats with a kind of scheduled regularity, looking forward to the next opportunity of lying on window seats, I felt justified in the belief that there was such a thing as the quiescent mind. I do not mean to imply that I reasoned about my classmates in any such critical or snobbish manner forty years ago; the snobbery is a later product. But such experiences as I had in the first months served to increase my inherent unadaptability to being «sociable» on a large scale.

College days thus constituted an effective kind of habit-forming routine, in which many careers were determined by taking the line of least resistance. Those happy years, so free from compulsion, certainly afforded an opportunity of becoming aware of the significance of will power and its uses. Pasteur proclaimed as the chief actuating force of a useful life «the will to work», which once in momentum can lead wherever the individual desires. Nevertheless, in so easy-going and secure a life as ours, it was natural and pardonable that some men should develop a genuine scepticism about the pleasure to be found in hard work.

The freshman teacher whom I remember as the most alive was Billy Phelps. He first made us appreciate Shakespeare and understand the qualities of great English prose. He made difficult subjects seem simple, and it is eternally to his credit that he succeeded by his plain, enthusiastic presentations in getting more reading out of students of average ability than any other teacher. It has always seemed unfortunate that during our first years, when the study of the classics was already on the wane, we should have had no opportunity of enjoying the guidance of Yale's foremost classical scholars. I was assigned to two mild, badly frightened teachers who, by their mechanical methods, proclaimed three times a week that the subjects which they taught were indeed as dead as the traditional door-nail. In Greek, the teacher was a mild-spoken, elderly, pale, white-haired gentleman, irreverently known as «Corpsy,» who was obsessed by the apprehension that his questions would never be answered correctly. He held in mid-air a neat little marking book with his pencil on the name just called, at the same time looking apologetically at his victim over his glasses. To spare the student the impending symbol of a flunk, he would answer the question himself after the briefest pause. «What is the case of this noun?» he would ask, and then add, «It is the dative, isn't it?» Whereupon the boy addressed would boldly answer. «It's the dative,» and get a good mark. In Latin we fared little better, for our youthful teacher would have been wholly lost in the streets of ancient Rome. There was in our section a cultivated classmate, Spinello, who, having had superior Latin training in a Catholic school, felt quite at home in that antique speech. One day after class he unjustifiably accosted the teacher in Latin. Was the poor man's face red, as he resorted lamely to the vernacular for a reply!

A popular collection of books was that of The Linonian library. It was accessible to all and consisted of the best selections from fiction, criticism, history and travel. The books placed in alcoves were dimly lighted by a single Gothic window; the quiet of the place made you forget the proximity of a noisy world, and its musty past was evident from a mellow, unventilated library flavor, which soon made the inquisitive newcomer feel at home. The books could be taken from the shelf with your own hands, and even carried to your room. In the surrounding gallery were the best magazines and journals, the popularity of which was especially in evidence on rainy days. Then the atmosphere of the place became even more compact and scholastic with the vapor rising from raincoats and dripping umbrellas. Those privileges were comparatively modest, but they served as an introduction for anyone who cared to learn the uses of the main library.

The outskirts of New Haven invited us to explorations of all kinds. The use of our legs was not yet limited to working the throttle or foot-brake of an automobile. We could make the acquaintance of picturesque spots for miles around, with their colorful beauty of autumn foliage, or their many heralds of a New England spring. In the first weeks I met Albert Keller, whose similar taste in studies and out-of-door exercise frequently brought us together. He possessed a bicycle and persuaded me to purchase a second-hand one; it must have been third or fourth hand, for one tire was perennially deflated. It also had the low-hung handle-bars of a racer, bent like a ram's horns. So that I might view more than the ground while pedalling, I turned the handles up like a bull's horns, and was in consequence almost disembowelled in the course of numerous spills. We rode leisurely over the countryside and spent many hours in shady spots discussing the past, present or future of our little world. We loafed entire mornings about the country estate of «Edgewood,» belonging to «I.K.G. Marvel.» This pen name of Donald G. Mitchell has grown dim among American writers, but his «Reveries of a Bachelor,» whimsical musings on man and nature, are symbolic of the difference between the undisturbed beauty of gardens and flowering hillsides in his time, and the improbability of being able to cross any country road today without being killed by a speeding car. Our walks through the rural village of Westwood, and the scrubby groves covering West Rock, still afforded a sense of undisturbed security and sylvan beauty.

Keller's and my favorite sport was tennis. We found an available court in the suburbs, scorned by excellent players, but good enough for us; our ancient tennis balls had long forfeited their resiliency and developed all kinds of erratic bounces. A trivial detail for some time put a damper on our game. The yard next to the court was ruled over by a bull terrier with a singularly unfriendly disposition. Since the intervening fence was not more than six feet high, well intended strokes frequently drove the ball into the brute's domain, and successful retrieving became a matter of strategy. The seats of our trousers were invitingly turned towards him every time that we leaped back to safety. But like many an enemy, he could be circumvented, and we soon learned that he would chase any object that we threw or pretended to throw. In the brief moment during which he had turned his back, we were on top of the fence, only an inch removed from his inevitable leap.

We took in the skating on Lake Whitney, which was not too far to be reached on foot if the unpredictable trolley was not available; or the boating and swimming in the Sound at Savin Rock or Morris Cove, notably in the fall, when warm summer days still left their trace in the waters near shore. During the indoor season of the winter months, I took up fencing and the useless gymnastics characteristic of the period. I lifted dumb-bells rhythmically and swung Indian clubs in monotonous circles. The director and medical examiner at the gymnasium was J.D. Seaver, called with typical undergraduate subtlety Gay Deceiver; he was a sedate personage with a sepulchral voice issuing from behind a patriarchal, most unbecoming beard. This lengthy excrescence tickled horribly while he went through the monotonous routine of listening to our insides and calling out our measurements to a recording assistant. He used only the human ear as a stethescope, which he squeezed unnecessarily tight against our naked form; one of my classmates remarked once after the operation, «Geez, how I hate to have his beard tickle down by bare belly.» The fencing was in charge of the most excitable Frenchman who ever wielded a foil, and he disarmed us as quickly by the flow of his imprecations over our awkwardness, as he did with an unexpected thrust. The art did not become popular and was pursued only by three or four classmates.

Favorite haunts of the overworked undergraduate were Poli's Theater and the Grand, homes of melodrama, variety shows and one-man performances. Among the latter, I remember hypnotists and sleight-of-hand magicians such as the «Great Hermann,» who could flick playing cards into the farthest gallery and pull anything out of his coat from a duck to a bowl of fish. He wore a flaming red cutaway, black knee-breeches, and with his pointed mustache and Van Dyke beard looked the true diabolical magician. Some of the melodramas, which we always patronized in large numbers, turned into incipient riots. It had become a tradition to hiss the villain and to applaud the stainless hero and heroine. Our untimely hisses and applause were resented by town boys engrossed in the plot, and the resulting set-to sometimes required the intervention of the police. The Puritan rectitude of the New England society which surrounded us gave vent to vigorous expressions of condemnation. A commentary made by a shocked New Haven matron, publicized in the newspapers, was to the effect that «as freshmen we first came to her home radiant in our innocence, as sophomores we appeared with pipes in our mouths, as juniors we didn't appear at all, and thereafter we went straight down to hell.»

The arrival of the famous hatchet-thrower and saloon-smasher, Carrie Nation, was an occasion for gay intrigues in which she was the guest of honor, although quite ignorant of the true nature of our hospitality. Carrie was the homeliest little frump that ever came out of the West. She was dumpy with broad hips and always on the go. She wore glasses on a ludicrously small pug nose. In every public appearance, even when walking along the street, she would stage a defiant attitude, swinging the hatchet which was the symbol of her way of life. She dragged it about as other women did their handbags. She would glare and shout at the crowds of heckling listeners in a shrill voice, and no police authority ever succeeded in intimidating her fanatical courage.

Carrie was received at Yale, which she publicly had denounced as «a hell-hole in need of reform,» by a carefully instructed delegation. We demonstrated the sincerity of our teetotalism by having a photograph taken with Carrie seated in the midst of some twenty students, each holding a glass of water. The negative, however, was retouched, converting every glass into a foaming beverage. Some of the group, while they were being taken, simulated various stages of intoxication behind her back, and the developed photograph would have been a fatal shock to that soldier of Prohibition, if she had ever seen it. The picture was displayed only in the greatest secrecy, and it was rumored that a New York newspaper which had got wind of it offered a large sum for the negative.

Concerts and plays were given at the Hyperion, the only theater of good standing and the only available auditorium of considerable size. I have forgotten most of the plays, with the exception of Oscar Wilde's «Lady Windermere's Fan,» and Shaw's «Arms and the Man,» with the versatile Mansfield as Napoleon. The noted comedian, Joseph Jefferson, gave us his outstanding roles of Bob Acres in «The Rivals,» and of his much-loved Rip Van Winkle. We also had the advantage of seeing many new plays, which prior to their appearance on Broadway were brought to New Haven for a trial night, the reception accorded them in the college town being considered a barometer of their fate in New York.

On the whole, we led a tame-cat existence. I can record no stormy or dramatic doings comparable with what I have experienced since in the battles of temperamental French or Spanish students, who often went so far as to upset their nation's political apple cart. New Haven was still a hopelessly quiet town, which fact alone made the midnight disturbance of a solitary drunk or two a conspicuous occurance far above its intrinsic significance. In fact, we secretly counted on the good will of an understanding Irish chief-of-police inclined to wink at our conception of academic freedom. His discussions «touching on and appertaining to the benefits of alcohol» were spiced with digs at the local descendants of the Pilgrim Fathers, whom he scoffingly called Puritans, and the Puritans, he added, «is like potatoes, the best part of them is under the ground.»

Some of our customary observances have long been abolished or forgotten, but they awaken pleasant memories in old-timers. I have mentioned compulsory morning chapel, called promptly at eight-ten according to the bell, but never promptly heeded by the students, for there was a mighty inrush to the seats for several moments after the appointed hour. Whether you received a tardy mark or not depended on the extent to which the appointed monitor would stretch his conscience. This chronic tardiness led a classmate to remark that he did not mind having morning chapel before or after breakfast, but that it was objectionable to have it come in the middle of it. The seniors occupied the center isle, and when President Dwight descended from the pulpit, and, in compliance with an ancient custom, walked out between them, each senior, after bowing to the President, fell in behind his bent and dignified form. The falling in was often like a football scrimmage about to carry the President off his feet, and only by miracle stopped short of his person by half an inch. President Dwight never varied his pace or changed expression to indicate awareness of the perilous rush at his back.

Is the sophomore fence still in existence, and is it still handed over to outgoing freshmen in a ritual of witty oratory and amusing vilification of the worthless members of the lower class? Alumni Hall, an unattractive brownstone building with wooden crennel-work giving it a fake Gothic touch, happily survives only in old photographs. Our examinations were held in it, and the alumni gathered in its main hall during graduation week. The tables and chairs were as time-worn as the building, and when it was torn down my classmate Herbert Gregory, luckily on the ground as a faculty member, secured for me one of the ancient hexagonal tables. Its top is scarred with scores of initials and dates going back into the sixties, and its rickety form may become an heirloom. In connection with Alumni Hall, I recall an episode from the last week of President Dwight's incumbency. He and President-elect Hadley were coming out of the hall after addressing a large gathering of alumni. It was raining and both presidents carried umbrellas; when Mr. Hadley opened his first to shelter President Dwight, the latter, whose ready wit was a byword, refused the proffered courtesy and opened his own with the words, «This is still my reign.»

Half-hour talks by President Dwight, given once a week, were a privilege which we enjoyed as seniors. I recall one of his themes, which dealt with the choice of books. He advocated that we read some worthwhile author every day, if only for ten minutes; this, if kept up religiously, would, in a few years, let us accumulate a wide acquaintance with many significant works. On another occasion he spoke of friendship and of the choice of such associates as might represent an improvement on ourselves, or again of such pleasant platitudes as the superiority of solitude over idle comradeship. He illustrated his point by recalling a certain farmer's habit of talking to himself; when asked the reason, the farmer replied that he had two, first, he liked to talk to an intelligent man and, second, he liked to hear an intelligent man talk.

Recollections of individual courses pursued during four years form the high light of a general picture. Out of the extensive list of teachers who dominated the scene, many become visible again with the living presence of that long ago. There were some rarae aves among them whose remoteness we could never bridge; others showed a more friendly and approachable disposition. Some of the very great appeared only on the fringes of the undergraduate world. They passed now and then like comets across the campus sky, but in our crass ignorance we saw nothing particularly remarkable. There was the very famous Willard Gibbs, who lived only in a dimension where mathematics and metaphysics clasped hands, where only a few initiated could ever follow and understand him. He appeared unobtrusively on the campus, a tall, slender man, dressed in a longish Prince Albert coat, a cropped beard with lifted chin raised, perhaps, in unconscious pursuit of a significant calculation. He walked leisurely with his hands clasped behind him. If addressed unexpectedly, he dropped from the clouds, and having spoken in a rather high-pitched, muffled voice, he quietly resumed his wanderings among symbols and signs.

A relative of the great Willard Gibbs was Yale's noted librarian, Addison Van Name. He was one of the last of a great race, selected to preside over collections of books because they knew what was inside of every one of them, and just where it could be found in the stacks. After his time came the librarian-administrator, who heads the organization of the library and, with the help of many others, controls the acquisition of more books. Like any practical head, he now directs the activities of an army of employees, from the pages who fetch and carry the books, to the specialists who classify them or the infinitely patient attendant at the reference desk, who hands out to queer strangers bits of information never before sought by any man. Van Name was noted both as a scholar and recluse, hardly known to us undergraduates, for he rarely spoke to anyone unless addressed. None of us guessed who he was, but he could be seen wandering about the library with his glasses on the end of his nose, his mind on some acquisition to the stacks and, thereby, to his own stacks of knowledge. Through the open door of his office the casual passer-by could see in the very center a round table covered with a litter of papers several inches deep, resembling an explosion in a printer's shop; only the librarian's supernatural memory seconded by his intuition enabled him to distinguish the geological strata of that pile and select the particular paper he sought.

The professors whom I knew more intimately were connected with the fields of language, literature, and history. Among them were C.H. Smith, professor of American history, a gentle spirit who earned our genuine devotion; Jules Luquiens, in French literature, of French Swiss origin, a man of the widest culture and an inspiring teacher; Henry A. Beers in English, with a quiet wit, to whom many of us owed a lasting interest in English literature; Thomas Day Seymour, father of Yale's present head, who was on more intimate terms with Homer than he was with the lower classes. And there was Tracy Peck, who was held to be a reincarnation of some ancient Roman, for whom Latin held no secrets. In the courses on Cicero and Pliny he always spoke courteously of «Mrs. Cicero» and «Mrs. Pliny,» which seemed to indicate that he must have known them in a previous existence. There was the queerish triumvirate in philosophy, cacophonously named, like some business concern, Ladd, Duncan and Sneath. A noteworthy public appearance was that of Professor Arthur Wheeler, who year after year was induced by Phi Beta Kapa to give a lecture on Waterloo. His description of every phase of the battle and of the leaders was exceedingly detailed and graphic, and the mention of Waterloo in later years was less likely to bring up memories of Napoleon or Wellington, than of a packed hall and the dominating, white-haired, handsome figure of Arthur Wheeler. The man whom we all held in especially affectionate regard was Dean Henry P. Wright, who with unvarying wisdom counselled us and set us in a straight path. All of these teachers will recall to my contemporaries peculiar traits or amusing incidents, some of which I venture to set down.

Sadistic students always find an appropriate label for some physical peculiarity in their teachers. Professor Smith was better known as «One-lung» than as a scholar in history. His long, slim figure with its unathletic chest and the fact that he lectured in a weak, high, metallic voice, may have accounted for the pulmonary epithet. Moreover, an intermittent cough, accompanied by a loud, beneficial clearing of the throat, was apt to interrupt his even flow of words on the American Revolution. Indeed, he occasionally asked that the window be opened, for he was inclined to address us in his overcoat, standing almost motionless near the platform. One morning he happened to be speaking of a famous debate in the Senate between Webster and Hayne; he had reached a climax in his usual falsetto voice with the words: «After Hayne had spoken three days, and no one believed that his arguments could be refuted, Webster rose and in stentorian tones began: (cough and spit) 'Will someone please throw up a window.'»

Professor Seymour, familiarly known as Goat Seymour, had the habit of injecting an «ah» between his words, notably when he was speaking deliberately or carefully translating his Greek original. When on one occasion one of the class attempted a version which, though couched in noble English, failed to convey anything approximating the words on the page, Seymour looked at the misguided bluffer a while through the side of his glasses and then remarked slowly: «Would-ah-it not be more-ah-to the point-ah-to be accurate before-ah-you try to impress us with-ah-your elegance?»

It was a tradition among students to wait for the teacher at the door of the classroom until the stroke of the hour, and then, if he was nowhere in sight, to yell lustily and disperse. Professor Luquiens, a newcomer to the ways of Yale, was greatly mystified by such youthful manners. Having once been guilty of a moment's tardiness, but having caught a glimpse of the tail-enders of his intelligent class in flight, he politely remarked at the next meeting: «When I am a moment late, be seated just as if you were grown up, and do not run away like a herd of frightened asses.»

Henry Beers was a closet scholar, whose lot combined too large a family with too small an income to permit him to travel. Every summer, when friends left for Europe, he «watched,» he said, «their lessening sails with an aching heart.» He thus never could match his incomparable knowledge of English literature with foreign journeys. Beers read his lectures from irregular sheets of paper, economically covered on both sides. The sentences continued their course from the bottom of the page up and around the margins along which he would pursue the idea with near-sighted eyes, his nose only an inch from the paper. As the climax might be captured in some far corner, his remarks had to be closely followed by those who were awake. On one occasion he was speaking of Wordsworth's unbelievable Peter Bell: «There was nothing original in the introduction of an ass into literature, but Wordsworth was the first (here there was a delayed chase of the conclusion around the whole margin) to make of the ass a moral reformer.»

The liveliest courses in Latin were those of Professor Peck, who had a knack of lighting up ancient paths with a ray of humor by associating his travels over the Roman world with the pages before us. We were reading one of Horace's Satires, in which the poet entertainingly describes a visit at Benavento in the company of the Emperor. With a touch of the epicure, Horace speaks of a toothsome delicacy, some kind of thrush (or *tordo* in Italian) which an excited innkeeper desired to serve to his august company. «When I was last in Benavento,» Peck commented, tilting back in his chair and tapping his chin with his pincenez as was his wont when elucidating the text, «I asked the waiter to bring me the well-known tordo prepared in the customary local style. The waiter looked puzzled and answered that they didn't have any such bird. To which I replied: 'But you used to have them.'»

Many controversies arose over the courses in philosophy, the unpopularity of which was no secret, and it is probable that only a handful of students would ever have taken them if they had not been prescribed for the senior year. Professor Hadley at a faculty meeting put the situation in his usual concise manner. When the question arose, whether philosophy ought to be left to the choice of the students, he said, «Those courses which when made elective would not be taken, must be made compulsory.»

The names which have the firmest hold on the memory of all Yale men, both as personalities and as great teachers, are those of William Graham Sumner and Arthur Twining Hadley. Sumner was our leader in all political and social thought. In his courses he was always prompt and in his seat ahead of the class, which was always a large one. His appearance commanded immediate respect. As he leaned forward in his chair, the bald surface of his unusual, dome-like head gleamed above his deeply lined face and high forehead. He seldom smiled, the logic and profundity of his analysis enduring no light interruptions. His authority was unquestioned, at least by us, and many details of his philosophy have become incontrovertibly imbedded in American life. He laid the foundation on which his followers and disciples continued to base their principles of social science. Sumner was labeled by some as a laissez-faire philospher, being thereby enclosed within a narrow definition unjust to the immense scope of his outlook. He was opposed to the «quackery» of a protective tariff designed as the sole means to prosperity; he disapproved of government interference in business because such interference would be shaped by politics and not by scientific procedure. His abiding contribution may be sought in his principles of education, which are scattered through his writings, and are still today the ones most fitted for a democratic society. He was a devout hater of «shams,» a term that often appeared in our notes, and he brushed aside with scorn «social panaceas» and improvised reforms. In the development of his favorite subject, which he designated at times by the terrifying hybrid of «Societology,» he often injected the question, «what are the facts?» His famous work, *Folkways,* is an abiding example of his ceaseless search for the facts to which he gave his life.

Recollections of Arthur Twining Hadley, professor of political economy, are a felicitous mixture of skillful lecturing and comic incidents. He was reputed to have been the most precocious youth who ever graduated from Yale, and in some of the stories which he told about himself he seems to have admitted as much. He lectured to his classes in Osborne Hall from a high platform on which there were a blackboard, a table, a paper basket, and, on the side, an arm-chair. Either the basket, or the chair, always got into his way, no matter where it was. Owing to his disconcerting performances, it was better to keep your eyes on your notebook. To follow the speaker all over the stage would have distracted you from paying close attention to the clarity of his exposition. He was in motion even when sitting down, his arms and legs unconciously flailing about as they accompanied the processes of his active brain. His discussion of an economic theory was carefully balanced, and he frequently indulged in his favorite rhetorical device of dividing his statements with the gestures proper to the words «on the one hand; on the other.» In the act of making the chief point, he would stride forward in long steps and, when about to plunge into the pit, he would stop only a fraction of an inch from the edge of the platform. There he would fix his gaze on the chandelier in the middle of the ceiling, and pause a moment in silence, with his right elbow and fist moving up and down like a pump handle, before completing his idea. Sometimes he would cap his point with an apt story, witty insertions which he would multiply when he noticed that some members of the class were inclined to nod.

An immense number of anecdotes, true and apocryphal, became connected with Hadley's name, some of which were based on his own reminiscences told at banquets or alumni gatherings. Irreverent Yale grads, whose name is legion, included an imitation of Hadley among their parlor tricks, and as I was one of them, I venture to recall two stories with which long ago I made hay in the sunshine of friendly gatherings. The reader will have to imagine the indispensable addition of his peculiar, elaborate intonations and unrelated, uncoordinated gesticulations. «Once, as a boy,» he said, «I wanted to make some gun powder. I knew what other boys didn't, that it contained three ingredients, charcoal, sulphur, and saltpeter. I knew that I could make charcoal from willow-wood and get sulphur from ordinary parlor matches. But when it came to saltpeter, I was up a stump. So I went to my father and I said, 'Father, is there any saltpeter in the dining-room closet?' And my father answered, 'My son, I don't know.' So I went to my mother and I said, 'Mother, is there any saltpeter in the dining-room closet?' And my mother answered, 'My son, I don't know.' Now the difference between my father's reply and that of my mother was, that when my father said 'I don't know,' what he meant was, 'I don't know what's in the dining-room closet.' But when my mother said, 'I don't know,' what she meant was, 'I don't know what saltpeter is.'» Another yarn was told concerning his early childhood. He had been caught with two little playmates in the garden without a stitch of clothing. «'Arthur Twining,' said my mother, 'what does this mean?' And I am reported to have said, 'Little Mary Gardner is Eve and Tommy is Adam.' 'And, Arthur Twining, who may you be?' And

I am reported to have said, 'I am the Lord God, walking in the garden in the cool of the day.'»

These recollections of my teachers could be spun out, but time did not lag and the memorable years at Yale swiftly came to an end. No doubt the sum total of my college days had added up more on the side of study and of books, so that I may have missed a number of friendships and valuable experiences. This loss has seemed especially regrettable to people who have bothered about my character more than I have myself.

The week of graduation ceremonies arrived. They included an unscheduled dramatic moment. Every outgoing class planted on the campus with a certain amount of ceremony an ivy, to commemorate its year of graduation. We had procured a cutting for our class from the grave of General Robert E. Lee. On the occasion of the unveiling of a bronze statue of President Woolsey, the speaker, Reverend Joseph H. Twitchell, Fellow of the Yale Corporation, infelicitously indulged in a bit of bloody-shirt waving. Having been a soldier in the Civil War, he worked himself into a patriotic fervor over our act of treason to the North, and exclaimed before a large public: «It would make this bronze statue turn its head in shame, to see this ivy from the grave of Lee climb the loyal walls of Yale.» The newspaper took up the scandal, but apart from the anger aroused among Southerners, our class ignored the Reverend speaker's inept fling, and the Lee ivy continued to climb the loyal walls of Yale.

The merciless class historian who summarized the shining qualities of each one of us at the last informal gathering of the '96 clan, made it clear that my way of life had been a misguided one. How was he to explain otherwise my disinclination to mix more freely with the members of the most extraordinary class that ever graduated from Yale? He was right; but he gave insufficient credit to my misguided career, since I had achieved at least a small but select number of congenial intimates who have, as far as I know, managed to keep out of Wall Street and out of jail.

As the end of the senior year approached, I hoped that through some unforeseen dispensation I would be able to continue my studies abroad. I had accumulated a small sum, enough for a bed without food, or food without a bed. I was looking around for a supplementary job, when the All-seeing Eye must have picked me up with its infinite range-finder, for some such long-distance influence brought desired results. Brother Will heard about my pipe dreams — it could not have been directly from me — and invited me to come to Munich, where he had an unoccupied room in his flat. Thus my dream was fulfilled and the fall after graduation found me ready to sail.

LIFE AT GERMAN UNIVERSITIES: MUNICH

Five years had elapsed since I sailed from Holland in September 1891. In the same month of 1896 I again reached Europe. This time my port of arrival was Antwerp. I was to meet brother Will in Leipzig a fortnight later, leaving the interval for a leisurely ramble over Belgium and Holland. At Brussels I made the acquaintance of a young Englishman likewise engaged in that pleasantest type of travel, the casual itinerary. Like the «leader of the Queen's Navee,» «he might have been a Russian, a French, or Turk, or Prussian, but he was an Englishman.» His contagious *wanderlust* led me to tie up with him for a few days, which we spent walking over the battlefields of the last Napoleonic campaign. He had a map of Waterloo on which were carefully indicated all the essentials which a loyal Britisher was to observe, so that he knew, to a few feet, just where Wellington stood, and where Napoleon. When I recalled Professor Wheeler's lecture on that battle and ventured to intrude a remark about the significance of the Prussian attack on Napoleon's flank, he waved that significance aside, and proved to me by his map that the victory belonged only to the Iron Duke.

At the end of the summer I returned with my brother to Munich in time for the opening of the fall semester. The captivating qualities of the Bavarian capital have always impressed foreign visitors, who found there in those years a singularly many-sided social life; it was a life which attracted men from all over Europe, in the fields of science, letters and art.

The flat occupied by my brother was a spacious affair; it had a studio cluttered with paintings and studies finished and unfinished; the walls were hung with portraits, landscapes, copies of old masters; you stumbled over plaster busts, plaster feet, easels; bulky black closets were filled with costumes and draperies, books and scores of miscellaneous objects. This was a sanctum into which I ventured to go only when asked, or when I was certain not to interrupt sessions of models, or working hours. There were three bedrooms, Will's, my own, and one next to the kitchen occupied by a Bavarian couple who, in return for their living quarters, attended to all of my brother's immediate needs and kept the flat tidy. The presence of this efficient couple created Utopian conditions never again to be duplicated in any existence on this racked planet. The wife looked after the laundry, which included mending, and replacing lost buttons. The husband, by profession a cutter or patcher, a lowish rank of the tailor's career, could perform unparalleled miracles with old suits of clothes by turning their shining surfaces to the inside. His skill was worth trying; it would make me more presentable in society, and put off the inevitable day of a new suit of clothes. So I made the experiment, persuaded by the state of my purse, and by the arguments of this wonder-working tailor. The transformation was successful, not so much because of the fictitious newness of my garment, but because close scrutiny of my friends made me feel safe in the midst of others also manifestly clothed in reverse.

The only shadow which hung over our unquestioning faith in the pure gold of this Bavarian couple was the impure quality of the coffee they served us at breakfast. Will occasionally set his cup down with the expression of one who suspected a foul deed. Coffee in Germany was in those days reputed to contain, at least in the restaurants, an unrevealed high percentage of chicory or of some low adventitious bean. In consequence the servants had been given orders with proportionate funds to buy only guaranteed actual real genuine coffee. Any investigation of our quandary might have revealed a happy bit of graft in the kitchen, but the remedy would also have deprived us of an indispensable couple, unmatched in any household in the entire metropolis. I personally found a way out by switching over to chocolate, Will trying to solve his own difficulty by purchasing the coffee himself. But a tailor who could turn an old suit into a new one must have considered it no trick at all to turn chicory into coffee. So he continued his sleight of hand occasionally, with a little profit and a pleasant breakfast for himself and mate.

We had in the household only a portable bathtub, a contraption of shining zinc in no way inferior to the Sitzbad of great princes of the past still displayed in their unhygienic palaces. This made bathing a cumbersome ritual, to be gone through with in all kinds of temperature. Winter days in Munich can be the dampest and chilliest on earth, and the hypothetical source of heat in my roon on such days was a tall, square Dutch stove called *Kachelofen,* a gaunt white creature which glimmered like a ghost in the dark. The servant fed it briquettes for hours, and even so the temperature rose more slowly than a mild fever. The flies could warm their sticky little feet all over its surface, a privilege denied to me, since my shoes slid off the glazed surface of the stove unless I sat slumped on the middle of my back and close enough to keep my feet on the level of my head. Since too many briquettes were already consumed in the kitchen, in keeping two Bavarians comfortable, and in brewing coffee not meant for us, I gave up the unequal contest, wrapped myself in blankets on chilly days, or did all the work I could at the public library. There, at least, the reading room was warm, not only because of artificial heat, but also the bodily temperature of the thousands of readers who in the course of many years left their accumulated warmth behind in a room where it was a criminal offense to open a window.

To return to the two servants, they spoke German in an unmistakable Bavarian peasant dialect, and when you had learned to understand that speech no idiom on earth could give you a moment's pause. It was good schooling, for it enabled me to feel at home whenever the dialect was likely to be sprung on the listeners at the theater, on the streets, among the students, and even in the lecture room, where Bavarian born professors were in the majority.

In my senior year at Yale I had decided to continue the study of literature. In Germany a student was drawn to a definite university chiefly by the fame of the man in whose field he desired to pursue his studies. There were at Munich, Hermann Paul, the foremost authority on the history of language, Franz Muncker, a specialist in German literature, Wilhelm Hertz, the noted poet and medievalist, Karl Theodor Heigel in history, Berthold Riehl in the history of art, and Johann Schick, prominent in the English field. Paul was an unforgettable character, excessively short, with a closely trimmed, brown beard, a fringe of hair on a very round head, and thick glasses through which peered barely visible eyes. This frequently gave him a dazed expression and recalled the words of another professor who said that Paul never ventured abroad in the late afternoon, because he did not see very well after four o'clock. Paul's morning class was a small seminar, following one taught by a very tall man who always ran the lectern up to the top notch. This was an annoying state of affairs for Paul. When his short rotund form appeared on the platform at the exact hour, he was first obliged to readjust the desk to his diminutive height. This he did by stretching himself on tiptoe to reach the adjusting key, and letting the book-rest down with a bang to the bottom. He would then look victoriously over the top and proceed to set in order an armful of books which he always brought to the class.

Our subject was the Nibelungen epic, and the first thing that we learned was that all the known editions of the poem were defective and so could be discarded. This subtle beginning prepared us for the information that there was a sounder and more recent interpretation by the occupant of the platform. Paul was a tireless investigator and looked the part, so we expected to be treated to an encyclopedic amount of learning. His manner of speech was Prussian, precise, clear and unhurried, of that subdivision of the different German pronunciations which gives *st* at the beginning of a word the sound of *s-t* and not *sh-t*; his enunciation being in every respect far removed from that of his Bavarian colleagues.

Franz Muncker, in contrast, was tall and thin, his clothes were not the best fit, and his oversized collar loosely encircled a rather long neck which a short beard did not sufficiently hide. His lectures dealt with the eighteenth and nineteenth centuries and attracted several hundred listeners. He spoke with eloquence and ease, never referring to a note. His fluent address was interrupted only by the trampling of applauding feet whenever he reached an impressive point in his discourse. I had had my first experience with this manner of expressing approval at Freiburg, so it was not new; but now I could intelligently share in the demonstration. A peculiar detail of his speech was a difficulty, shared by others from Saxony, in distinguishing clearly initial B and P, or D and T. So he often spelled out names of importance which began with those consonants. For the sake of clarity he used the Greek alphabet, which he pronounced as *peta* and *telta,* leaving to your imagination the inference that the names in question began with B and D. Muncker always gave unstintingly of his time and earned the devotion of an army of students. He and his wife frequently entertained this army, on which occasions Frau Muncker would go to the piano and make a fine old grand rock with her technique for an hour. She was very short and exceedingly nearsighted. Whenever she played from the notes, her nose almost touched the score, gliding over the page with the same speed with which her hands flew over the keys. At these entertainments there were students from all parts of Germany; they represented every category of society, every dialect of the national idiom; there were men of means as well as those who welcomed the refreshments as a timely supplement to their customary frugal diet.

An unusual combination of the distinguished scholar and original writer was Wilhelm Hertz. He was first and foremost a poet. He came from Swabia (Stuttgart), the cradle of many German poets, a contingency which Hertz himself attributed to the climate and natural beauty of his Schwabenland. In class he reminded me of Professor

Beers of Yale, both in the manner and the matter of his lectures. As teacher of literature at the Institute of Technology and not at the University, he spoke to small compulsory classes interested only in scientific fields. The fact that I was actually a devotee in his field made me a rara avis on his branch of the academic tree. I profited by my rarity in having him quite to myself at his house, or in an occasional walk with him through the English Garden. He lived only a few years after my Munich days, a modest and retiring spirit, and the last greeting from him contained a moving expression of gratitude for the loyalty and friendliness which I had maintained in an indifferent world of scientists.

My program included a course in the history of Europe after the French Revolution, and another on the history of art. The first was taught by the most jovial of the faculty members, Karl Theodor Heigel, a tall, powerful figure, reduced just enough in frame to make a refined kind of Falstaff, if you substituted beer for sack. As a son of Munich and a Bavarian in every fiber, he was worthy of his birthplace, not only because of his partiality to its noted beverage, but also because of his share in its intellectual achievement. He displayed his convivial character by occasionally attending our *Verein,* a students' club at which we spent one night a week in song, impromptu speeches, and concerted drinking-bouts. Heigel spoke his native Bavarian at all times. If I had not had practical experience with that dialect in conversing with my brother's servants, I would have been unequal to the rich and comfortable flow of his language. When the spirit of our meetings had become sufficiently injudicious, I would give an imitation of Heigel's dramatic lectures on the fate of Danton or Robespierre. In his sonorous Bavarian dialect, which became more pronounced at such moments, an eloquent phrase of Mirabeau acquired a local color not calculated in its French original. Our distinguished Bavarian was knighted during one of our terms, and a thunderous applause welcomed him at his following appearance on the rostrum.

The professor of the history of art, Berthold Riehl, apparently had no slides to illustrate his lectures, so he brought a huge bunch of photographs to his classes. The attendance was fairly large and only those in the front rows could get a glimpse of the pictures as he held them up to us. At first glance he passed them around, but desisted from the practice very soon, having possibly observed that some never returned from their intended circuit. In a city crowded with artists, he was bound to be looked upon as a mere «critic» who could not paint, at least not much. B. Riehl was the son of a well known historian and novelist, W.H. Riehl, whose short stories were once upon a time used as texts in our American schools before their dullness was discovered. So it came to pass that gossip spoke of the older and younger Riehl as Father and Son, malice adding the Holy Spirit was lacking. I was grateful to Riehl's course, nevertheless, for directing my attention to famous paintings, and to him personally for giving me hints of what would be required in my finals. I also seized more eagerly on the opportunities offered to wander among easels in the studies of Will's friends, to smell the paint of fresh canvasses and witness with my own eyes the evolution of pictures exhibited later at the Glass Palace.

In the limited time given me to get my degree, not all of the courses could be new and intensive work. So a cinch course in a familiar English field, offered by Johann Schick, came in pat. Schick was a brilliant speaker and passed with ease from German to English, but not without that occasional slip which gets the best of men down. When on one occasion he had pronounced *mead* as *med*, mislead by meadow, he caught himself and used the occasion to demonstrate the cussedness of a speech in which the spelling is no clue whatever to the pronunciation. As regards initial *th*, even Schick, who had mastered single occurrences of *this* or *then,* floundered when suddenly confronted with a long string of *th*'s, such as «though the truth had been thoroughly threshed out»; there he succumbed and relapsed into *zo* and *ze*, as Germans generally do. He was too well versed in English ever to miss out on the pronunciation of *though, enough, cough, plough,* etc., but a classmate of mine was completely sunk, when he attempted to read about a farmer «pluffing wiz his pluff.»

There was a timeless atmosphere in our heremtically sealed lecture halls. You had the privilege of living on the very air breathed in and out by previous generations. Owing to the inclement winters of Munich and to the German's proverbial terror when he suspects the presence of a draft, the window-frames throughout the university were thickly padded at the first sign of fall. The only oxygen admitted thereafter into that deep and dense atmosphere of accumulated learning was perforce through the occasional opening of a door. When this process went on too frequently, as at the beginning of a lecture, cries arose: «Es zieht!» (there's a draft). This lasted until Spring came over the land. Even then the students sniffed the fresh air with suspicion, as it was sure to be germ-laden and subversive of the healthy odors in which they felt at home. This peculiar traditional atmospheric pressure in educational halls has remained an unstudied influence on the sweetness and light in German thought and style.

The richest source of a free education was the accessibility of dozens of daily papers and illustrated magazines in the restaurants and beer-halls. All over Munich good eating and mental pabulum were thus dispensed in a happy alliance. What could be more profitable all around than serving standard dishes and the most recent news together? Any resident of Munich, with his inborn leaning to sausage or a cold plate, potato salad, Vienna Schnitzel, plus a full stein, could unhesitatingly enter any eating-house and find more than his heart's desire. The first thing he did was to peruse the bill of fare, then, having satisfied his immediate bodily needs, he made straight for any one of a dozen newspapers suspended on the wall. If he got there a little early, he might even bag two or three at once, and so assure himself of the latest news contained not only in Munich papers, but in those of Berlin, Leipzig, and the other chief cities. Thrifty Germans, for whom it was more economical to eat in restaurants, seldom subscribed to a paper; they were nevertheless well informed because of this singularly efficient process of making news available to everyone gratis, over a glass of beer. If the beer had been gratis, what an intellectual paradise it would have been!

The eminent character of German newspapers before the first World War deserves a brief word in any record of the times. Their size generally ranged from four to eight sheets, strictly limiting the editor to essentials, and giving a broad similarity to the appearance of all the foremost dailies. The front page contained the latest dispatches, all the news of a general interest, together with a scholarly article on some current question. Editorials of a political color were to be found in the important party organs. Berlin, Munich, Frankfurt and Leipzig published some of the most distinguished and influential dailies. On account of the restricted size of the papers, the reader could quickly get the gist of current events; there were seldom any reports of scandals or murders, and no comics. The report of a crime was in all of the respectable sheets relegated to the back; it was succinct and without a sensational note. I often heard severe criticism of our own papers, the excesses and the license of which would have been condemned in Germany by the public itself. Expressions of good or bad taste did not seem to Germans to be a matter of freedom of the press, but of national culture.

These dailies made pretty serious reading and you would rarely have discovered any humor, intentionally funny. For political jokes or jibes you went to *Kladderadatsch,* and when you saw a native looking harmlessly amused over his beer, he was reading the *Fliegende Blätter.* These sheets enjoyed freedom of expression; if the Kaiser's person was quite generally respected within the statutes on lèse majesté, outside of them neither he nor anyone high in authority escaped the thrusts of adverse opinion where serious national or international questions were concerned.

How pleasant the *Gemüthlichkeit* or cosy, easy-going life of that vanished Munich world was may be inferred from this unexciting record. Unhurried living was the keynote of those who moved within the various artistic, literary or scientific professions. Their members foregathered in groups at regularly reserved tables in restaurants, or in halls which offered all the facilities of eating and drinking also; this sine-qua-non in itself justified any kind of meeting. Munich's reputation of being the chief art center of Europe was reflected in the impressive Künstlerhaus, or artists' club, a hearth at which the leading figures of Munich came together; Lenbach, Stuck, the younger Kaulbach, Marr passed daily through its doors. The yearly exposition of paintings and of sculpture at the Glass Palace displayed the significant results of their work, and no other city afforded the public such opportunities of becoming acquainted with the peculiar state of the fine arts in that decade.

What the artists thought of one another's work was a horse of another color, and I got an inkling of these cross currents at informal meetings in the low-vaulted cellar of a beer hall, attended by brother Will's personal cronies. I was all ears, and what I heard about contemporary painters and paintings when these foregathered pals unburdened their souls on art in general and on certain artists in particular was an earful. Discounting bits of malice, there were good talks not only about individuals, but also on styles and techniques of the time. All this helped to get me away from Riehl's academic approach, to a more genuine appreciation of the older masters. When I saw a man in an exhibition suddenly go up to a painting as if about to smell it, I now inferred that the proximity of his nose to the canvas only meant that he was studying the painter's brush-strokes and other subtleties of technique. This I also learned to do in a less professional, olfactory manner.

Attracted by the obvious compatibility of plain food and drink with higher converse, in other words, pleasant confabs, a lower group of my personal friends likewise drew sustenance from the above compatibility. In keeping with an old university custom entirely commendable and therefore worthy of being reintroduced today, four or five of us met at about eleven in the morning, to partake of the traditional *Frühschoppen,* a diminutive glass of beer, served with *Weisswürstel,* a small white sausage, toothsome and satisfying since it supplemented the deficiencies of a meager breakfast consisting of the usual coffee and a roll. Butter was at all times an expensive luxury, which we eschewed as did all thrifty natives. These brief relaxations were known as *Ausspannung,* unhitching, a subterfuge for an hour's loafing. Under this starvation regime, we had luncheon at two, coffee with coffee-cake at five, dinner at eight, topping the day with a last tasty morsel at midnight, after a show.

The cost of our inserted repasts was incredibly low, as well all restaurant prices at the time. It has been frequently stated since the age of Tacitus' *Germania* that the Germans have always been given to gormandizing. That historian alone does not suffice to make the accusation historically sound, and as a generalization it is misleading. If you added up the various consumptions of each day, beginning with breakfast at an ungodly hour, the sum total was probably not as monstrous in quantity as in calories. The Germans looked well fed, but their avoirdupois was due more to the inflating effect of the divine Munich nectar than to excesses of worldly ambrosia. Besides, afternoon coffee and cake in some open spot like the shady Hofgarten was a social occasion for whole families. They could meet their friends at the same time. On the other hand, well-to-do families enjoyed the privilege of inviting guests to their table at home. This social superiority derived from an economic advantage which permitted the employment of various servants. At such dinners it became clear that even the ice-chest had not yet been invented and that, as a result, no household ever kept bottled beer. When this drink was preferred to wine, a servant would be dispatched to fetch it sparkling and cool from a near-by restaurant. By this generous and delicate touch, perfect hospitality was assured.

In my early Cincinnati days, my father had insisted that I attend a gymnasium in which the class was taught by a muscular German gentleman called a Turnmeister, as graceful as a ramrod, whose native slogan with all his classes was «chest out, belly in.» Our resulting posture was a caution. He may have toned up some flabby muscles, but he made me acquire a lifelong distaste for Indian clubs and dumbbells. German youth was of the gymnasium type, not yet having turned collectively to athletics, as it did in later decades. Those who felt the need of exercise took to the Alpenstock and toiled through forests or up the high mountains, lugging a bulging Rucksack, and lifting their heavy hobnail boots against gravity only to view the landscape through powerful binoculars. Thus they were able to bring back tales of hiking achievements that filled the assembled family with speechless admiration. My lack of enthusiasm for such excessive exercise made me wait until the Munich rains had let up sufficiently to permit early morning outings on my bicycle. I rode forth generally with some friends to get the bracing air of nearby fields and woods, and we ordered our coffee and a roll anywhere under the open sky.

In town the air was always full of Kunst and Kultur. Student cards furnished by the university included the special privilege of a reduced admission price to concerts, opera and theater. This often meant that we could get only a *Stehplatz,* standing room, but we were spending only fifty pfennigs, or a mark, to witness a classic masterpiece of the theater, or to hear a concert or an opera sung by the finest voices in Germany.

Through friends of Brother Will, I met Paul Heyse, the novelist and poet; he had settled down in Munich after having been a much traveled citizen of the world. He lived in a rambling house on Luisenstrasse, surrounded by an extensive garden, across the street from the studio of the painter Lenbach, and a stone's throw from the Königsplatz, a classic square of stately buildings which simulated Athens or Rome. Heyse kept open house every Sunday afternoon, and on fair days the assembled guests were seated in the garden, or chatted in groups under the trees. A novel and very engrossing feature of these gatherings for me was their manner of dress, which represented the fashions of many decades and nationalities. There was the old tradition to be lived up to that Sunday clothes were of a choicer vintage than those worn on weekdays. So from the depths of a closet the regulation garment was brought to the light. Men and women alike appeared in disparate styles, ranging from museum pieces to recently imported fashions; the prevalent outfit suggested strictly home talent. Any peculiar taste would remain inconspicuous to the assemblage as long as it did not exceed the actual deadline of the outmoded or outworn. This seemed to be about thirty years back. As for the men, their solid boots and stovepipe pantaloons bagging at the knees were visible under noble cutaways or Prince Alberts. This display proved irrefutably that styles need never change if a specific suit of clothes can only be made tough enough to resist the wear of three or four decades.

The personality of Paul Heyse dominated these social gatherings. In spite of his seventy years, he still retained the vigor and impressive posture of a tall, robust frame with a fine head covered by a shock of greyish hair. He had a round face with large, prominent eyes, which he fixed without blinking on the person to whom he was speaking, as though he were looking through him. This would have been disquieting, had it not been for his placid, gracious manner. One day Heyse mentioned to me one of his hobbies which he had pursued for years. It consisted in sketching some of his friends. When he asked me if I could find the time to come and sit for him, I mastered my embarrassment and did so on several mornings. The time was divided between sketching a little and talking much, and during the occasional hours spent in his study or in the garden I had a glimpse of the wealth of interests that may be accumulated by a man of creative power when it is stimulated by wide travel and privileged associations. His father had been a teacher in the household of the distinguished Wilhelm von Humboldt and later became professor in Berlin. Heyse himself had attended the University of Bonn, where his chief studies had been the literature of France, Italy and Spain. Some of our familiar talks, during which he spoke at length of writers of those countries, were of a deciding influence on my determination to specialize in those same literatures. I heard for the first time some illuminating opinions on the writers of Spain, of whose works I had up to that time not read a single line in the original. Heyse mentioned his continuous reading of Cervantes and Calderón, and he spoke with enthusiasm about Spain's great ballad poetry. Of the latter he and the poet Geibel had published an anthology of select translations into German, still among the best of their kind. He spoke intimately of a noted scholar, Adolph Friedrich von Schack, who had been his neighbor in Munich for many years. Long afterwards, when I had become well acquainted with Schack's history of the Spanish drama, I recalled the profitable hours spent in Heyse's study. Thus you can never foresee where small tributary streams may swell the main current of your ulimate career.

I had frequently sat for my brother when he needed a victim to substitute for the real figure, or to supply a particular posture of the human body for a painting. I had concluded that immobility and silence were the prerequisites of all such sittings. Heyse made no such demands. The strokes of his crayon were always accompanied by questions and commentaries which kept our talk going. He asked what I was reading and enlarged his query with suggestions of related books. He spoke of his intimate friend, Jacob Burckhardt, and his works on the Renaissance; he told me of the History of Rome by Gregorovius, a writer who had also been a resident of Munich and so became a living personality. Above all, our talks taught me how great an interest may attach to recorded humanity, booked and bottled humanity of every vintage which can be brought out of its ancient cellarage with all its fragrance unimpaired.

The popularity of this aged idealist was presently to fall on more critical times with their rapidly changing taste. The art of the novel as Heyse conceived it gradually became converted to the new aesthetic of naturalism, with which he had little patience. The course pointed by French novelists, even the milder realism of Sudermann, was anathema to Heyse, who continued to the end of his days to uphold the principle of classical beauty, which meant to him also whatever things were decent and of good report. He was, after all, a German Victorian, and would have applauded the aged Tennyson's bitter protest against «wallowing in the troughs of Zolaism.»

«The world is changing fast,» he said to me during one of our last meetings, «and soon I shall be treated as scrap-iron.» When I arose to leave, I put my hand inquiringly on a massive high desk near a window. He explained, «That is my favorite place, where I can write standing up. It is a pleasant change from sitting too comfortably in a chair. I can stretch my legs, and in a less cramped position my ideas flow with greater ease, and I tire much less quickly.» I later copied the idea and had for many years a high desk in my library. Most of my reading for pleasure, or a large part of it, has, however, been done in a reclining position, as befits pleasant self-indulgence. I heartily recommend it, but it is up to the gentle reader either to remain alert or to fall asleep. This habit has forced me to curse heavy tomes, and I hope that some day a reading civilization will arise which shall sentence to hard labor all printers of howitzer-like volumes. Then we shall have only delightful small volumes, readily slipped into a side pocket, to be taken along on every occasion, and read on trains or boats or walks or, best of all, lying down. In a world of distasteful duties, it should always be easy to get at a readable book.

The picture which I have given of Munich life would not be complete without the inclusion of a genuine American scene maintained in the midst of its German surrounding. A warmly hospitable home already mentioned in an earlier chapter was that of the Peck family from San Francisco. A large number of friends, chiefly compatriots, continued to gather there as of old. Orrin Peck, his mother and his sister Janet were generous hosts who entertained friends of every nationality, although English was the chief language spoken. As guests of every profession were welcome regardless of race or color, I recall an occasion when there appeared two negresses, who were both singers. They had performed at a variety show and being hopelessly stranded in a foreign city, they were promptly invited by Orrin Peck to their home. This hospitable act occasioned no astonishment in cosmopolitan Munich. The negresses were mother and daughter, both filled with much ready talk, and as puzzled over German ways as if they had dropped on the moon. Their manner of dress was something more than colorful, as was their speech. When fresh youngsters on the street stopped in front of them and said, «Grüss Gott, Schwartze Dame» (Good day, black lady), they took it as a tribute to their celebrity. «But why,» said the mother, «do dey all speak German? I heerd de chillen talk, and it's a pity to make'em talk German when dey would talk English, if you only lot 'em alone. I heard one boy say to another 'Komm her' just as natchl, and den dey go to work and make 'em speak German.»

The winter was now slowly vanishing. In the English Garden, the earliest green leaves were awakening on the bushes and trees. My brother asked, what I was planning to do during the Easter holidays? «You will have some six or seven weeks of vacation. Would you like to run down into Italy and take in an Italian spring? I have just sold a picture, and you know you don't have to stop at the Palace hotels.» This may have sounded like a non-sequitur, but it was a compact way of indicating an unexpected source of revenue and the best way of keeping within it. It was the realization of a hope that I had not envisaged. While planning to start out by myself, the undertaking was made more feasible and pleasant by the arrival of an old Yale friend. Edward B. Reed. He had no fixed itinerary, so we could plan a journey together for the greater part of our Italian visit. We decided to get away the latter part of March, in the happy year of our Lord, 1897. The semester was drawing to a close, the unacademic talk in the halls turned on early visits to the home town. The restlessness of the classes resembled that of the flocks of pigeons in front of the university, always poised for a flight to some other spot. We got together the most necessary articles for our hand luggage, which had to be kept light, for those were still days of uncertain cabs and droschkes. Equally light was the amount of my Italian. So I equipped myself with phrase-book and pocket dictionary and swallowed on the run large doses of indigestible Italian grammar. The Italians who were destined to hear our speech could unwittingly increase their knowledge, if they did not get some free entertainment out of our efforts. We loaded our memory with stereotyped questions about food or prices or directions of the compass; but such linguistic equipment always turns out to be wholly beside the point. Natives have been given to a fatal speed of utterance from the cradle, and in proportion as they grow up their conversation gets needlessly full of words. The answer to a simple query is not yes or no, but swells into a personal history. Presently you acquire courage; with more glibness of tongue and the improved wariness of your ears, which have grown in length with the constant effort of listening to the foreign idiom, you feel less strange in a strange land. You even become friendly with the railways. When, in keeping with the resources of your purse, you repeat an infinite number of times the unupholstered experience of a third class carriage, you develop in good time a marvellous resistance to hardness of seat, in all kinds of weather, by day or night. Besides, these trifles do not matter if you are really on the road to Italy. For were we not at long last in a carriage marked with the magic word, *Verona*?

A TOURIST IN ITALY (1897)

We were soon in the heart of the Alpine range. Over narrowing meadows flocks of birds were on the wing, and further south the birth of the new season was evident in the flowers which appeared higher and higher on the hillsides, as if drawn by balmier airs and longer days. But the mountain tops were covered with winter snow and the stations of the Brenner pass still wore their white hats, often at a funny angle. The rapids of icy waters gathering from the highlands increased on the lower Italian slopes and raced by the train in a growing volume.

Ned Reed and I made a privileged entrance into the ancient city of Verona at midnight, which was illuminated by a great moon directly overhead. This gave the houses in the narrow streets through which the station bus rattled indistinct shapes and exaggerated height. A feature which brought us to earth in those precipitous entrances into Italian cities was the sudden appearance of the excise collector; he would pop his head into the vehicle at the city gate, shout «*la dogana*» and demand what commodities we had to declare, meaning tobacco or liquor or any kind of food. He looked us over scornfully as third class tourists and seemed uncertain as to what products we might be smuggling in. The people whom he generally held up and turned inside out were the long-suffering countryfolk with their sacks of supplies for the early markets.

Even a pillow filled with gun-wad and clean damp sheets inviting rheumatism could not interfere with the sleep of two weary travellers. The next morning found us refreshed and ready for any fate. It was our first experience with three superimposed worlds, ancient, medieval and modern. There were, too, the reminders left by famous individuals in the historical and artistic records of Verona, spread everywhere before our eyes. We wandered along the banks of the river Adige, with its floating mills and waterborne commerce; we passed through ancient gates and crossed bridges already trodden by the busy humanity of distant ages. Towers and soaring housetops looked down from the surrounding heights or crowded one another in the narrow passageways. In one of these we came upon the house in which one of the two celebrated lovers of legend had dwelt, Shakespeare's Juliet, the scene of whose story is laid «in fair Verona». Doubting Thomases of course have always passed the revered spot contemptuously, but we stood shoulder to shoulder in speechless absorption of the elevated façade, with our heads thrown back at a painful angle, commensurate with the vertical view imposed by a cramped street. At the supreme moment of our romantic concentration some contemporary Juliet threw something down on us from her balcony, and if we had not snapped out of our trance in good time we might have found an early return to the hotel necessary. Her performance may have been intended as the most effective method of discouraging so many peering tourists, providing at the same time an entertaining interlude for the natives.

The showpiece of Verona is the Roman amphitheatre, happily preserved and intelligently restored in recent times. From the topmost tier a superb view takes in most of the city and its picturesque setting, notably the vast ramparts of the Alps to the north. Our quickened imagination readily peopled the arena crowded with spectators. We recalled the gladiatorial combats held there, the chariot races, the contests with wild beasts alternating with the burning of Christian martyrs. In the days of the Empire, as Browning puts it, «the monarch and his minions and his dames viewed the games,» a bald vernacular way of saying that the Emperor viewed his dames, while the dames viewed the charioteers. Thus from ancient rulers through medieval princelings to Napoleon exalted personages graced the amphitheatre, to say nothing of many American visitors, from Buffalo Bill and his Indians, who performed here, to Ned Reed and myself.

We left Verona with a store of novel images and experiences pressed down and running over. The morning mists were lifting lazily, and we found ourselves in the midst of the fresh green landscape of the Lombardy plain dotted with occasional white blossoms. Plows were opening the ground for spring sowing. On the fringes of farms squatted an occasional stumpy willow or some scraggy mulberries, reminders of the silk industry of the region. A brief stop at Mantua may have been dictated by the pious wish of paying homage to the poet Virgil born thereabouts, and celebrated by Mantuans in a monument and the name of a Piazza. Since his time the town had washed its face a bit. But the ancient poet could have recognized some of the littered unsanitary streets in which no urgent activities were spurring the citizens to accelerated motion. The wide Piazza Vergiliana was filled with indolent strollers and many reclining, somnolent bodies which, if they jostled one another, did so unconsciously as they turned over in their prolonged noonday siesta. Out of this unkempt environment there arose several stately façades and imposing walls; they were the remains of bygone pomp and power once lodged in buildings the size of which strained the imagination. Most of the paintings of the noted Mantegna, who added to the glory of Mantua and the Gonzagas, her ruling dukes, have been obliterated through neglect or the hand of time. But his grave in San Andrea, the finest of all Mantuan churches, abides as an enduring evidence of his presence there.

With some experience to go on we now chose our lodgings first for cleanliness and then for price, instead of the other way around. The hostelry at Milan, our next stop, was advertised as «commercial», with the possibility that mine host was bent not only on doing business, but also his guests. The place proved satisfactory; at our first meal we had an opportunity to make use of the vernacular by ordering some rare Italian dishes which turned into spaghetti or rice. The waiter, who was probably also host and cook, listened to our Italian patiently, with a somewhat pained expression; only at the kitchen door he stopped and asked in our own inferior language: «Do you like your rice well-cook-èd?» Such experiences are humiliating and justify the travelling Englishman who addresses all the world only in the idiom of his tight little island.

We had our first glimpse of the Milan cathedral under a bright moon, an unusual stage effect. We saw a gleaming edifice of lace-work in marble with subdued reflections in the windows, scores of statuettes wherever the eye turned, and overhead numberless pinnacles crowding about dome and spire. Conceived in Gothic, carried forward in the Renaissance, and completed in days that had no genuine feeling for either, the cathedral is a pattern of conflicting designs. Equally disparate, the figure of Napoleon in Roman garb can be discovered among those of saints and heroes and pinnacles surrounding the dome.

In Milan a visitor soon becomes conscious of the pervasive presence of Leonardo da Vinci, whose conceptions in their finished and unfinished total stagger the imagination. He was a wizard on whom nature played a scurvy trick by first endowing him with infinite creative urges, and then permitting his gifts to interfere with one another. Because of this super-abundance of inspirations, and due to his habit of pursuing fleeting ideas or merely sketching a caprice, the completion of many a work was relegated to a day that never came. Yet the fantastic endowment of Leonardo with its vanished dreams and fragmentary achievement suggested no finality to the unlimited capacity of the human spirit. It recalled to me a notion expressed by Goethe. Since nature had enriched his long life with such vast experience and knowledge, she could not logically cut off his mature being at its culmination, and so by implication owed him immortality. There in Italy something of this eternal spirit became apparent. The portraits of the dead speak to you, the statues or the inscriptions on their very tombs keep alive their names and deeds. The books which they wrote are preserved, and the manuscripts which they illuminated have a beauty and a permanence that outlast the grave. The venerable church of San Ambrogio in Milan seemed a companion of Time in its intimacy with a thousand years of mankind. Its walls had witnessed the crowning of forgotten Emperors, and its chiselled dates told of a yesterday fabulously distant. It has always been a source of regret to me that some meddlesome sacristan will put you out when twilight comes, even locking the doors with enormous keys, as if the house of God feared thieves. No doubt in the silent half-light of those tombs ghosts walked undisturbed and they could, if not interfered with by narrow human regulations, tell us tales unrecorded by any written line.

Having taken in as many of Milan's ancient landmarks as Reed or I could comfortably digest, we decided to spend a day on Lake Como. Many of my friends have been an urban lot, excessively attracted by town life; the communications of such, according to St. Paul, corrupt good manners. I have, therefore, found frequent excursions into the countryside a happy antidote. Spring was in evidence on all sides at Como. The nipping air of the early morning gave way to a warm sun by noon. There was still a marked contrast between the somber coat of mountain-sides which enclose Como, and the carpets of flowers spreading over the valley. Hedgerows with tiny blossoms surrounded secluded gardens, but the distant summits were still covered with snow.

At this point companion Reed, moved by an unsuspected urge to indulge in maritime adventure, decided to take the small steamer to Bellagio, situated at the head of the lake. This would give him the opportunity to boast later of a wider experience; it left me to my own devices and the less daring program of sticking to my immediate neighborhood. Along the shore women were washing clothes; children took up the primeval pursuit of the stranger, begging for a copper; a regiment of bersaglieri was tramping in accelerated pace along the road and vanished singing around a curve; birds and more birds soared and sang under the open sky, a domed cathedral of measureless dimensions filled with music inspired by the season forever new.

Fortunately the things which the human frame requires set a limit to the poetic state; rapturous moods give way to ravenous impulses, and the lure of the outer world yields to the needs of the inner man. Under such circumstances even a mountain of spaghetti becomes a dainty dish to set before a king. The artistry of preparing food and the poetry of pouring out wine surpass, under appropriate conditions, the other kinds of art or beauty which an Italian journey may offer.

When Reed returned from his voyage of conquest we swapped experiences and agreed that we would gladly continue our lotus-eaters' reveries and stay indefinitely at Como. But we had to pursue our way across northern Italy. Little towns, museums, processions of old masters crowded our memories, proving that leisurely observation is indispensable to appreciate the numberless works left by skilled Italian hands. When we dropped into bed at Genoa nothing less than forty-eight hours of sleep seemed adequate to restore the use of our ruined pedal extremities. It was not certain when we aroused ourselves to inspect some of Genoa's colorful narrow streets, or bestirred our patriotism enough to recall that a certain Christopher Columbus might have wandered about the place, lost in meditation over the prospective discovery of our homeland.

Here we had our first glimpse of the Mediterranean. We wandered under crooked walls overhanging dingy shops which drew the light of the sky down into their narrow streets by means of reflectors projecting from the ground floor. Electric tramways carried us in their weavings through a network of alleys, up and up around housetops and hilltops, making a motley and ever-changing panorama. Here were hundreds of years packed into cramped houses that buttressed each other as they followed the contour of the hills where chance and not a preconceived plan had set them: a city unlike any other in Italy and probably in the world.

We now turned south to Pisa, our train making an impressive run through countless tunnels, every one of which added a dramatic note of suspense to the journey. Whenever we passed out of the darkness into the light we either looked upon a gleaming stretch of sea, or into colorful gardens with villas in the midst of spring blossoms. Pisa made a striking contrast with crowded Genoa. Here were open cheerful streets and gleaming ivory-colored buildings set in the midst of green meadows. The harmony which unites into such a balanced and effortless whole, a cathedral, a baptistery, a formal burial ground and a leaning tower, achieves an unmatched spectacle. A priest in a long red gown crossing the white expanse of the flagstones between the buildings added a touch of color to the background of light and dark marble. Every tourist mounts the leaning tower ostensibly to enjoy the fine view of Pisa and of the Arno flowing by into the sea, but he will invariably drop a stone from the top platform over the projecting side also. This act will prove anew that bodies fall according to some scheme once discovered by the great Galileo on the same spot, and in the same manner. We tried it and our calculations did not materially shake Galileo's law.

On re-entering our hotel we met a newly arrived, weary compatriot who was making supreme efforts to get further service out of his exhausted feet, and as we matched our impaired extremities with his, we consoled him with the prospect of worthwhile things to be seen in Pisa, notably a tower which actually leaned thirteen feet off the center line. «In my present state,» he replied in despair, «I wouldn't walk thirteen feet to see the crown jewels!» And off he went to bed.

We acquire the cheerful habit in Europe of looking for the graves or tombs of famous men; already inclined to pursue the great while they are alive, we continue the custom to their final resting place. So we spent a day near Viarreggio, on the Mediterranean shore, where the sea had taken the living body of the poet Shelley. When his lifeless remains had been given back, they were there consumed by fire in the presence of Byron, Leigh Hunt and other friends. The poignant sentiments which move one on such occasions, led me to pick and preserve some flowers growing at the foot of an unimposing monument raised to Shelley's memory in a little square of the town. Having dismissed these associations with death, we paid tribute to the sunlight and the long warm beach by a dip in the rolling surf; this was followed by an indefinite stretch on our backs in the sand, as we looked at the sky or the fishing smacks which dotted the bay, and thought of nothing at all.

On our way to Florence we included the town of Lucca. Many epochs of history were there discernible: an ancient amphitheatre, medieval churches surrounded by venerable city walls. The great arena had been absorbed by the colorful activities of a vast market; shouting venders of fruits, flowers, vegetables and fish took the place of the ancient heralds of combats, creating an incomparable bit of local color, which also meant local odors, as characteristic of these towns as their infinite beauty.

A professor at Oxford once told me that having had much difficulty in arousing in his son an interest in the barest elements of culture, he packed him off to Italy, actuated by the hope that its magic surroundings might bring about what paternal solicitude had failed to achieve. After travelling about a bit with only lukewarm reactions, the son finally reached Florence and sent from that city the most enthusiastic account that his father had ever had from his pen. It was recorded on a post card and read: «Dear pater, there is not very much the matter with this place». To be as effectively laconic is my predicament.

I presume that the little inn which we selected has long since disappeared. Already in those days it had a decrepit air about it. The name was Albergo di Spagna, and as a shelter it combined dark rooms with a restaurant offering various inscrutable dishes. At all events, we generally ate out. The advantage of a central location meant much to two travellers who had already done more walking than the average letter-carrier does in a lifetime.

There is a halo over Florence which distinguishes it from other cities; I do not refer to the mist which frequently hangs over it in the morning, but to that impalpable crown bestowed upon the community by the consensus of history in recognition of its achievements in so many fields of human endeavor. After venturing forth you unconsciously repeated to yourself, this is actually Florence. There were also two views, the limited physical scene, and the vast historical or spiritual prospect beyond your grasp. The first filled the eye, the second flashed everywhere on the mind; the physical scene could be taken in best from a lifted hillside, but the historical aspect accompanied you wherever you went. Florence was not metropolitan in the ordinary sense. The various commonplace attributes which go with any sizable city had no meaning in connection with this timeless community. Her inhabitants of past centuries are still present there and speak through the visible creations which once came from their hand.

At first we wandered somewhat planlessly about, coming by chance upon a typical flower market which brought the countryside and its riot of color into the city streets. Soon we found ourselves on the classic Ponte Vecchio with its time-honored row of shops. They were filled with buyers who moved about in an atmosphere hardly changed since the days long gone. Having reached the left bank of the Arno we continued up to the height of San Miniato to get the coveted view of the city. This is at its best in the afternoon when the setting sun lights up the panorama from the west.

I was inclined to divide an endless list of Florentine churches into two classes, those that were sufficiently lighted to be enjoyable, and those too dark to let us discern any of their contents. Two of the latter class were the spacious church of Santa Croce and the domed cathedral of Santa Maria del Fiore. Theirs were gloomy interiors indeed. In this connection it will be recalled that the contemplated assassination of the Magnificent Lorenzo dei Medici had been planned to take place in the cathedral during a solemn service; if the interior of the edifice was at that time equally nocturnal, any such plot might conceivably have been carried out in its gloom undeterred.

Florence is a treasure house of the early Renaissance. That supreme epoch had a luminous creative youth. With great names and their works on every side, there came to my mind a chain of books and men made real because they had been the substance of recent acquisitions in class rooms. Thus noted Italians were converted into presences, and we walked through streets some glimpses of which may have been known to Dante, Boccaccio, Machiavelli, Savonarola and Galileo. But not every popular belief was to be taken at its face value. Fabrication and credulity go hand in hand, and for every intriguing story there is the receptive dupe to whom «the house in which Dante lived» indisputably becomes that very house. But incredulity also raised its head among the Florentines themselves. The attendant on the lookout at the top of Galileo's tower, that ancient Torre del Gallo above San Miniato, brought forth the telescope «through which Galileo discovered the moons of Jupiter» with the air of a skeptic. «Fa buio», «it's pitch black», he remarked, adding, «with that instrument he could never have seen our own moon». Guides as a rule do not express such doubt about the authenticity of their historical ware: once in Edinburgh I was one of a group which a patriotic highlander was conducting about the city; when he had pointed out a number of balconies from which Mary Queen of Scots had once gazed, a doubting Thomas whispered: «I would give a sixpence to see a balcony from which she did not look». Every Scotchman can hear the word sixpence, even in a whisper. Without a moment's hesitation our guide led us to a nearby corner and pointed: «Yonder is a balcony finished a week agone Saturrday».

A pleasant interlude was created by the arrival of brother Ferd with his friend Robert Morss Lovett, both on the faculty of the University of Chicago. They were making a brief halt in a bicycle trip through Tuscany and gave us the benefit of their advice and experience in capsule form for subsequent use. I remember that he especially cautioned us to drink wine always instead of water, an essential philosophic *Grundprinzip* applicable to all the years of one's life.

Electric tramways were already replacing the horse-car, the casual use of which took us wherever it chose to go and enabled us to inspect undisturbed nooks of Florence. Our last two undertakings intended to crown our stay were the intimate view of the city from the top of Giotto's campanile and the vaster panorama stretching below the terraces of Fiesoli. A few hours' stroll brought us into the midst of lilac bushes and walls covered with wistaria vines surrounding concealed villas. Many of these belonged to dinstinguished foreigners who were ancient residents of the hillside. The view from the terrace of the Monasterio di San Francesco is supposed to be one of the noblest experiences in the world. This is undoubtedly so, but there comes to me after all these years a possible comparison which may not hold all the romance and historical scope of that supreme view of Florence; it may even be considered an intrusion of our western boasting. From my window here in Berkeley I can take in the expanse of the Golden Gate with San Francisco Bay stretching north and south many miles with the setting sun riding on the top of the coastal range.

On our journey to Rome we passed through pine forests which the western sun crisscrossed in dark parallel shadows; with the coming of the twilight a half-moon stood in the sky. The train was very late, a commonplace detail in those days, and we arrived near some witching hour of night. A hack on which years of service had left their mark bore us to our hotel. The cabby emulated his impetuous namesake, the late king Jehu of Israel, by driving his chariot furiously. In fact, all the hacks left the station careening wildly on two wheels, an impetuosity which suggested not so much the paternal eagerness of the drivers to get back to wife and child, as to a long-deferred glass of vino del paese.

On the train we had been cooped up with a young Frenchman about to be ordained. Going to Rome meant to him the realization of a cherished dream: to visit at last the established center of his faith, the home of the Popes, Saint Peter's with all the triumphant glamour of Christianity, to view endless churches, processions, displays and recurring festal days of Saints. To a heathen like myself it represented a world of which I had seen next to nothing. Munich, to be sure, was a Catholic city in more than one sense. Politically and religiously it was attached to the power and influence of the Church, but socially it was noted as a liberal and broadly cultivated center where allusions to the dominant faith were not always kindly. Rome, on the other hand, everywhere meant the Center of a Roman Catholic world.

Our first objective was the Forum; there we tried, like every gaping college graduate, to connect what we saw with fleeting memories of Caesar and Livy, of Virgil and Horace. These academic tidbits proved of little use, and we had to lean heavily on our more reliable guidebooks. Real miracles have been worked by those archeologists who, starting with only a few broken stones and a great deal of imagination, have recreated sites and emplacements, with the streets and squares in which life can once more be visualized as it was two thousand years ago. But there was also an aspect of that ancient spot which had escaped all ruthless agencies: from the Forum we entered what were once the gardens of the palaces of the Caesars; the palaces had left hardly a trace, but April walked there unchanged as it had in all ages before Rome began.

Letters of introduction to natives may afford a welcome break in sight-seeing; they may also supply a guide for ignorant foreigners in search of worth-while sights. Some Munich friends had urged me to be sure to call upon a professor in Rome whose cordiality they said I would find equal to his bottomless erudition. He was supposed to know things about Rome unknown to anyone else. So I decided to knock at his door and tactfully hint at my need of a directing hand. While inquiring the way to his address I learned by successive steps more and more about his fame as the maker of a dictionary. After decades of labor he was reported to have reached the letter «m», which, after all, was halfway through the alphabet and a mark of progress, if not of final achievement. I have never seen his name on the finished product.

He lived in a flower-filled inner court, and the door was opened by a servant, who, having wiped her mouth on her wrist, and her wrist on her apron, let me in. I squeezed my way between walls of books through a passage leading into a library. I took a chair with my back to stacks of volumes piled horizontally beyond arm's reach. All around were layers of publications rising skyward; some of them I was sure swayed in unstable equilibrium, having been set in motion by my footsteps.

No reception could have been more cordial. The host had a typical professorial exterior; tall, aquiline, bearded, scrutinizing when he chose to fix his glance. His wife was relatively short, plumpish, kindly, and clearly pleased with any interruption of her routine tasks. I resumed my seat under the cliff of books while the signora ordered the servant to bring some coffee. Whether the gentle ways of the *serva* or a draught had caused the door to slam after her, I had no time to determine. The pile of books behind me swayed out of plumb and broke over my head and shoulders. Both host and hostess jumped up crying: «Dio, Dio, Santa Maria, are you hurt?» Fortunately these keystones of the dictionary were unbound, and I could frankly laugh the episode off. But the wife looked disturbed and confided to me later: «If only books were something to eat» (she must have thought of some old cheeses or storageable hams), «or some useful possession! As it is you may be drowned or crippled by them in your own home.» We decided at once on a brief tour of some interesting places, suggested by the host. I told them of my companion Reed, so we stopped to pick him up at the hotel. What we then saw has long since faded from my mind, but the peculiarities of our fellow men remain with us through all the years. We set out from the hotel on foot. Presently the thoughts of our guide, who was one of the most absentminded of men, must have reverted to the quest of some word blocking the progress of his dictionary. He forgot all about us and forging ahead seemed lost to his urban surroundings. When his wife became aware of his absence he was already in the next block. She immediately broke into a brisk trot calling at intervals: «Ma Pietro, Pietro mio, we mustn't lose him». So we stretched our legs and finally managed to catch up with him. Plucking at his coat his wife brought him back to earth, and he looked down at her with surprise and pleasure saying, «Why how strange! How do you happen to be here?» Then he looked up and saw us on either side of her. This restored his sanity, and exclaiming «Dio mio, the museum!» or whatever it was that he had at first aimed at, he again became our cicerone.

We owed to our informed guide a better acquaintance with details of history, with ancient bits of architecture, with less known treasures of the galleries, and would gladly have made more extended use of our new friends. We wandered again over the Forum with increased knowledge and turned with redoubled interest to the ancient scene of the heart of Christianity symbolized in the modern Vatican City and Saint Peter's colossal dome. After viewing church upon church we put our feet to better use by walks along the Appian Way, attempting to capture something of the outskirts of ancient Rome. We rambled over the campagna and lay a long time in the deep grass listening to the skylark, invisible under the noonday sun. When we mentioned our venture into those picturesque marshlands to our host, he threw up his hands in horror and exclaimed that we were now saturated with the germs of Roman fever. Friend Reed assumed a retroactive virtue, saying: «I warned you that we should keep away from the campagna,» with other folkloric absurdities. But no ill followed, presumably because the sun of spring was seconded by the resistance of our own antibugs derived from yards of spaghetti and heaps of risotto washed down with prophylactic drafts of dago red.

We were now ready to leave Rome, perhaps more so than in the case of Florence, which seemed to have a greater and more integrated magic. Companion Reed had been seized by some touring relatives who pounced upon him off his guard as we were innocently engrossed in some picture gallery. Since I am a poor hand at travelling with strange groups, we planned to meet again in Venice, and I headed for Naples alone.

In Europe the foremost cities are nearly all in far northern latitudes, so that to a Parisian, for example, Italy belongs to the far south. Actually Naples is only on the forty-first degree north latitude, about that of New York City. But my own sensation of speeding south was occasioned by noticeable changes in the landscape and in the people themselves. The spring had turned into an exuberant early summer, the life and routine habits among the south Italians had slowed down. As in southern Spain, through ancient usage men have acquired a preference for relaxation or sleeping in the shade to laboring in the sun. I say men advisedly, for the women appeared to be doing most of the work. This distinction became clear in the stations before we reached Naples. Toiling women wheeled grimy cheeses and grimier looking bread under our train windows; only people new to these strange articles classed as food, or those who required bread and not a stone to live, were tempted to buy. The vender, or rather vendeuse, of the bread would clutch a loaf in her hands, wave it aloft, and at some nod saw off a slice and thrust it on the knife's point through the window to her client. A fellow American, indifferent to the mother-earth mixed in his diet, took a slice, and having put his teeth but once into the unsavory mess exclaimed: «God, I wonder what I bought this time!»

A tourists' slogan of long standing has been «see Naples and die», which, I conjecture, meant in those years, see the Bay of Naples while you live, but stop in Naples at your peril. The Bay is the work of the Divine Hand, the city, of the Neopolitans who actually enjoy living there. The greater part was an open-air world of unwashed poverty. The aspect of the labyrinthian streets and squares reminded me of the steerage of ocean liners of long ago. I walked through waste-strewn thorough-fares with orange peels, and orange piles for sale. Goats with their kids were being driven up stairways to be milked at some fourth-floor entrance. Men and boys were asleep on the curb. Beggars bestirred themselves only long enough to stretch out a hand for a copper coin. But there was also music and singing that issued from cellars or passage-ways or shady spots. Thus life was taken restfully to offset the occasional exertion required to exist. The combination of bodily ease with entertainment makes bearable the recurring necessity of lifting an arm to quell the pangs of hunger. A lazzarone, whom I approached to carry one of my bags, replied without stirring, «I have already eaten» (ho mangiato). So why worry before another day?

Although my hotel was listed under «recommended» in the guide-book, a plague comparable with that of Egypt lay in wait for me in the bed. The creatures may not have had the size of the frogs with which the Lord smote the borders of Pharaoh, but they sufficed. I resolved to migrate. The alluring view of the bay, the islands set in an azure sea, Vesuvius idly smoking on the horizon against a spotless sky sponged out every annoyance and I decided to move at once to Capri.

To be truly alone you can do no better than travel. The peculiar blend of tourists who crowded the small boats plying among the sights of the bay of Naples filled one with a sense of self-sufficiency. Having escaped from the city with one's life, it was good to be safe on deck. But you discovered that land-beggars had turned into mermen and lived in the sea. For the entertainment of innocents abroad, these am-phibian creatures dove into that more than briny deep for their sustenance. When they brought it up in their mouths, it turned out to be the popular copper coin sought everywhere, here tossed into the bay by the foreigner to satisfy this marine branch of the beggars' guild. We finally cast off and some strolling singers, who also turned out mendicants in disguise, struck up «la bella Napoli», the only number in their limited repertory.

Nature all around the bay had played into the hands of tourists' agents and their venal henchmen. It became a source of never-ending amazement that the human mind could devise so many petty games of graft. For our great fairs we have invented Eiffel towers, Ferris wheels, Parachute drops, and the people fall for them. At Naples nature has invented only endless beauty and everywhere you paid the grafters for its enjoyment. The Blue Grotto at Capri, a thing of magic to be viewed quietly and alone, has for decades been invaded by shrieking mobs distributed over scores of tiny boats, each of which holds three or four persons. The boats have glass bottoms which per-mit a view of the exquisite rainbow hues on the rocks and in the water. Yet by looking down I could see only the huge feet of two German tourists whose Rucksacks effectively blocked any other view. After bumping each other and then the walls of the grotto to the peculiar satisfaction of the visitors, all the boats with their crews were again rowed ashore, where no one could land before he had disbursed the outlay of a whole day's subsistence.

Having escaped from the descendants of the forty thieves, I found a happy refuge in a hotel situated on a hillside, with a view of the Mediterranean over the tops of some orange trees. It was now late afternoon with a cloudless sky. So I made my first objective the hilltop where once stood a villa reputedly the residence of Emperor Tiberius. It is now a ruin covered with vines and had been converted by some scientific farmer into a shelter for cows and the ubiquitous Italian goat. This creature figures prominently in every Italian journey. The climb had been a simple task. I mounted by a short path leading through passageways cut into the hill and up over steep stairways; these landed me on flowery terraces, diminutive flat spaces covered with capricious patterns of gardens and orchards. Many walls were concealed by roses and wistaria.

On the supposition that every effort to lift the human body must be compensated for by dividing the ascent, however gentle, into stages or stations of refreshment, my progress was presently interrupted by a wine-shop, or more exactly, by a dark native girl, who beckoned from a doorway and lured me to take in an unusual view of the sea and the beach below. Having succumbed to the prospective sight, the next step was the purchase of some refreshments, whereupon I was led into a room in which several girls were dancing a kind of tarentella to a small gathering of gulls who had flown to the same spot ahead of me. The faces of the guests were flushed with the goodly vino rosso of Capri and I realized that any romantic mood was out of place. So my next move was dictated by plain funk, limited funds and equally limited Italian speech. By keeping my eyes fixed on the beauty outside, rather than the beauties inside, I managed a quick getaway, and fled to the top of the cliff. There I found refuge among the grasses which almost concealed the remains of a light-house, once commandingly placed. Far out on the water I could count the sails of idle fishing boats; bees hummed among the flowers and innumerable swallows wheeled about me, so close at times that I could have touched them in their flight.

To the northeast lay the brown promontory of Sorrento, standing forth in the evening sun. Twelve hundred feet sheer beneath me, too far to be heard, the water was lapping in the crags, its rhythmic motion evident only to the eye in recurring crests of white foam. After an unobstructed sunset there came with the twilight the sound of bells calling from church steeples below. The late hour brought with it the usual lapse from poetry to prose; the chimes carried hints of food rather than devotion and prompted a speedy descent to the hostelry.

At table I found myself seated with three men who turned out to be a retired Russian doctor, a German officer on leave, and just an Englishman. During the entire meal the latter kept his identity to himself with an expression which said, 'I am learning what you are, and you are trying to guess what I am'. When self-revelations and friendly exchanges are on a reciprocal basis, they add to the richness of these chance associations. Otherwise one could converse as profitably with a portrait on the wall. After the meal our Englishman fell back on the congenial company of his reticent pipe and exchanged our company for solitary meditations on the hotel veranda. The three of us who remained decided to enjoy the night under the open sky. We climbed past the village of Anacapri to the foot of Monte Solaro. A belated group of girls on burros, with a guide, had stopped on our path with a display of much merriment caused by the burros named Raphael, Michael Angelo and Yankidoodle. Why these animals are ever used for conveyance is a riddle, as they seldom understand that motion is required to take you from your starting point to your destination. In the open country they enjoy the landscape, partaking freely of the twigs or grasses or thistles that fringe their path. A timely return to your own meal never crosses their minds.

We had discovered at table that the three of us could pool some English, more French, and German enough to make companionable our ramble under a starlit night. It was another example of the benefits to be derived from travel. The chance meeting of unattached men wandering over the earth in a relaxed, receptive mood represents a phase of liberty which has not been sufficiently stressed in the Bill of Rights. It stands out in sharp contrast with the bondage hanging over one obliged to stay forever at home or the slavery of the poor fish who travels with a family periodically torn by conflicting desires or engaged in tracing lost pieces of baggage. Our schools should make solitary travel obligatory, to be undertaken as early as possible.

I spent the last day on the top of Monte Solaro. The cargo of tourists had not yet arrived and the natives stood forth in their own values. Peasant women in gaudy colors carried their loads up the hill upon their heads; a group of children passed singing as they filed down the path silhouetted against a background of silver sea or green hillside. Lizards, ubiquitous Capri citizens, flashed along walls as you come into sight. While returning from the beach of the secluded piccola marina, to which descended a flight of stone steps carved out of the mountain, I heard again the urban din of a beer hall and foreign voices which showed that the regulars had already come. Always desirous of inquiring into the sources of any revelry, I found myself in front of another refreshment station where everyone was quenching an imaginary thirst. I followed suit as my thirst was genuine. Even these coarser notes could not mar the general picture of this earthly paradise. On the return boat the strolling musicians exchanged «la bella Napoli» for «la diva Capri», divine Capri, in which every opinion could agree.

Filled with foreboding of such Neapolitan hotels as were within the scope of my purse, I tried my luck with an inn on the road to Herculaneum and Pompeii where I had planned to spend the next days. Any choice would have been immaterial, as I always left the hotel early and returned late, too tired to quarrel with bedfellows, however small. This time fate proved more kindly and I slept in peace.

Pompeii is a paradox. As I stood for the first time in the heart of this ancient city, my imagination carried me quickly through the significant stages of its existence. A Roman town, vigorous with life ages ago, became in a few hours a buried city; not a dead city, only a sleeping community. With the passing of the centuries, it rose, an uncovered city, and became a re-awakened community. No ancient city yields as realistic an image of its daily living as this. On the other hand, we can see in mediaeval prints pictures purporting to reproduce the contemporary aspects of Italian cities, but drawn from memory, without any regard for proportion or distance. But at Pompeii the grim and smoking creator of the local scene still stands watch over his ancient handiwork. With an occasional menacing blast from his furnace he has continued to remind the tillers of the vineyards on his flanks of his presence. His threats have also been a tribute to the courage and indifference of those sons of earth who century after century have continued to wring a livelihood from the mountain's volcanic soil. When I spoke to them no sense of insecurity affected their unconcern. On a yesterday almost two thousand years ago, with no fore-warning commensurate with the ensuing disaster, the eruption burst forth in a quickly descending night. Pliny the Younger, whose letters had brought a human note into our Yale class-room, tells of the eruption which he witnessed across the bay of Naples: how the region was buried in a thick cloud of darkness pierced by lightning flashes and illumined by an incandescent glow. From its depth were hurled stones and lava; mud-streams were formed by a torrential rain falling on the mountain-side, the sea was violently churned up with both land and water about to return to the uncreated beginnings of the world.

Surrounded by the picturesque remnants of white walls, in the warmth of an early morning sun, no horror of that fatal catastrophe strikes the mind. The ancient inhabitants can again be pictured in the pursuit of their daily routine; the shops are open, the pious resort to the temples, hawkers and venders can be heard in the streets, servants pass in and out of the houses. Everywhere the worn stones of thresholds or street-crossings, or the ruts of wagon wheels were still visible. Life stirred within the patios where fountains once played and the household pursued its various tasks. Here and there a whole window-frame came to life and was filled by a living figure. From ancient paintings on the walls and from mosaics on the floors the imagination could derive sufficient material to rebuild and revive the essentials of daily Pompeiian existence.

These sunny communities of the indolent South suggested to me a pleasant philosophy of Utopian living as I was lying at peace in a shady spot. We really need few things to make up a satisfactory world. They are sunshine, food within reach of your arm, wine in an unstinted quantity, water to cleanse the body and, possibly, a little wherewithal to secure the other four. Some misguided people get involved with religion or politics and are ever at loggerheads with the Deity or the City Hall. Others feel the irrational need of indulging in violent exercise. An American wit once said that he got his exercise as pall-bearer to friends who took exercise. My philosophy, therefore, is based on a life of repose in which a few necessities are to be distributed a bit more equitably than at present. This would require merely a new scheme of distribution. In southern Italy such a land of promise could be devised, making the folly of all controversies arising from settled philosophies as plain as the nose on one's face. Such meaningless catchwords as 'I think, therefore I am' (clearly false when there are so many who exist without thinking), or 'innate ideas and empirical ideas' (there are those who get along without either) would disappear forever. Then someone could invent a new slogan proclaiming my world the best of all possible worlds.

But at that time this Italian paradise also had its serpent. It took the form of the guide, who in those years when the tourist world was still young, functioned without official vigilance. He was especially wily in his exploitation of the stranger within the gates; he took him around and took him in. After a few days of unmolested rambling about those newly discovered cities, I thought that I ought to pay my respects to the old monster Vesuvius. For this a guide was an inescapable dilemma. There may have been an honest one. Most of those of last century have long since gone to their doom, the open crater of Vesuvius suggesting an appropriate end. I once read of a tourist who pushed his guide into the volcano. The unasked services they rendered and the split fees they extracted in their secret interlocking chicanery were, for long, my most humiliating memories. My guide was a charming youth who underneath a convincing exterior concealed many years of successful banditry. My financial shortages have always been due to a kind of adolescent incapability to scent the furtive ways of mankind. I was prepared for a reasonable amount of guile, but I had exacted no written contract from the man and the horse which he put at my disposal. I have as a rule left a margin in my travel budgets to make up for a deficiency of intelligence and the resulting deficit. On this occasion I was handed from one specialist to another under the pretext that there was no other legal way of reaching the crater; the legality consisted in paying an additional fee at every break in the journey called a new stage in the ascent. As a result the sum agreed on at the beginning had to be multiplied many times before I was given my liberty to return to civilization. The horse I rode was thoroughly initiated into the game; it accelerated its gait on approaching any one of the lairs where wine was for sale, but solely to the guides. Tourists had been warned that any drinking prior to or during an ascent in the heat of the day would without exception bring on a stroke of apoplexy. This did not apply to the guides who constantly appeared to be dying of thirst, and of course there was no water on the slopes of Vesuvius. At the close of the ordeal I learned that even the horse had drunk wine at my expense.

There was however a credit column to the day's journey. Everywhere on the lower slopes of the mountain men and women were at work in the vineyards; here and there stood fig-trees clad in bright green. When these were left behind the ashes and slag of remote eruptions increased under foot. The rudeness and desolation of the scene cut by the torrents of stark lava gave an inkling of the destructive forces at work in the bowels of the crater. Once on the summit, as a supreme climax, I turned my back on the terrors of Vesuvius and took in the whole superb bay of Naples, one of the fabulously lovely panoramas of this earth. A perfect sunset closed the day's adventure, and I gathered enough courage to return to the hazards of neapolitan hostelry.

By this time I had spent more time and certainly more centesimi than I had originally estimated as sufficient for my itinerary. Visits to the Naples museum to see the ancient bronzes and household objects salvaged from Herculaneum and Pompeii had to be cut short. I managed on my way north to include among things worthy to be seen Bologna, Ravenna and Venice; Bologna, for being the site of one of the oldest universities, Ravenna, because it held the tomb of Dante, and Venice for being Venice. At Bologna I could still recapture glimpses of mediaeval and Renaissance times. Long ago the university was a distinguished alma mater of students who flocked there to revive the study of Roman law. In some of the more venerable streets and squares I could still form a mental picture of those motley gatherings of natives and foreigners who carried their knowledge of the laws to all the corners of Europe, establishing the foundations of an orderly society and providing the legal backbone of its government. In nearby Ravenna Dante's remains lie buried in a sombre and unworthy tomb. Standing before it a devotee of the poet could for a brief moment recall the visions of his Divine Comedy and see in them the exalting implication that the tomb did not mark a definitive end, but only a resting place for our dust, that beyond it an undefined hope of another *Vita Nuova* beckoned to men.

I reached Venice on a church holiday. Arrayed in her gayest attire she was as spectacular as an elaborate stage pageant. It was Venice, «where the merchants were the kings, where Saint Mark's is, where the Doges used to wed the sea with rings». It was easy to think of such fantastic ceremonies in those Arabian Nights' surroundings where the sea supplied the streets, where the cabs in which we had everywhere else risked our lives were happily replaced by smoothly gliding gondolas, propelled by colorful gondoliers instead of suspicious-looking, not always sober drivers. Stately palaces rose from the water, and the residents became sea-faring at their very doors. This was the mighty republic which «once did hold the gorgeous East in fee».

The scene was a mixture of reality and magic. The canals, big and little, swarmed with oddly shaped black boats; the banks were alive with jostling holiday crowds; above you, over the bridge, streamed passersby, among whom were foreigners speaking all the languages of Europe. The Venice of yesterday was acting the host to the world of today. Having arrived at the high tide of the tourist season, I was lucky to find a garret room in a small hotel. Nevertheless, from a small window I could take in the entire harbor; at twilight the strings of lights on the Great Canal began to be duplicated in the long mirror below.

Comrade Ned Reed had also arrived, so that we could resume a common itinerary before returning to Munich. We crowded into brief days the routine obligations of the hounded sight-seer, beginning with the square of Saint Mark's. There everyone's first acts were charitable ones, divided between feeding the pigeons who have made the piazza theirs, and bestowing something on the ubiquitous beggar; pigeon and beggar lived similar lives in their dependence on the bounty of foreigners. Only after such preliminaries one could proceed to examine the motley qualities of the cathedral. In its dazzling features East was joined to West, Byzantine details, cupolas and mosaics were combined in a miraculous oriental fabric to serve an occidental Church. Venetian pageantry was likewise evinced in the great paintings of Titian, Tintoretto and their peers exhibited in Churches and palaces; the very saints stood forth in a show of Venetian pomp, and the Virgin Mary proclaimed herself a native Venetian with her embroidered garment and the elaborate head-dress of some fair mortal who long ago sat for the painter's conception of Our Lady.

I have read adventure stories told by travellers of earlier centuries, who recount the difficulties they had in getting about safely in fair Italy. They speak of magicians, an ancient variety of swindler, who practiced their wiles on innocent foreigners and so made a living wage. The lineal descendants of this ineradicable tribe were, in the nineties, to be found in numerous Italian towns. In Venice they camped with characteristic self-effacement on the square of Saint Mark. They lured the stranger by some magic into buying objects of which he had no need whatever, and gave him in small change for good money a handful of fake coins, redeemable nowhere on earth. When Ned Reed and I wanted to get a final view of Venice from the top of the campanile of Saint Mark, we repeated this engrossing experience twice, first at the bottom and then at the top in the guise of fees, one for admission, and one to look when admitted. These esoteric proceedings brought into play much slight-of-hand work on the part of the ticket-seller below and of the guide and friend aloft. The end of such a perfect day left us poorer in spite of our possession of specimens of coins from all over the world. The campanile collapsed a decade later under the weight of accumulated crime. A friend who saw it a dozen years thereafter, rebuilt in its full vigor, reported that the guides and venders of old had vanished for good, having been eliminated under the massive tower when it fell. I still possess a boxful of coins presented to me on that journey.

On our return we succumbed to the lure of one more stop, Padua, another venerable university town. We limited our visit to the church of the Madonna dell'Arena, with the extensive frescoes painted on its walls by Giotto. The small chapel is set in the midst of a garden, the circular walls of which are formed by the ruins of a Roman amphitheatre, giving the church its name. The intimate size of the chapel made it a unique spot in Italy, for we could imagine the painter at work on his scaffolding as he depicted his gentle pious scenes against a background of simple daily life.

At Padua a veritable chain of great names lights up the past. There Giotto had been Dante's host, and, like all painters, he must have asked his guest to sit for him, an interesting situation which we might as well take for a historical fact. Not many decades thereafter Petrarch came to reside in the neighborhood, and those who have weighty opinions in these matters add that England's Chaucer appeared on the scene at that auspicious moment. On my own authority I affirm that while the two poets were happily tippling together, Chaucer, in an unguarded moment, took from Petrarch «the tale of Patient Griselda», under the misguided impression that so unbelievably dull and wholly unbelievable a tale would please the marriageable girls of England. At all events, to give the story authority, his Clerk of Oxenford insists that he got it from a worthy «clerk at Padua, Fraunces Petrark the laureate poet»,

«Who is now dead and naylèd in his cheste;
I pray to God so give his soule reste.»

Chaucer has written better verse than this which reveals only details of interest to morticians. The additional pious invocation for Petrarch's future state justifies still another opinion that there was a real friendship between the two poets. It is the accepted way of reaching sound literary conclusions.

A night train carried two weary and satiated travellers back to Munich with miscellaneous acquisitions, contained both in our baggage and in crowded memories. Many details of that experience have survived through the years, and the beauty of the journey has been a luminous background to much that I have learned and seen since. The Italian scene, with its endless display of human achievement, was a new world; it revived a historical past which had had repercussions over the entire earth, both in the realm of fact and of the imagination. Some of it was gay and colorful and evanescent, but mostly it told of intense living and doing, inspiring sober and thoughtful moods; all in all a brief journey, but in it «my heart had great experience of wisdom and knowledge».

A FRENCH INTERLUDE: THE SORBONNE

It was uphill work to get back to my academic routine right after the Italian adventure. Various courses begun in the fall term had to be completed in the spring and summer. I also had to gather the material for my doctor's thesis from countless notes. The annoying early-bird habits of two of my professors who scorned the blessings of sleep prompted them to put their classes at seven o'clock in the morning, but the extra physical effort required of me to meet this obligation had a spiritual compensation. I could pretend that I belonged to the class of useful citizens whom I met on my way to the University. They were the respectable bread-winners whose daily labor was sustaining those who were still asleep at that hour and who, when awake, would eat the bread. But June in Munich also inspired week-end hikes up the picturesque valley of the turbulent Isar. We loafed along its gray-green precipitous current by the hour, and, truants ourselves, we watched the idle boys who risked their lives wading in the whirling stream. Those busy days of mingled application and play also brought home to me the distinction between the urge merely to work and the urge to create something new. In that process of self-analysis I discovered my limitations, and gradually comprehended what I could do, or ought to do, with such gifts and opportunities as I had at my disposal.

The fruit of my particular tree of knowledge was to be a comparative study in German and French literature, taken from the field of the theatre. Consequently a first-hand acquaintance with the background of the subject made it necessary for me to continue my work in France as soon as feasible. The itinerary which I planned was to take me to Paris in a leisurely and round about way. It included the upper Rhine region, Alsace, and the French borderland. I was eager, also, to return to Heidelberg and renew the happy acquaintance with mother's relatives begun in my first European journey.

I had barely got over their cordial greeting, somewhat prolonged at the station and continued at the house, and had comfortably established myself, when I remembered a rash promise made to Munich friends that I would convey their «hearty greetings» to a certain Heidelberg family. The sooner I got through with it the better. So I nerved myself for the call, discussed with my relatives the proper hour, put on the stiff regulation collar, borrowed a pair of gloves just to carry in my hand and started off. I presently found myself at the proper door, and, a few moments later, in a large overstuffed parlor shaking half-a-dozen elderly persons by the hand. Then I had to take the guest's usual seat on the sofa, to be reached only by edging around a table which successfully barricaded any access to it.

In a moment of silence when none of my hosts seemed to think of another question concerning «Amerika,» the door opened and a beautiful girl with dark eyes and hair entered. She turned out to be the granddaughter, daughter and niece of persons already in the room. I realized with the susceptibility of an immediate admirer that this was a case of tyrannical parents, who did not countenance the association of young people unless they were flanked and backed by vigilant elders. We managed, however, to exchange a few words. My next visit was hardly more successful under the inescapable gaze of Blue-beard and his watchful family.

My astonishment was therefore great when, on the following morning, I found under my coffee cup a note brought by the milkman, whose beat covered the needs of her family and mine. The letter tactfully conveyed the news that a certain young lady could be seen walking up the picturesque Philosophenweg at a certain hour to take in the beautiful view. Not having played the bold Knight in the past, I had to pluck up my courage a second time and face fate. I saw her on that lovely hillside which overlooks the whole valley with Heidelberg and its castle, but in my terror of Bluebeard I could only keep thinking how had she got out, and how would she get back undetected. I was about to utter some poetic platitudes, when she suddenly jumped up from the bench where we were sitting, clanked her invisible chains, and suggested a retreat while there was still time. We got safely within a block or two of her house and said a hasty good-bye. I waited a long time for the cry of the nabbed fugitive; but hearing nothing, I relaxed for the first time and beat it for home. Her absence had no doubt been discovered, for I received only the most laconic note of farewell and I never saw her again. So nothing came of our brief meeting and briefer messages except fleeting memories. But this is not a sentimental journey, which requires a very special pen. Whatever sentimental details may creep into these pages will be attributable to some external agent and not to me.

In my studies I had consumed much time over Goethe, so I made my first extended stop in the environment of Strassburg, where some of the happiest days of his youth were spent. Goethe has left us a longish and at times terrifically dull story of his life, travels, and conclusions on aspects of art, literature and science, including many details about what he said and did, also when he did not say or do it. That makes the tale no less true. Among his early years he included the moving account of his love for Fridericke Brion, who reciprocated his passion, unaware that Goethe's higher social station made his marriage to a simple, pretty, country girl improbable. Recalling this story, I visited Sesenheim, the village in which she lived. It had retained all the idyllic qualities which long ago had made such an appropriate background for his very genuine although passing love. Many of the landmarks of Goethe's days were still to be seen, somewhat renovated and probably improved upon: the church and the bench on which the lovers sat, presumably hand in hand, not exactly listening to the sermon; the arbor in which Goethe says they chatted forgetful of the flight of time. The arbor had been pretty thoroughly rebuilt, its floor worn out by the footsteps of more recent lovers who had rehearsed the pattern laid down ages before Goethe rode into town on horse-back eager to meet Fridericke. Her grave is in the cemetery of a neighboring village. The simple epitaph devised by admirers of the great poet asks us to believe that the reflected glory of the great man she loved suffices to give her immortality. But this vicarious glory omits the fact that she died a forgotten spinster who might gladly have exchanged the meaningless credit of a future fame for the cash of a bit of earthly felicity. I wandered over the fields and meadows scattered all around Sesenheim, and beheld several latter-day Friderickes tossing hay or carrying baskets of fruit on their heads.

Strassburg in those days served as an excellent borderland introduction to the people and country of France. You heard both German and French in the streets and could infer the inner conflict of a province which has been handed back and forth repeatedly between two cultures and two loyalties, and which always looks back and forward with mingled regret and insecurity. The aspect of the city likewise bears the imprint of both German and French arts and customs. Ancient houses with elaborate half-timbered façades and ornate window-frames recall Germanic structures of the Rennaisance. The magnificent Cathedral has a long history of mingled Germanic and French styles. In my travels I always got involved with a cathedral whenever there happened to be one about. On this occasion, before I realized it, I was feeing a guide at the foot of one of the great towers to obtain access to the lofty platform from which the whole world was visible. The prospect was worth the effort which was necessary to mount so many stairs; it constituted a flight worthy of the daws who dwelt in the hollow spaces afforded by Gothic style, and who were blown about the tower whenever they issued from their nesting places. Carried by the same wind the clouds were racing over a blue sky; below in the square there were many human ants crossing the Cathedral Plaza. The single finished spire makes a disquieting impression as though the builders had been chased away, without previous notice, by war or pestilence, leaving behind the truncated tower-base with an expression of expectancy, as if the masons were sure to come back to complete their unfinished job.

The guide books tell you to look for the names of famous men among the hundreds scratched all over the walls of the tower platform. It occurred to me also to add my name with the proper date; its discovery should put my biographers on an unexpected trail in my career. As I proceeded into French territory, the character of town and country-side underwent a gradual change. The tempo of life slowed down, the efficiency of the German industrial civilization made way for the less hurried easy-going agricultural world of la douce France. The neatness east of the Rhine was replaced by a certain indifference for thoroughly swept streets and squares. I later had occasion to remark on the noticeable discrepancies between outward Paris and the provincial cities, and was told: «Paris is our only city and for her sake the government neglects all the nooks and corners of France.» Yet one got to love those small French towns, so remote from any pressure of thoroughness in the daily routine, so unregimented, unsanitary and free.

Seeing Paris for the first time was like entering an imaginary capital of the world. In no other great city are you absorbed as quickly. You have no sooner taken a temporary lodging in the very heart than you begin to live the life of Paris. Having alighted at a station near the center of the city and having been duly packed into a cab with bags and trunk I was immediately engulfed by the waves of Parisian life. Ahead of me was an endless string of cabs. Seated on the box of each was a stuffed cape surmounted by a glazed topper with no visible head inside. As I proceeded slowly into widening streets and through great squares with vistas of trees and arches and wide avenues of impressive buildings I became conscious of being in the most beautiful city on earth.

My first lodging was a quiet pension in rue Hamelin not many blocks from Napoleon's triumphal arch on the Étoile. It was kept by a Madame Guillaume, an elderly French lady of culture, and a thorough Parisienne. She was the widow of a general who had lost his life in the

Franco-Prussian War. An occasional visitor at the table was her only son, a lieutenant in the army, who assisted his mother in running the establishment; this he did chiefly by entertaining the mixed assortment of boarders with amusing stories which he told in what one of the boarders called excessively «fast French», that is, too fast for us ever to catch the point. At all events here I first learned to swim linguistically, having acquired the buoyancy I needed under the direction of a well informed spinster who combined an uncertain age with much teaching skill. She gave a number of us daily lessons in slow French which I gradually succeeded in speeding up for practical purposes in a city where occasions to speak were never lacking.

The topics of daily French life, reflected in conversations and newspapers, were chiefly of a political nature. By chance I had arrived at a moment of profound national disturbance. The Republic was still young. The many conflicting opinions expressed regarding the efficiency of the government were an indication of the insecurity which the entire nation had felt ever since the *débâcle* of 1870. France was apprehensively conscious of her more powerful German neighbor, so recently a victorious foe. In her need of a friendly ally to bolster her prestige she was at the time wooing Russia. The Czar had already visited Paris in state to confirm an alliance between the two nations, and in the fall of 1897, the President of the French Republic in turn visited the Czar in Petrograd. When he came back to Paris he was received with the most noisy demonstrations of patriotism conceivable. We waited for hours along the great boulevards to see the chief magistrate pass, surrounded by his entire government. The gorgeously arrayed chiefs of the army and navy, followed by diplomats and dignitaries of every kind, rolled by in decorated carriages, proclaiming the revived prestige and the glorification of the Army of the Republic. The much heralded alliance was announced amid a picturesque clatter and glitter of masses of French cavalry, flanked by miles of red military trousers which were drawn up along the sidewalks, with the colorful addition of uncounted tricolors, banners and streamers, fanfares and salvos and cries of vive-la-France.

There was one fly, and that a large one, in the ointment of all this military splendor. That was the Dreyfus scandal. Under a relatively calm surface, Parisian life was seething with the hatreds and antagonisms engendered by «l'Affaire». It was a happy circumstance for me to arrive in the very midst of a national commotion, about to rock all Parisian society. To understand it, I first had to become acquainted with the antecedents of current events.

Two aspects of contemporary French thought were receiving

more and more prominence, socialism and anti-semitism. I had heard a good deal about socialism in Germany where it was on the increase and affected many discussions in the Reichstag. Socialism in France had not yet become a practical coherent force in the political arena. On the other hand, anti-semitism was dividing French society, especially in Paris where the cleavage was everywhere in evidence. It was fostered above all by the upper military cliques. These cliques were reputedly clericalists or monarchists, according to their social bias, and by implication anti-bourgeois and anti-semitic. Generals and Cabinet officers had been publicly accused in the press and on the platform of being incompetent and undeserving of the public's confidence. Consequently the popularly esteemed army and the young Republic were held to be in jeopardy. Reputations had to be salved, betrayals of military secrets to Germany had to be traced, a scapegoat had to be found to silence the violent attacks made on the War Department. The anti-semitic craze readily attributed to the Jews a plot to undermine the prestige of the army. This whole political mess gave birth to the Dreyfus case.

Captain Alfred Dreyfus, it will be remembered, was an Alsatian Jew employed in the war office. He was consequently selected for the role of traitor, and crimes admittedly committed by an unknown personage were given the color which best fitted his situation. The case is forgotten today, but it split France wide open throughout the nineties of the last century.

I had moved into a little room in a hotel near the place de l'Odéon, in the Latin quarter. It was on the fifth floor, there being no sixth; it faced the street and also looked over neighboring roofs with their clotheslines of white linen waving in the breeze, their lazily smoking chimneys animated by the visit of occasional birds. Well I remember an early winter evening in January when I had just returned from my hideout in the National library. Cries began to grow louder in the street below: Émile Zola accuses the War Department and the General Staff. Zola proclaims the innocence of Dreyfus and names the real traitors. Newsboys were running through the square with the evening edition of Clemenceau's l'Aurore. We rushed to the street in a body, snatched the fresh copies and devoured Zola's famous letter beginning «J'accuse». Its contents have been dramatized recently by Paul Muni in an excellent movie, and are therefore familiar. If the rumors of widespread treason in the war office had up to that moment been kept underground, the uproar stirred by Zola's letter brought both truth and lies into the open. Zola had mentioned by name every officer whom he considered a participant in the miscarriage of justice which in 1894 had degraded the innocent captain and sent him for life to the penal colony on Devil's Island. Zola was promptly sued for libel to which the army chiefs had to resort to uphold their honor. It was a foregone conclusion that the trial would end in the temporary discomfiture of Zola; but it also brought to light more details which the commanding generals had striven to surpress.

Episodes of the French Revolution were now re-enacted on many street corners. Regiments of soldiers paraded the chief boulevards, shouting mobs mulled about the court while the trial was conducted. Newspapers violently expressed the conflict of opinions which turned Paris society into a stormy sea. The events which immediately followed implied only a temporary victory, since it had been won through fanatical patriotic faith of the people in the army chiefs. Then the drama slowly unrolled as it unmasked the real criminals; a forger's suicide, the universal denunciation of the government's policy of concealment brought to a head in the next months the growing demand for a second trial of Captain Dreyfus. How he was, under political pressure, once more pronounced guilty, then pardoned and subsequently cleared, how the valiant Zola did not live to see the outcome to his «J'accuse», needs no rehearsal.

But the poisoned atmosphere of Paris had in the interim contaminated social life and broken up friendships. Invitations to dinner were accompanied by the plea to refrain from all allusions to the Affair. One heard of meals at which a controversial opinion was answered by a well-aimed sententious plate, and friendly sittings were disrupted amid shouts and recriminations. Having on one occasion been invited to the house of a professor at a Lycée, who happened to be a personal friend of Zola, I remarked that the guests had been carefully selected for their pro-Dreyfus bias. I myself was looked upon as an ignorant and silent participant. The case was given the freest airing, and I heard details which found their way into the printed record only in later times. Even when Frenchmen agree, an exciting subject is argued with a note of violence. There were no casualties on this occasion, but such a contingency might have added greatly to the dramatic experiences of my winter in Paris.

My chief interests have generally been confined to the puzzling composition of individuals, so I have never acquired the slightest competence in rehearsing current political or social theories. The slogans plastered on all the walls of Paris proclaiming liberty, equality and fraternity for mankind, seemed to me pretty academic. The many irrational doings on every street corner negated the few rational ideas expressed in print. The French have given a greater variety to expressions of liberty than any other people and they furnished plenty of examples of the extremes to which liberty may go in those very days. At the one end there was the aspiration set down in a bill of rights emblazoned on walls all over France, and at the other end was the conception of personal liberty of the whimsical Frenchman, who one day knocked off the silk hat of M. le President innocently taking a Sunday stroll in the Bois de Boulogne.

Parisian life has always had an immense reservoir of varied interests, and a newcomer could do no more profitable thing than tap that reservoir as often as possible. Since the classes at the Sorbonne and the College de France did not open before the end of the fall, I used the intervening time to familiarize myself with the face of Paris. I walked miles, I rode on the top of the leisurely horse busses through every conceivable part of town. Those were the days when you did not ride in the darkness of a subway, since that evil device was still in the first stages of digging. This process was apparent in some streets, not from vast gaping holes, but from small openings in mother earth, at the rim of which, occasionally, appeared a small cup; the cup when turned over would leave what looked like a large worm cast. When I asked what the phenomenon might protend, I was told by a proud lingerer, «Ah monsieur, c'est le métro; they are working on the subway.» Continuing my walk I came to another opening where a wooden drum with a crank was being slowly turned and a thin cord rolled on the drum by solitary manpower. Now and then a toy bucket would appear and more hatfuls of sand would be turned out. I asked a workman, absorbed like myself in looking on, why they brought up such small loads at a time; he looked at me in surprise, pointed to the cord and said, «Ah monsieur, more would be too much.» Some years later I compared this kindergarten process retrospectively with the construction of the New York subway, in which tons of rock were blasted out of the earth with the aid of dynamite, and then removed by huge dredges that bit into the rubble for nothing less than a truck-load at a time. I found out subsequently that the leisurely French process had been justified by the nature of the soil on which Paris reposes. It is alluvial, brought into the plain by the river current, and being wholly free of rock formations, it could be dug out with a trowel and passed out in piddling quantities.

Everyone has reason to mourn the gradual disappearance of the horse bus, now replaced by ill-smelling, wholly unreliable auto-buses, and by a network of subways reaching over the entire expanse of the city. In the métro you travel like hurried moles and no longer see the entrancing sights of Paris, which we of old could view. On the top of the deliberate busses you were one of the populace, you heard their conversations, you saw everything that passed on the street, you stopped and looked into shops, you witnessed a dozen brawls, both on or off the conveyance. In no other way could one scrutinize so many unvisited nooks of Paris, so many ancient buildings that have now disappeared. Here and there you delayed long enough to read the plates on façades indicating the residence of some famous personage. All of these were details which, experienced together, made up the history of the city.

At the suggestion of the head of the pension in which I first stopped, I visited what native Parisians, oozing pride in their city, called the most worthwhile spot to be found in all Paris, namely, les Halles, probably the vastest central food market in the world. The time to view these immense, glass-covered halls was at the crack of dawn, when products from all the fields of France were arriving to be unloaded, displayed and purchased by the thousands of small shopkeepers already on hand long before daylight. Nowhere else could the absorbed sight-seer become more quickly convinced of the supreme importance of filling the human stomach. Here were vegetables set out as far as the eye could reach, legs of mutton hanging from hooks in such quantities, that every animal must have had as many legs as a centipede to produce such a number. Enough butter was displayed to cover all the bread of Paris and enough loaves of bread to make a mound as high as the Eifel tower. Where were the hens that laid a billion eggs? I have always prided myself on my ability to distinguish good cheeses. I beheld there the deeply moving spectacle of many unknown kinds to which I was immediately introduced. To complete the picture there was the vintage from many a province in both grapes and wine. The quality of the latter must have been superior, for the owners themselves had already tested it. This was evident from many tinted noses and animated voices. For an eye not satisfied with cheeses or legs of mutton there were all the varied fruits of the autumn season and flowers no end which you might have seen later in the day tucked away in little corners of Paris, for sale at three times the price originally paid here. The human scenes surpassed those of nature's products. Sales, quarrels and bickerings, excited protests over some exhorbitant price created little interludes, no doubt reenacted without a change every morning, and all of it was Paris.

There was a marked contrast to the common humanity concentrated at les Halles in the select humanity which crowded French theatres and operas. This was no less Parisian. I remember especially one night when Louis Metcalf and Charles Decamp, two Yale friends, and I contrived to be supers at the opera house, an entertaining experience eagerly sought by native and foreign students alike. I think the opera was Aida which required a lot of Ethiopian or Egyptian soldiers. No three men could have been a worse assorted lot. Our oriental military misfits with tin breast-plates and long pikes were not calculated to give us even a semblance of martial bearing. After a lot of silly marching and counter-marching we stood in the background of the stage long enough to get a perspective of the pit of the opera crowded with a dolled-up public. Far above this social élite of Paris, in the gallery, we could just see the Parisian intelligentsia.

Our daily life was not all cakes and ale. I had to tackle the work which brought me to Paris and gradually to become acquainted with the chief libraries. Some of the episodes which I recall in this connection could have taken place only in some vaudeville, or in the French capital. At the Bibliotèque nationale, richest in old books and manuscripts, I was from experience elsewhere familiar with the atmosphere, both that which you had to breathe, and the spiritual kind. I was becoming used to the leisurely procedure by which books were handed out; it seemed only a shade speedier than the method I had seen in action at the libraries of Berlin and Munich. There you dropped the title of the books you wanted into a special receptacle on the afternoon of one day, with the fair prospect of getting them as early as ten o'clock on the following morning. At the Nationale you handed your slips directly to an attendant who took them with a dubious air, as if any success in obtaining those particular books required luck, persistence and a naïve faith in the particular call-number given by the catalogue. You brought enough other work to fill in a few hours, and then, if favored by chance, you might look up to find the victorious attendant depositing some volume with a «tenez voilà, monsieur», in a tone which implied the outcome of an arduous quest. In Germany patience had always been the accepted prerequisite in view of the well known library regulations, and no German reader would have dreamed of speeding up what was to him a long established, inviolable procedure. Not so in France. There the great Revolution still lingered and broke out sporadically. One day, in the midst of studious quiet, a slender man not too well clad, with a burning look in his eye and his arms excitedly raised, stood up on his chair and addressed the reading room: «My long-suffering fellow readers; I arrived this morning when this institution of burocratic inefficiency opened its doors. It is now two o'clock. I handed my slips at once to yonder ill-paid attendant and then sat patiently down to wait. What has happened? Nothing. I have waited one hour, two hours, more hours, and what has happened? Nothing. Finally I shall tell you. I have been handed two books. Were they the books which I requested? Certainly not. They were books which no one would think of requesting. They were brought to demonstrate the imbecility and inefficiency in vogue here and which can be remedied only by destroying this entire place». This had all been stated with typical French clarity and in perfect style, and the oration was punctuated by salvos of applause. Reference to the ill-paid underlings brought applause from them likewise. There had been no interference during the scene. The kettle had simply boiled over and the fire had in the process been quenched, as happens in these French flare-ups; after much excited whispering and a general agreement with the protest on the part of the readers, slips were handed in and books made their tardy appearance as usual.

At our hotel I made friends with Julien the garçon who had the care of my room, brushed my clothes and polished my shoes. I learned a great deal from him, not only of the peculiar lingo of Paris, but also of popular customs and of Parisian daily life which always turned up endless surprises. With an innocent trust in the unfailing courtesy of Parisians I had accepted at theatre windows or in restaurants a goodly number of fake coins. Among them was a prominent and villainous pièce de cent sous, a five franc piece which proclaimed its leaden character to everyone but myself. Julien could not have been more annoyed if the false pieces, which I left on my table instead of hiding my disgrace, had been passed off on him. Their presence must have lowered me in his esteem. He was easily the sharpest garçon in all Paris and I had every reason to like and trust him. I knew that he liked me and the regularity with which I handed him a monthly tip. His sense of morality caused me a qualm only once when I came home to find all the false coins gone. I never knew whether they had disappeared singly or all on one night when the stars were set for the perfect crime. At any rate, a day or two later the impeccable Julien appeared before me with a smile and handed me a dozen or more francs in honest coin of the realm. When I looked puzzled he pointed to the table indicating a clean sweep of the fake money. «I got rid of the five franc piece first», he said. Julien was so constantly full of things new to me, that my attitude of 'say that again' was not new to him. «Yes», he said, «I passed it on a bus conductor last night as I was sitting on the outside, in the dark. That made five francs. The rest was easier, as there were only single francs or fifty centimes pieces which you mix with others, all quite simple (he meant, if you are a clever garçon like myself) to get rid of.» When I lamely questioned the ethics of his particular method, Julien laughed boisterously: «Monsieur, it is the way of Paris. I hand the conductor five bad francs. He feels the coin in the dark, he accepts it, he either passes it again on the same bus, or hands it in au bureau. Who can tell where it came from? It is again sent forth and keeps changing hands. Why should we keep it for ourselves and stop its normal journey? Jamais de la vie. Hereafter, Monsieur, keep your eyes open and trust no man or woman who hands you change. Even a person above suspicion is by the custom of the country likely to give you a coin which he does not like.» Thus a casual little sermon delivered by a hotel garçon may contain a practical element which even Schopenhauer would have accepted as a necessary constituent of his philosophy of Worldly Wisdom.

The opening day for the meeting of classes arrived. The prerequisites for enrollment were not very exacting, since practically all courses at the Sorbonne and at the Collège de France were open to the public. The crowd which had assembled in the newly built halls of the Sorbonne looked a bit motley to me, and very unlike the student bodies that I had seen in Germany. There were young-looking boys and elderly women; such a phenomenon as the appearance of females, especially such as were no longer in the heyday of youth, would, in the sacred academic halls of Germany, frequented only by males, have been comparable with the sudden alighting of an extinct awk. Coeducation made victorious inroads there only in later decades. The peculiar gatherings at the Sorbonne were characterized by more than differences of sex. There were also many nationalities, to judge from appearances and from the languages spoken in the corridors.

The Sorbonne, today an imposing array of buildings between the rue des Écoles and the rue Soufflot, was then in its first stages of reconstruction; older halls, some of which had been erected in distant centuries, had become entirely inadequate. The unique and unanswerable reason which normally makes Europeans demolish ancient structures much used by the public, such as university buildings or hospitals, is that they have become nothing less than a deadly menace to public health. Semi-occasionally, as a last resource, improved appointments have been installed in venerable buildings, as at Oxford or Cambridge; but more generally, as in Italy and Spain, the old edifices were considered past praying for as breeders of the plague, and were, therefore, regretfully pulled down. But even the latest peculiarly inadequate subterfuges, labeled concessions to progress, which had been incorporated in such public buildings as the Sorbonne, were by and large another evidence of the national indifference to what we in America euphoniously call comfort and rest. This inability to plan adequate conveniences must be in the blood of European architects; no matter where they have been permitted to erect schools and universities it is the same story.

The confusion among the prospective students was very great; it took several days for the flood waters to run off and let every applicant decide what courses he did not want. This result was generally reached by means of trial visits to the classes, by observing the professors in action and incidentally discovering the popular subjects. Since I was there to learn something of the French language and literature and to obtain the guidance of specific scholars, my choice was more readily made. For the history of the French language I chose Ferdinand Brunot, still winning the spurs and hiding his youth behind a ten inch beard. He turned out an admirable teacher. I attended lectures by Ernest Lavisse, the famous historian, and by Petit de Julleville, who spoke to a large mixed audience on the history of the French theatre. His discourse was of a popular nature, full of conversational turns and pleasant literary details regarding the stage.

My liveliest choice which gave me unqualified pleasure at every class meeting was the critic and essayist Émile Faguet, a professor of the Faculty of Letters. He met his classes twice a week and discussed a number of plays by the chief classical dramatists. Faguet was a medium-sized man of solid frame with uncombed unruly hair, piercing eyes, an unimportant nose and a straggly mustache. His gestures were deliberate; as he made each point he would hold an arm poised in mid-air, with thumb and index joined, and when that arm tired he would fall back on the other. He was clarity and precision personified. We had to read carefully beforehand the plays which he proposed to consider, so we could intelligently follow his analysis. Faguet was the most *spirituel* of all my teachers, his wit and acumen turning a scholarly hour into a profitable and often entertaining experience.

In striking contrast to his brilliant performance was the rather neglected appearance of the man. He ought to have had a valet to attend to his shoes. According to whispered gossip they were cleaned chiefly by wiping them on opposite legs of his trousers a moment before he entered any door. When he came into the class he was always preceded by the janitor who carried a glass of water flanked by a couple of lumps of sugar. This was placed on the desk before the distinguished man took his seat. Every motion of Faguet's hand toward glass and sugar represented a particular stage of his discourse. When he slowly moved the glass of water to the middle of the desk the peroration was about to begin. When he leisurely dropped first one lump of sugar, then the second into the glass and began to stir the liquid, we could look for the last telling sentence. When he lifted the glass we would be told the scope of the next reading; when he drank it off to its sugared dregs we knew that the curtain had come down for the day.

An internationally famous scholar was Gaston Paris. He was a preeminent interpreter of early French literature, a supreme teacher who combined lucidity and incisive analysis with a rare imagination and a colorful approach. The pearls which he cast before our miscellaneous gatherings in his public course were frequently wasted. Only specialists could follow his white plume through the complexities of an ancient and difficult field. He was a typical scholar, slender, of distinguished features with gray hair and beard, an aquiline nose on which rested a pince-nez with an exceedingly flexible spring. This spring permitted him to fold the two lenses into a single glass which he held close to one eye before he bent down within a few inches of his text. He too was preceded by the janitor with the statutory glass of water and two lumps of sugar, but he partook semi-occasionally of this nectar when a normal pause in his material permitted such an interruption. I have thought of introducing this pleasant habit in our class rooms, but none of my colleagues have ever in any way resembled «the good Sir Percivell, who drank the water of the well.»

In Germany one could supplement one's education by a perusal of the many excellent sober daily papers. The Parisian dailies on the other hand were intended pretty generally for particular political groups. Only the better ones, such as *Le Temps, Le Journal des Débats, L'Echo de Paris* and *Figaro* supplied miscellaneous and profitable reading. Notably the feuilletons, brief essays in various fields, written at regular intervals by noted men kept one abreast of current thought and events. My communicative concierge, Julien, or some waiter who had become friendly because we frequented his table, would call our attention to other popular sheets which appealed to their class. At times we could hardly fail to see some shrieking article in Rochefort's *l'Intransigeant* or in the rabid anti-semitic *la Libre Parole*.

The sparkling theatrical reviews written by such men as Faguet, Lemaître, Brunetière or Sarcy were an education in themselves. They formed a comprehensive index to the many plays performed throughout the season. Admission prices to most of the theatres were moderate and we always had the choice of the gallery, or standing room, or the most uncomfortable *strapontins*. These were seats with springs, fastened to the end of each row, which could be let down in the middle of the aisle. They were a most villainous invention, for, apart from blocking the passageways and being an obstacle in case of fire, they would jump back unexpectedly the moment you got up; then the house would be filled with the clatter of rebounding strapontins that sounded like a machine gun. Your pleasure was also dampened by the indignant glances of the person who occupied the end seat in your row. You felt that he hated the sight of you for crowding him in his seat, already a tight fit.

Nowhere in the world was there ever such variety of shows produced. You had the choice of Molière and Racine down to the latest of living French authors. If you were lucky enough to get in, the first night (première) of a new production became an unforgettable event. My aged programs even list two translations from Sophocles and a number of plays by contemporary foreigners, among them such widely different dramatic performances as Bulwer Lytton's *Richelieu,* and D'Annuncio's *la Ville Morte.* In the latter Sarah Bernhardt played one of her greatest roles. At the Théâtre de l'Oeuvre a notable company of actors played untried ventures, and it was there that I first saw some of Ibsen's plays, *Hedda Gabler,* and *John Gabriel Borgman,* and Gogol's *l'Inspecteur Général Revizor.* The roster of actors and actresses included some of the greatest names of the stage. Among them were Sarah Bernhardt and Madame Réjane, Mounet-Sully and the unequalled Coquelin, all of whom played parts in both modern and classical masterpieces; it was their superb impersonation which caused particular plays to run night after night. I recall especially such dramas as *Madame Sansgêne* and *Cyrano de Bergerac.*

We also heard good music in Paris. Cheap subscriptions (abonnements) admitted you to the popular Concerts-Colonne at the enormous Châtelet Theatre. On the other hand, the Concerts-Lamoureux afforded the choicest selection of classical works. An old habit always landed me in the topmost gallery and I saw famous directors both native and foreign. Felix Mottl appeared in person and Richard Strauss directed a program of his own compositions. I heard for the first time the foremost violinist of those days, the Spanish Sarasate, also the pianists Cortot and Harold Bauer, who were then at the beginning of famous careers which have extended into our present time. Years later I met these musicians in Barcelona, at the home of Pablo Casals who had become an intimate friend.

The opera of French Composers attracted me less, though it was performed with commendable verve at the Opéra Comique. I have never been an enthusiast about opera, which I considered a peculiarly irrational mixture of music and theatrical absurdities. The great music of opera is most satisfactory when played at concerts and without the distraction of complicated stage machinery. I have witnessed no end of unexpected mishaps not only in Wagner, whose stage devices frequently invite disaster, but in such innocent inventions as *Freischütz*, and the *Magic Flute*. Of opera Voltaire long ago remarked that whatever isn't worth saying, one may sing. (Ce qui ne vaut pas la peine d'être dit on le chante). Which goes for me too.

The pith of my education was fostered in daily visits to the book stalls. From my window I could look down on the Odéon, under whose arches was set up a most comprehensive array of books, new and old. Their open display attracted a numerous public which never seemed to buy anything. Dozens of idlers, including myself, pawed over the long rows. We read large portions gratis, and pounced especially on volumes just off the press. There were beautifully bound sets of French classics, paper bound copies of the latest novels or of successful plays; there might even be a rare edition of a famous work at a tempting price.

Next in order was the education furnished by the casual inspection of hundreds of yards of bookstalls set up along the left bank of the Seine. The volumes were of every age. The men and women who had charge of these curious assortments were also timeless creatures. In all seasons they could be found either seated on something improvised or walking up and down in front of their stalls, hoping against hope that a book lover might appear and break the monotony by some purchase. Sometimes they varied their routine toward midday by unwrapping a bit of bread and cheese or drinking some coffee from a tin; and French coffee served to the ordinary citizen requires no obloquy of mine to describe its unfitness to be called a beverage.

Of the books displayed, the vast majority were waifs. They showed by their imprint, if it survived, that they had come from every land and covered more mileage than the crusaders. Many had neither title nor jacket. Others were odd numbers of same set; their comradeship had been forever dissolved by the unforeseen vicissitudes that so often scatter human belongings to the four winds. Miracles have occurred in the discovery among these vagrants of a missing volume which could relate a singular tale of many adventures. I myself have picked up old prints and quaint maps and often lamented the limitations of the franc which could not be stretched to cover more purchases from the quaint bouquinistes of the Seine.

Student life in Paris bore no resemblance to that of the German universities. Any judgment of it had to be superficial, and more social than academic: you saw the students in their comings and goings, not so much to and from the Sorbonne, as in and about the restaurants and cafés. Apart from their personal distaste for regular class-room attendance, there were two other reasons which drove the men into public places; first the absence of any dormitory system, Student-Union, or club in which to congregate fraternally and second, the wide-spread indulgence of French fathers, notably Parisians, who conceded to their sons complete independence, and freedom from parental vigilance. In consequence, many young people left home and resided on the «Left Bank of the Seine,» in dozens of streets near the University, known for their rooming facilities, notably in hôtels-garnis which took in rather heterogeneous lodgers. Collectively they were much younger than the body of German students, less serious, less tractable and, in their meetings in the street or in the restaurants, more demonstrative, noisy and uncontrolled. It was, therefore, natural for a foreigner to infer from the temperamental nature of that scholastic body that academic tasks were resting lightly on the shoulders of most of them.

The restaurants and cafés of the Latin Quarter had the attractive aspects of all live pageants. They were sometimes dramatic, always animated. I recall an eating house run by an Alsatian, which we frequented with great regularity. The wife who symbolized the French household goddess Thrift followed a good native tradition, by holding the fort behind the pay-desk. She kept the accounts and disbursed to her husband with the proper precaution such funds only as were necessary to run the establishment. He was thus enabled to attend to the irksome buying and bargaining and catering, and no doubt had to give a strict account to his vigilant better half.

We had many happy evenings there, notably when American friends arrived and joined us at our regular table. I recall the advent of Frank Mather, then on the faculty of Williams College and later at Princeton, a cultivated and stimulating talker in matters of art and letters. In the field of art the culinary always came first. French cooking, gigot de pré salé, creamed spinach and the like were compared with the inferior dishes offered everywhere else in the world. From these lofty discussions we descended to an exchange of impressions of the plays and books and doings all about us. In return for the benefits which a newcomer might confer in the higher realms we initiated him in the choice dishes of the menu and introduced him to our witty Alsatian waitress. The most attractive feature was the small sum we had to pay for an excellent meal; our dinners amounted to one and a quarter francs, and a meal of one franc seventy-five centimes was for a capitalist or a gourmand.

Student night-life began about twilight and ran its course through all the happy hours when the sun discreetly remained below the horizon. The doings of the Latin Quarter in those years suggested to overworked imaginations a kind of tangled and promiscuous existence, all kinds of liberty and fraternity with a conspicuous intervention of womankind. Its life was reported to be one of questionable ethics and subterranean morality which shocked the superior foreigner and lured him to inspect it at close range. Readers of «French» novels skimmed through the first pages, intent on discovering the chapter which paints life in the Latin Quarter, where they would always become absorbed by the tale. Obviously, cafés or restaurants after nightfall gradually unfolded their peculiar social features. The women of the boulevard, like everyone else, enjoyed admission to the cafés with the tacit understanding that they restrain their advances which of course they never did. Their presence added to the income of the place; it stimulated the sales of food and drink. Such ephemeral associations as were formed on such occasions by the students seemed to me the most unalluring on earth. In that little world of a dozen nationalities and various races, white, yellow and black, the problem of ethics did not strike an observer as much as that of health, decency and physical cleanliness. In such situations, exacting routine occupations are a help, and keep you from lingering by the way. And so those particular Latin Quarter memories are among the vaguest, the least significant of my fruitful and busy sojourn in the French capital.

Winter winds were giving place to the faintly perceptible warmth of approaching spring. This meant more concentration and less procrastination if I wished to have something to show for my pains by the summer. As I mused over the discomforts of my pleasant lodging I was often filled with wonder at the helpless attitude of all Europeans who manage to survive through their chilly winters with indoor temperatures very little unlike the outside. In the lofty top-story of my quarters the bleak winds had played at will in utter disregard of my comfort. Chillblains and frostbitten fingers and toes were just around the corner, so I decided to indulge in the luxury of some briquettes, those slow-burning contraptions of pressed coal-dust, the questionable efficacy of which I had already experienced in Munich. My fireplace had not been used in decades, perhaps never, and the old chimney must have been amazed at being put to such an unheard-of practice. My concierge Julien could not believe his eyes at the sight. His speechless amazement was born entirely of his French thrift, and he plainly suffered on seeing good francs going up the chimney in smoke. This did not prevent his coming in frequently to give me good-day, and, incidentally, to praise my diligence, while warming his hands over the fire.

I had planned to leave Paris by the end of July and travel a few weeks before beginning my last term at Munich. The days were hurrying by as I attempted to gather the many threads of a year's sojourn. My main difficulty was how to resist the lure of seeing and doing so many things which the flight of time was threatening to make impossible. When Julien, whose aim in life was the fullest amount of leisure possible, hinted that I «travaillais trop dur», I gave in to the beckoning of out-of-door Paris in May and June. Whenever I could, I loafed about the Luxembourg gardens or in the Bois de Boulogne. The shifting scenes of children again at play under the vigilant eye of their bonnetted nurses inspired a growing distaste for work, and I occasionally wasted hours watching the youngsters float their boats on the ponds or chase their hoops along the paths right into the first pedestrian. Idle grown-ups sat reading on the benches under the trees, spring fever was in the air. During successive days we took a boat down the Seine to Belleville or Saint Cloud and ate unforgettable meals in the open, where the breeze lifted the gleaming white tablecloth. We ventured into a restaurant of ancient repute which only opulent guests could patronize more than once; this was the Boeuf-a-la-Mode, near the Palais-Royal. What its fate has been in later years I do not know, but it was once a land-mark for strangers ranking in signifance with Notre Dame or the Louvre. The boeuf-a-la-mode served there was probably the progenitor of all pot roasts, although the descendants, as is usual, do not measure up to their ancestor. It must have owed its origin to some inspired convent cook who in his spiritual surroundings acquired his skill under divine guidance. A meal there was enough to remember Paris by for all your days. Nowhere else were there ever served such hors-d'oeuvres, such potatoes, such peas and carrots and onions, such desserts, or such burgundy.

I had unusual views of Paris during the spring in long walks at night. The home of a distant relative was also distant from my lodging by several miles. He lived on the other side of the Étoile and had given me a standing invitation to take the Sunday evening meal with him, which always included a game of chess afterwards. This was a hobby of his, to which his intimate friends had to yield or stay away. One game generally became two, and to get the picture of the chessboard out of my head I walked home by anyone of many ways. There were various avenues leading from the Étoile to the Seine, continuing to the Latin quater by a dozen historic streets. It was often after one o'clock when my bell routed Julien out of his improvised bed by the front door. He was too discreet to ask questions, and I would hardly have succeeded in making him believe that I had, in my own company, been having the most satisfactory glimpse of Paris under lamplight and starlight that anyone could desire.

Everyone whose melancholy fate it is to leave Paris after a year's sojourn should visit the tomb of Napoleon before his departure; he would there read and understand the Emperor's last request, engraved over his resting-place, 'that his ashes be allowed to repose on the banks of the Seine among the French people he so deeply loved'.

A DOCTOR'S DEGREE: BEGINNING A TEACHING CAREER

The spring had been disturbed by the outbreak of the Spanish American War. At the beginning I proclaimed my patriotic fervor by talking loudly of going home at once to enlist. But presently my American friends abated their cries of vengeance against the dastardly foe and the slogan «Remember the Maine» was heard less and less. My own immediate return was not ordered by either military or parental authority. So I remained abroad to complete the final stage of my studies.

In the late spring my sister Elizabeth arrived in Paris. She made an unsuccessful effort for a week or more to get used to my Latin Quarter mustache and black flowing tie. At last I could bear the agony expressed in her face no longer and shaved the vile appendage off, to her volubly expressed relief and thanks. The tie survived for several years. When draped on a human form, it resembled the sympathetic crape fastened to the front door knob of a bereaved home. I occasionally brought it out into the light to recall its showy past, until it was finally consumed by moths.

Before Elizabeth's return home, we decided on a brief ten days excursion to England where we managed to get a glimpse of London, of Stratford-on-Avon, and of a cathedral or two. We squeezed an unbelievable number of sights into a few London days. We began with a solid British breakfast of very dark concentrated tea and Yarmouth bloaters, or kippered herring, or delicious whitebait; we made the acquaintance of that unforgettable stone-cold English toast, prepared ages before, and given ample time to absorb some of the London fog. We took in the British Museum and the Tower of London; we rode miles on the horse busses, and after the National Gallery there was still plenty of time for Carlyle's house in Chelsea. But we would always get back to Oxford Street at the proper hour to order fresh strawberries and Devonshire cream with the same tea, and in the face of complete exhaustion we would end the day with a show. We drove to Warwick Castle and Kenilworth and we spent two days in Stratford. I recall a bus which arrived there laden with tourists. The poor things were turned loose by their guide at the door of the church of the Holy Trinity with the peremptory command, «Five minutes to see Shakespeare's grave.» As regards English cathedrals, their study and comparison later occupied me in an amateurish way and lured me to pass an occasional summer in England.

After this brief interlude I returned to Munich where I had to put my nose to the grindstone and my pen to paper. The notes which I had taken for my thesis in the course of two years would have filled several paper baskets. In the midst of the torment of composing my «dissertation» it occured to me that the achievement of a degree is considered by our universities an unnecessarily important step in a teaching career. Many a student feels that his thesis is a task that must be speedily got over with, so that he may get a job; it is a stone to be rolled up a hill entailing labor as uninspired and hopeless as that of Sisyphus. I have continued to believe that the writing of a thesis is unrelated to the career of the teacher. Its peculiar, so-called «originality» does not resemble the creative originality of one who writes easily because he is moved to do so. I myself was far from ready to put anything definitive into a printed form. But however insignificant my thesis might turn out, it had in compensation yielded me many educational by-products. I had traveled in various countries absorbing as much culture as I could digest, and the degree had been throughout a minor incident only. Miscellaneous reading, the chequered experience of living in the company of cultivated men had constituted the main process out of which I might ultimately evolve thoughts and conclusions of my own. If they turned out good enough to put on paper from time to time, or worth presenting orally to classes, that was all that I dared to hope for.

When the great day set for my examination approached, I received an official notice regarding the various preliminaries connected with my appearance before my examiners. To be thoroughly impressed with the formality of the occasion it was customary for the candidate to dress in a swallowtail coat in open daylight, with a white tie, white gloves and a stove-pipe hat. As far as I know, no German has ever been asked to write a thesis on the origin of that comic outfit, which everyone contemplated without batting an eye. The dress-suit of the candidate was generally a borrowed one so that a successful fit was the exception and not the rule. In my own case the collar was too tight and my gloves two sizes too big. My tails looked like Charlie Chaplin's, and when I put on my silk topper brother Will remarked, «Take off that hat occasionally and rest your ears.» In sharp contrast with their victim's clothes, those of the professors looked like the oldest which they possessed — the kind that never had a pressing in all their worn existence. Thus at three in the afternoon I oozed starched formality as I set out to meet the ordeal. The impressive fact was that I had before me at one and the same time all the professors whom I had seen at a distance and admired singly. My situation seemed comparable with that of Daniel in the lion's den. I expected some preliminary growling, whereupon the brutes would quickly dispatch me. Anyone would have looked rather helpless in the presence of such a bevy of distinguished and erudite men; they epitomized before the learned world the various fields in which I was to be examined, namely language, literature, European history, and the history of art. The first growl turned out to be the happy suggestion that I make myself comfortable and remove my gloves. If I had been asked to include my collar and tie I would have been more comfortable still. To my surprise I found myself in the presence of kindly and considerate examiners; they may have got my number early and remembered the old adage that out of nothing nothing comes. At all events, they did not bore into my weak spots, but allowed me to hold forth on matters relatively prominent in my memory. Many commonplace facts vanished at moments when I needed them most and I was grateful that some of my replies did not arouse loud laughter of derision. Herman Paul, whom I dreaded especially when I recalled his tart and destructive criticisms in class, proved the gentlest of lions and actually purred at some of my successful guesses. Muncker and Schick fastened their gaze on my bulging starched bosom and charitably led me into well known paths. Riehl seemed impressed by my careful scrutiny of the particular pictures in Italian and French galleries which I had previously discovered to be his favorites. This detail contributed to the successful outcome of an ordeal of three hours. Thus, I laid the foundation on which I have built that rambling edifice called an education.

The peculiar destiny of my thesis must, like that of all masterpieces, have been written in the stars. I corrected the proof sheets while the printing of a few hundred regulation copies went merrily forward. The completed work had then been safely stowed away by the printer in his storeroom, bundled and packed to meet the presumptive demand which would presently arise. Then my reputation was saved by what fire insurance policies call an act of God. The printer's shop with all of its priceless contents went up in flames. I survived the shock with some three or four copies which by chance I had taken away the day before and have thus salvaged for posterity. Carlyle had a similar experience with the manuscript of his French Revolution; he courageously rewrote his book. My work did not seem of comparable significance; besides, the printer folded up, my own courage was at an ebb, funds to reprint were non-existent. So the three or four surviving copies of my labors plus my sheepskin have ever since represented the outward and visible sign of two busy, fruitful years. My interests turned later to a different field and those studies became ancient and often unrelated memories.

A final picture of my student days deserves to be recorded. German universities relinquished their venerable customs slowly. One that was conspicuous in many academic centers was the *Mensur*, the practice of duelling. It did not enjoy equal prestige everywhere and was more in evidence in smaller cities like Heidelberg and Bonn than in Munich. It so happened that some of my Munich friends had left for the University of Heidelberg. Since they were members of a prominent duelling fraternity, I was enabled through their intercession to witness a duel in that famous old institution. By its enthusiastic sponsors the «art» was always proclaimed a trial of courage, a commendable «Cavalierly practice» called *Ritterliche Uebung*. It did not seem to me more sanguinary than some football games at Yale in the famous days of Heffelfinger and the flying wedge, when after every signal the ground resembled a Roman battlefield. But as an artificial conflict, the improvised combat looked like a bit of bloody medieval sword play. All of the steps leading to the final meeting had to be taken in accordance with certain statutes and regulations. A member of one brotherhood deliberately «insulted» the member of another, both having been previously selected by a fixed procedure; the «insulté» then challenged the insulter and, after the usual details of the entire affair had been arranged, the two combatants could meet and proceed to cut each other up by rule. The blows were also limited by rule. The wounded warrior was then stitched and bound up by an attendant surgeon. Throat and shoulders were heavily padded to protect the jugular which, if severed, would be beyond any rule. But the top of the head, the top of the ear or the side of the face were exposed and inviting, and could be successfully laid open. When the slashed surface had been sewed up the number of stitches were carefully counted, as they were of prime significance in determining the relative merit of the duelists and in assigning the victory. Many German students carried to their graves great scars which, far from being considered a most unfortunate disfiguration, were held to be a permanent source of pride and an eternal badge of courage.

As the irrational world moved on, it increasingly seemed to me that I had passed many years in a Garden of Eden destined to become legendary. The privileges which I had enjoyed in that long ago through some kindness of fate, the harvest of memories which has since enriched my days, constantly prompted the question whether similarly pleasing communities of congenial workers would ever arise again. Obviously what today looks like supineness on our part in the face of the social evils which were already in evidence does not, in all fairness, vitiate the record. We were aware of the international political conflicts and social clashes in the making. But we considered it permissible none the less to lead an existence peacefully absorbed by the spiritual values that seemed worthwhile. That Munich world consisted, as far as I was aware, of a community of idealists who were satisfied within a minimum of material goods. They were creative men who sought whatever fulfillment they could attain in themselves first, and thereafter in the stimulating association of others.

It was now time for me to realize that I had devoted several years exclusively to spending money on the improvement of my so-called mind. The day of earning my bread had arrived. On my return to America I offered myself on the auction block to the highest bidder for newly sprouted teaching talent. It was the middle of the academic year, there were no immediate bids, so I had to content myself until the spring, when the fancy of college heads lightly turns to thoughts of hiring and firing instructors.

It was fortunate that I could be at home. Father had passed away in the previous fall and a bereaved household would bear heavily on mother and my sisters. A few quiet months followed, devoted to becoming acquainted with the family. This process is always pleasant and profitable, in spite of those slightly annoying qualities which members of a family feel free to vent on one another. I had ample time for leisurely reading. My own collection of books was still insignificant. I possessed sets of English novelists, a complete Carlyle whom I had read entire, some volumes connected with my European studies, and a number of the world's classics.

The German and French fields with which I had made myself familiar left me with a vague dissatisfaction. I was not attracted by the prospect of having to go over a lot of ground already covered by others. The search for a new plot in an old field might be an arduous one; it might leave me in a pocket and not on an open road. On the other hand, I had been frequently puzzled by the fact that Spanish writers and Spanish civilization were seldom drawn into a discussion. In Germany only Paul Heyse had spoken of Spain with understanding. In France the people had reechoed Victor Hugo's opinion that «once in Spain you are no longer in Europe.» Spain might have been on the moon. So I took up Spanish seriously to get a first-hand idea of the Peninsula and of the part which Spaniards had played in Europe and America. Father had traveled through the Spanish southwest where he had picked up an old anthology of Spanish prose; I got hold of a battered Spanish grammar which served as a basis for my preliminary efforts. In earlier New England Spanish studies had already been fostered by Ticknor, Prescott, Longfellow and others; their renewed flowering began about the turn of the century, when American scholars again made an effective contribution to a fuller acquaintance with all things Spanish, the Spanish American War being a powerful contributory cause.

As far as teaching was concerned, I was still tied to the studies which I had just completed. So I accepted an offer extended by Bucknell, a small denominational college, to teach French and German. The college, at Lewisburg, Pennsylvania, bore the proud title of university. It was a coeducational, self-sufficient institution hidden amid prosperous orchards in the picturesque, rolling landscape of the lower Susquehanna. The president at the time was Dr. J.H. Harris, a tall, impressive personality with a broad loosely-hung frame. He had proved himself to be a practical administrator, which implied that he was also a successful legacy seeker. He gave the campus a flourishing aspect by adding a number of buildings and various improvements. As the head of a denominational institution, he was also a prominent religious figure in the state.

The small midwestern towns which identified themselves with the educational institutions in their midst were much the same — they all had their peculiar local pride, with unassuming friendly customs. They observed the loyalty due to their particular churches by attending Sunday services with regularity. In their culture and daily thought they had preserved something of the America of pioneer days. Like their grandparents the «townfolk» kept up the liveliest interest in one another, and no member of the community could escape the kindly intervention of the neighbors in his personal affairs. This was entertaining enough in itself, if you shared the town life without snobbish reservations and indulged in no invidious comparisons with larger cities. Most of this «small town stuff» has probably disappeared in the acceleration of modern life, so a record of my own experience with the social life of a typical community may seem worth preserving.

On my arrival at the station I was met by a young student, the representative of an organization which took strangers under its wing. He led me to the home of a widow of Pennsylvania-German extraction, who kept a boarding house of shining neatness. Some of her rooms were already let to members of the senior class with whom I soon became friends. One of them, David Pitt, rose into prominence as a preacher and occupied the pulpit of a large metropolitan church. His fine career after he had left college reassured me that his early resolution to follow a religious vocation had not been undermined by my presence. We met again many years later here in Berkeley, where he had been invited to preach. Having seen his name in our daily paper, I hastened to attend his service. At its close I greeted him without mentioning my name and apologized for having intruded my reprehensible person into the piety of an elevating morning. A shout of cordial recognition removed the veil of years and led us to recall our many religious discussions of the Bucknell days.

To the Germantown extraction of our landlady we owed the excellence of the cooking, but to the presence of teetotalism the absence of all beverages of alcoholic content. From her many connections with town and church we derived the information necessary to keep us abreast of worthwhile rumours. Her budget of news gathered in the course of her shopping or after evening prayer meetings was comprehensive; it left no one out, it rectified reports of the previous week and introduced new items for future rumination. She had a vivacious disposition and when outside of the house she was as mobile as a squirrel gathering nuts. She did all the marketing and showed a detailed knowledge of the marketing of others. Inside the house she was a capable and motherly soul, resembling the devoted barnyard fowl which runs about intermittently pursuing and teaching her chicks, inquiring where they had been or what they had seen whenever they returned to their own corral. As the meals that she served were unfailingly appetizing, abundant, and miraculously cheap, we were on the verge of eating the good woman out of house and home. It was therefore a foregone conclusion at the end of the first semester that she would proclaim her prospective bankruptcy together with her inability to continue to set before us those daily flesh-pots of Egypt. But she charitably agreed to go on providing us with our breakfasts. Rather than undertake the futile search for a comparable boarding house, we accepted the offer of three very elderly women to cook the remaining meals for us. They happened to live next door, but their proximity did not compensate us for the inferior unbalanced diet which they set before us. Abundance gave way to bare sufficiency; the varied and savory cooking to which we had grown accustomed now consisted of a depressing monotony of dishes, among which I remember the constant reappearance of boiled potatoes, stewed meat and apple pie. We ate everything uncomplainingly. Our undeniably healthy appetites were aroused, on the one hand, by the stimulating country air, but they were restrained, on the other, by the humility of our new household, in keeping with which we gave due thanks at every meal for whatever we received.

In the center of the town there were several churches of different denominations situated on the opposite corners of two main street crossings. Our landlady attended one of them; the women who daily restricted our diet at meal time attended another. Such a situation was bound to muddy the springs of our information. The news brought to the breakfast table was sometimes refuted by the details imparted to us at dinner. After a little experience we managed to weigh and sift essential items, having derived additional correctives from our own immediate contacts about town and in the college. These cross-currents of social opinions to my knowledge never marred the friendly relations or diminished the spontaneous hospitality of the little town.

Among the students I found the atmosphere one of pleasant comradeship. On the campus as well as in the classroom I was impressed by their maturer ways. They swallowed long assignments with a ready acquiescence that I have often missed since, and the earnestness with which they applied themselves to the study of impossible foreign languages revealed a grim determination to do or die. When I had weathered the difficulty of having before me a number of students older than myself, my apple cart rolled on more smoothly and I disposed of my ware to a tolerant class with growing enthusiasm.

The French classes went forward easily. They were not all elementary and I could undertake some advanced reading. My recent experience in Paris helped me to transfer some of the novel French manner and method from the banks of the Seine to the banks of the Susquehanna. If I had copied French gestures, worn a monocle, and hired the janitor to set before me at the auspicious moment a glass of water and two lumps of sugar, I would no doubt have shaken that unworldly institution to its religious foundation.

In the case of elementary German, it was a vastly more difficult task to introduce daylight into the character of that language. I could utter a string of German words without worrying about the inverted order of engine and caboose in that linguistic freight train. But teaching the structure of German to an incredulous group of novices required more eloquence and persuasion than I could muster. I lacked the intricate and detailed art of elucidation needed to analyse that grandiose edifice of endless genitives and datives, of delayed past participles and gratuitous infinitives. While insisting to the class that it was possible to say a thing clearly in German, I found myself admitting in the next breath that it was easier to be complicated and obscure. One section of serious students, inclined to view the German language without a sense of humour, would look on my careful disposition of peculiar forms on the blackboard as pure legerdemain, especially when I reached the noble forms of *dürfen* or *können,* I can, I could, I had been able, and the rest. «Suppose now,» I would continue boldly, «I hitch an infinitive to the expression 'I would have been able,' such as 'to teach,' or two infinitives 'to teach him to read,' what happens to the past participle (gekonnt) of the main verb? It becomes an infinitive also (können).» The class was on the verge of receiving this absurdity with contemptuous laughter. I bolstered my shaky position by assigning the explanatory pages of the grammar for the next lesson and dismissed the class with misgivings of my own. I was more shaken after class when a lingering student approached and, implying that there were no listeners and that I might as well come out with the truth, asked: «When you are actually speaking German, what really happens to können?» I spent another hour giving him endless examples, but he left me dejected (that is, we were both dejected) as he muttered: «They call that a spoken language?»

As an educational luminary my light has been of the reflected kind emanating from notable students. In one of my classes of that memorable first venture, I had no less a person than Christy Mathewson of immortal baseball fame. He had come to Bucknell from a minor school on a fellowship. Already a prominent athlete in those college years, he would have been a source of greater pride to us all had we guessed the glory of his unmatched pitching career. His admirers were presently filled with sorrow, for ill health pursued him and his death in his prime shocked the baseball world. He was buried near the school where I had known him for so brief a time. Whenever during his great days I proudly displayed a photograph which he had given me, envious baseball fans hinted at the possibility of my getting a few extra deadhead admissions to his games. I still think of him as an unpretentious and friendly giant seated before me in the last row.

Having been confined by wintry blasts and mounds of snow, the coming of spring seemed more than ever a happy contrivance of nature. A similar transformation took place in our baser human nature, and we needed no urging to exchange our stuffy hibernation over a stove for loafing in the new sun and clearing our congested minds of unimportant ideas. Spring fever moved lazily up the land and we watched with approval as the orchards and hillsides put on their garbs of pale green. Week-end hikes and picnics followed, and we went up into the foothills to watch the loggers at work in the lumber camps; we rode on the tiny trains which carried the logs down into the valley and sat with the loggers as we all ate our lunch together at the noon hour. There were also educational trips of discovery. Two or three of my students were budding naturalists and April meant the stirring of many varieties of bugs and beetles; song birds began to arrive and early wild flowers gradually put in their appearance. So I absorbed information with little effort watching the others turn up stones or wade into boggy sheltered spots for every kind of renewed life.

The tracks of various railroads ran up and down the river valley; lying on our backs we would watch the endless freight trains, hauled by two laboring, pounding engines and scores of cars as they appeared and disappeared around some curve. We would count the number of cars in competition like kids, or swap sandwiches, or drive off straying cattle when they nosed too close to us and interrupted our peaceful siesta. It could not have been very different in the idyllic days of Theocritus, not so long ago.

The faculty, on which I found some congenial friends, deserves a cordial word. The teaching bodies of our small midwestern colleges, snobbishly called «fresh water» by seaboard graduates, have played a large part in the education of the American people. Their service has been insufficiently remembered and extolled. They have included distinguished men of remarkable ability who began their careers with high hopes and ambitions and who might in other surroundings have achieved a name in the world. In their particular academic surroundings many of them have become anchored by any one of many chains, by growing families, by lack of professional stimulants, by administrative duties, above all by the absence of adequate library facilities. Inevitably their larger hopes and prospects have slowly disappeared over the immediate horizon and they have consequently devoted themselves to the routine education of their students.

In this connection Bucknell was in many respects superior to other small colleges. It had financial support through its religious affiliations. It possessed an active administrator in Dr. Harris. It offered a satisfactory curriculum for the bachelor's degree. But it had in my time a most meager library, and I soon took the course which must have been pursued by other teachers also, that of substituting various activities for the quest of books. Although this course might not be beneficial to study and scholarship, it did serve to consolidate the community in its friendly social relations. It helped me personally to establish some cordial associations of happy memory with members of the faculty.

Dean Franck E. Rockwood, Professor of Latin, was a cultivated scholar, and in spite of his retiring character exerted a fine influence on the student body. He had had years of experience in observing the life of our small colleges. He spoke now and then with warmth of the sterling qualities of the undergraduates. But he had missed the significant association and stimulating daily contact with classical scholars like himself. It therefore became inevitable that he would ultimately be drafted for the administration of the student body, and in the course of the events he had adapted himself, like other colleagues, to his community which managed to get along very well without the rest of the world.

Professor E.M. Heim taught Economics, and I was early drawn to his unobtrusive superior qualities of mind and character. He had wit and a sense of humor which buoyed him up under cramping conditions. His family was a haven of hospitality, frequently offering me a meal because I managed to hang around near the dinner hour. The excellence of the food was made more striking by the animated presence of a youthful relative whose female pulchritude had a high rating with me and was, as Jane Austen might have put it, the subject of much favorable comment on the part of others.

One of the teachers of French was a Gascon. He also taught in the school of Music. The number of his years was not known to anyone. He would nullify the rules of French pronunciation which I was trying to instill in one class by an entirely opposite practice in another. He had the habit of sounding silent final e as they do in his native province in France, and I therefore had the delicate task of persuading my confused students that «un-e petit-e fill-e» need not be pronounced with that mess of gratuitous syllables. He also disconcerted me by his failure to appreciate my wholly refined sense of humor. I ventured to repeat to him legitimate Parisian jests which I had brought fresh from overseas, but they must have seemed far-fetched for they never got a hand from him. To keep to the fore his connection with the teaching of music, he would hum to himself as he walked and the chance buzzing of a bee in the halls would be followed by the appearance of his ageing form.

There were two young doctors in the community; one was connected with the gymnasium and in charge of the athletes; the other was busied in the town or drove about the countryside. The latter was also assistant to the veteran local physician who was still consulted by everyone, but had turned his night calls and distant visits over to the assistant. On one occasion I had betaken myself with a cold to the old doctor who at once prescribed a cure-all which he kept ready-made on an office shelf. He persuaded me to take a spoonful right there under his eye. He must have given me Sloane's liniment by mistake, for it burned all the way down and I went home to die. I at once appealed for a soothing syrup to the assistant. He told me that it was not to be had in town, but that he knew where, and we became fast friends. He had to cover many miles with his buggy every day, and he and his horse blindfolded could have found any farmhouse or roadhouse in the country. On occasion he would stop for me week-ends early in the morning, and I would grab something to read while I was sitting in his buggy and waiting for him to kill or maim some patient. I too got to know that countryside and all its common ailments. «I ought to be half a dozen men» the young medico said once. «I could profitably combine a surgeon with an internal medicine man and a clever horse doctor. I ought to have a cure for dogs and cats and be able to put the sawdust back into a pet doll. Half the time these people don't remember why they called me or what member of the family was to have first turn. You wouldn't suspect it, but I am chock-full of spiritual advice. As a rule, they eat too much and then sit moaning in a rocking chair on the front porch. If I prescribe a needed laxative, it has to be alcoholically camouflaged and more potent than the patent medicines they all swallow. Then the neighbor feels the same ailment coming on, and my prescription is consumed in a jiffy.» I told him to go to school to the old witch doctors, and he might earn higher fees. Naturally we always found time for a noon-day respite with the proper refreshment to make easier those happy, arduous days.

An epoch without automobiles, without movies and without speed now seems incredibly remote. I sometimes think I would gladly have it all return. That pleasant social relation between town and gown with all its tame simplicity has no doubt passed and few remain to recall it. Since I had attached myself especially to the student body, I was often invited to their entertainments. My recollection is that we spent evenings until the late hour of ten o'clock playing charades and games rather than cards; with the latter I have been a drag more often than an addition. Smoking was practically unheard of on such occasions, even among the men, and as far as drinking was concerned, I have never been without a glass of anything for so long a stretch of time as in that happy year. We talked of the people we knew; we set up and knocked down reputations and personalities; we discussed such current events as casually drifted into our ken, for news from the outside world came to us chiefly on the morning train with the arrival of Philadelphia papers. The subject of religion was broached chiefly from the point of view of regular church attendance. People took for granted that everyone had a routine faith and approved of the invention of Sunday and of going to church. Inside of that self-satisfied and unconsciously circumscribed horizon I often became aware of how far removed our American life could be from my limitless European surroundings of the previous years.

Having been satisfied with my teaching, Dr. Harris asked me to continue on his faculty, but the intervention of my friend and teacher at Yale, Gustav Grüner, had procured me an offer to teach German in the Sheffield Scientific School in New Haven. I mulled over the distasteful prospects of once again drilling a class in German word puzzles, but I finally decided to accept the renewed opportunity of study at Yale. It was not an easy decision. I had a genuine affection for Bucknell and some of my friends hinted that I would be missed. But to be in New Haven again meant old friends, a library, notable teachers, and stimulating associations. Moreover, the stars might some day meet in a favorable conjunction and open the door into the Spanish field which had become my absorbing interest.

I was, above all, eager to get away from the risk of becoming exclusively a teacher of elementary language forms to students who have outgrown the monosyllables of the nursery by a couple of decades. I have never reconciled myself to our pretense of success in making grownups converse in a foreign language so that their conversation really contains matter fit for grownups. I have consequently maintained that the chief objective of language teaching should be a competent reading knowledge of foreign works. A student who has an intelligent grasp of the language before him is educationally far ahead of the one whose time has been wasted in piecing together mechanically a few speech forms. While the fluent reader has acquired ideas and culture, the hesitant speaker has got only a smattering of doubtful practical value.

By this turn of events I was to make a second entrance into the life of Yale eight years after those September days when I first appeared on the campus as a freshman. Some may question the wisdom of such an excess of school atmosphere as I have hitherto recorded. They may even consider my return to Yale a kind of vicious circle characteristic of the limited academic mind. But they have not heard the half of it, for all that has passed seems to me now only the beginning. I might have gone out into the world and learned something of a «practical» nature, if only for the sake of such an experience. But I could have dropped the lure of study and of books no more easily than I could have dropped a live wire. No doubt I have occasionally been envious of people who have achieved practical, tangible results, but it was impossible to follow them for my own bent held me by the scruff of my neck. Sometimes we can get away with these limitations by associating with practical, active persons who have managed to keep abreast of the moving world. By this clever method we successfully hide behind our friendships, using them as a kind of protective coloring, and when we are occasionally discovered in the company of our betters we get a higher rating than we do when left to our own devices.

Toward the end of my first year as a useful money-making citizen I counted my savings to see if they could be stretched to reach across the Atlantic and back again. With the additional assistance of guide books and the advice of friends experienced in the strange ways of Spanish hotels and boarding houses, I was at last to get my first glimpse of the Peninsula. Three months would give me only a nodding acquaintance but it would pave the way in other years for a more extended residence.

A friendly correspondence with American scholars in the Spanish field began and their advice served me in the practical disposition of my itinerary and in the preliminaries of my studies. I was indebted especially to Albert Kürsteiner, a careful and painstaking linguist and professor of romance languages at Indiana University. He sent me from time to time lists of books and fortified me with letters to his friends in Madrid. His intervention procured for me congenial shelter and skilled help in the acquisition of the spoken speech. Another unique scholar whose friendship was at first confined to profitable letters was the Dutchman Fonger De Haan. He taught at Bryn Mawr College and was without question the most brilliant as well as the most eccentric of all my associates in the Spanish field. When we looked for him at Bryn Mawr we would be told that he was in Holland. When we had been reliably informed that he was visiting his family in Holland, he would turn up in Madrid. He actually did appear in Spain during one of my first summers there and I benefited by his helpful direction for many years thereafter. Our younger set which gathered around him in Madrid was impressed by his vast learning, but we had constantly to be on the alert in apprehension of his unpredictable actions and jugdments.

I took passage on a venerable freighter bound for Gibraltar. We stopped at the Azores to take on the world's best pineapples and at Madeira for cargoes of varied fruits. We reached our destination as prescribed for that trip by the grace of God, but on its next voyage some overstrained boiler exploded and the old ship went to the bottom. When in retrospective gratitude I mentioned the catastrophe to a friend, he irrelevantly brought up the old saying that those who are born to be hanged will never be drowned.

SPAIN FOR THE FIRST TIME

When I first beheld the Mediterranean during my Italian journey, I had looked at its beauty in romantic admiration only. At Gibraltar my interest had acquired a wider scope. I had swapped educational horses in midstream, but I was not yet well acquainted with the character of the Spanish horse which I had decided to ride. I had made a start in some historical reading on Italy and Spain and was now earger to know more about the whole Mediterranean world. Obviously, when I first saw the Spanish coast I had only the merest hint of all there would be to see and learn later.

In those very days the British Prime Minister, Lord Salisbury, had pronounced Spain a moribund nation. Spain may have seemed so from the vantage ground of Gibraltar: from there the might of the British Empire could look down scornfully on the recently beaten and humiliated Spanish people. But those people could have found ample amends for the insignificant slur of a British Prime Minister in my admiration and my faith in their regenerating dynamic vitality, if they had only known about them.

Gibraltar in the summertime betrayed the proximity of a torrid Africa. It called for a cork helmet and a cool drink. The dancing and vibrating air of the confined streets was that of an outdoor oven. The protected lobby of the hotel, though stuffy, was a restful haven after climbing over accessible portions of The Rock in competition with the Barbary apes at home on the upper wooded slopes and terraces.

In the company of two American friends who had official business to transact I called on the American consul. This was at that time a Mr. Sprague who had been appointed in a dim forgotten past by Franklin Pierce and had become attached to the Rock of Gibraltar through half a century of incumbency like an abalone, until a recall from Washington released his hold. The consulate was a good specimen of protective coloring, fused with its background of rocks and scrubby trees, and of equal age. The room into which we were conducted was filled with revered keepsakes, and from one wall protruded a small flagstaff with the stars and stripes. At the far end of the room stood a slender, very elderly figure which might have been Franklin Pierce himself: retiring, clean-shaven and dignified. The prominence of the flag started the conversation on a patriotic note, and I carried away chiefly an impression of the unbroken chain of historical events. Here was an insignificant episode which still tied us to days before Lincoln and the Civil War.

Exclusion laws may keep out human beings, but unfilterable life defies control. The hotel, which tried to exclude the heat, was less successful with the creatures that crawl or fly, but have in common their bite and sting. On account of their presence everywhere in southern Europe, it would have been inaccurate to accuse them of narrow nationalism; I frequently met their near relatives in many places in Spain.

Spaniards, Italians and Frenchmen have always felt a profound dissatisfaction with the money printed or coined by their own governments. In those days you could go nowhere without having thrust upon you specimens of secretly homegrown bills and coins which looked innocent enough until they were handed back to you by some one with more experienced eyes and ears. A good ear was important, for all through Spain the clerks in the shops had the provoking habit of bouncing on their counters every silver coin before accepting it, or of carrying it to the light like a new-born infant to detect any congenital defect. In Gibraltar we exchanged our good American dollars for good British pounds, which in turn were transformed in every transaction into highly suspicious-looking Spanish money.

From Gibraltar we took a little harbor steamer on which the baggage was stowed first, and we then found standing room among boxes, bags and trunks. Our destination was Algeciras, where Spain begins. Although the land we saw also belonged to southern Europe, there were great differences to be noted between Italy and Spain. Many of these differences are not easily put into words and concern subtle distinctions of race, customs, or language, or of outward appearance which betrays only a superficial similarity. Immediately recognizable differences are the outward aspects of houses and streets, the intonations and the voices of the people, who at first do not seem to be uttering a Latin speech. Their language has a background of gutteral roughness with musical intervals. It is less than the Italian a language of song, and bel canto forms a marked contrast with the open-voiced, oriental singing of the Spanish people.

On the boat to Algeciras an American fellow traveler had turned up with suspiciously bulging coat pockets. Noting my questioning look in their direction, he felt obliged to reveal a scheme of bold smuggling. He was a smoker, he whispered in my ear, of the pipe only; and I at once saw that he was looking forward to many days of happy indulgence in his shameful vice. He had purchased great quantities of English pipe tobacco dirt cheap, he added triumphantly, and his stock had been calculated for many weeks of travel. Not being a smoker, I could virtuously point with a warning finger to the approaching shore and to the customs officials who were already craning their necks for prospective smugglers. He scornfully bet me a dinner that he would not pay a single copper in duty. «Watch me,» he said, «and learn.» Once on shore, we formed in line and passed through a stile at which stood two official watchdogs whose only recognizable insignia were two ancient military caps, hardly sufficient to dignify their slovenly appearance. They wore old patched clothes and rope sandals; they had no collars to their shirts like most of working Spain, whether in winter or summer, but wore the usual loose neckerchief floating under their unshaven chins.

I walked close behind my friend so as to follow with my own eyes the events by which I was to get a good dinner. The customs officials as a rule looked only for alcohol and tobacco, things without which the noble male cannot find contentment anywhere on earth. To detect liquor they would seize every piece of baggage, and if mere pawing it over revealed nothing shaped like a bottle, they would swing it through the air, listening intently for a betraying swish inside, and then pass the owner onto Spanish soil. For tobacco they would lackadaisically question the newcomer; if his suitcase looked like a carrier of contraband, they would order it into a nearby shed for inspection. My friend of the bulging pockets carried a red herring in his hands in the form of a tiny bag of tobacco about the size of a ten-cent pouch of Bull Durham, and a thin package of cigarette paper. Pointing at his large portmanteau carried by a local serf, he shook his head, at the same time holding under the official's nose his red herring with that convincing gesture which said this is my entire supply of tobacco. And the official, God's original dupe, waved him through the stile. Having vicariously turned pale in anticipation of my companion's unavoidable arrest, I made the official immediately guess that I was the inexperienced smuggler «dans cette galère;» so he ordered my bag to the customs-shed for inspection, while my friend calmly smoked his first pipeful.

Obviously men who had the habit of smuggling tobacco into strange lands never carried it in bulging masses on their person. Such bulges could only be useless personal property, and if the traveler also had the innocent look of a modest smoker — here the little pouch and the cigarette paper came in — his smooth, unimpeded admission was assured. Thus it rained only on the just; although I had nothing dutiable, I paid an indirect tax with the dinner which I had to buy for my companion, and he had his tobacco free besides.

We wandered about Algeciras and its port in the cooler night air and caught a morning train for Ronda, our first stopping place. The chief problem when traveling in Spain by rail was what class to choose. As a rule my purse determined the wise choice of third class. In Andalusia other factors entered into the picture. First and second class compartments are cushioned and generally softer, but the windows which must be kept open for the faintest breeze let in more dust than refrigeration. The dust soon fills the upholstery and remains indefinitely in all the crannies where also lurks the already mentioned diminutive enemy of the human race. This makes the wooden benches of third class cooler and freer of any hiding places. But this advantage gained by taking third was diminished by another custom of the country. The travelers would bring with them all their belongings, animate and inanimate. Thus we presently found ourselves seated with baskets of cackling fowl and an unconfined pet black-bird which alighted on the rack over our heads; we sat with vegetables, sausages and «botas de vino», wineskins, piled high around us. Third class was always crowded in utter disregard of the physical law which says that two objects cannot occupy the same place at the same time. The adjustment of any superfluous human bulk to the limited space of the compartment would be accomplished amid protracted vociferations, protestations and compressions; but the first jerk of the departing train would invariably end the uproar and squeeze the latest entrant into a seat.

Such situations made it clear to me that to become acquainted with the real Spain I must travel third class. There was never a moment of silence in that submerged group of humanity and not a detail of the life of the people was ever omitted. Generally, all would talk at once. A mother would explain at length a list of illnesses which had overtaken her child of three sitting on her lap and sucking a piece of *tocino*, a shapeless strip of bacon. I learned about family joys or difficulties, the price of eggs and of *garbanzos,* that indispensable chickpea; how meat and wine had soared. Everybody would listen sympathetically and nowhere have I ever experienced a kindlier sharing of our human lot.

Travel over long distances in third class had other interesting features. The best train, if not the only one, always left in the evening and arrived in the early morning, stopping, puffing and clanging at every village in the guide-book. If the traveler was lucky enough to have only a few fellow passengers in his compartment, he could stretch out on the hard bench for part of the night, put a bag or a coat under his head, cross his arms and sleep better than a king. In later days I added the picturesque alternatives of traveling to many nooks and corners of Spain on ass-back or in diligences. These misnamed coaches had nothing diligent about them and their trips were often suicidal ventures. I have never seen one among dozens that looked as though it could survive another trip. The custom of taking on excess persons and baggage, so annoying in travel by train, was an inheritance from those ancient four-wheeled road-runners. Sometimes an hour before their departure they were already overloaded, creaking and off center. Their motive power was derived from four or six over-worked, underfed, ageless horses or mules or a mixture of both; as they labored uphill accompanied by the curses of the *mayoral* or driver, the vehicle hardly had the appearance of a moving object. Downhill it made up for lost time by never running on more than two wheels at the same moment. Pious women would always cross themselves exclaiming *Jesús* or *María Santísima*; which I too learned to do.

Traveling on donkeys was more leisurely but less soft. No blanket could ease that seat, and it was never clear to me why an ass's skin filled with grass and ground-up thistles should be so hard. But that melancholy beast was frequently the only means available to reach out of the way places; so it has acquainted me with highways and byways leading far back into the dim history of national customs and traditions.

From Algeciras to Ronda the view from the train is a good introduction to the Spanish scene. In the baked landscape the little white-washed houses with their flapping curtains for doors caught the eye. There was no other sign of life. The niggard part played by the water which managed to survive in its descent from the hills explained the scant food yielded by the soil and the attendant struggle for life of man and beast.

The shifting scene grew more imposing as we entered the lofty Sierra of Ronda. Cork and olive groves succeeded each other, vineyards dotted the hillsides, orange trees ran in rows by the side of ravines. The engine shrieked and plunged into a string of tunnels. During intervals of light we could look, for a moment only, into deep chasms or up the sheer sides of cliffs hanging over the road-bed. Here were no possible sites for smoking industry, and the rugged grandeur looked forbidding even to the sport of mountain climbing. But a resolute people had formerly turned the country into an impregnable defense against invaders. The local history is full of ancient wars and the landscape is still crossed by surviving sections of walls; ruined fortresses on hilltops are eloquent witnesses of the sieges of long ago. Now the heroic heirs of former warriors were the smugglers to whose trade these impassable ways formed no obstacle.

It was hard to believe that a train could stop so often, until I remembered that it was a rare daily phenomenon which had to take care of the whole country-side in a single trip. Villages hidden in distant valleys cut off from the world had to be given an outlet also. Moreover this unique train combined the functions of passenger, freight and cattle train. The passenger section, being the least important, had to learn the virtue of patience as it waited for hours in railroad stations; but when the traveler at last arrived at his destination many hours later, he had learned more of Spanish life than was ever recorded in books. During the entire journey I could observe human beings intent on pursuing their daily livelihood, and the struggle of finding a seat on the train had been only a part of the struggle to live that very day. Most of our traveling companions clearly had no other clothes beyond those on their backs; the only food they were sure of was the loaf of bread which they were eating at the moment, or the fruit or the wine they carried in their baskets.

In the stations there were numerous barefooted men, women and children. I noticed a boy who still wore the brim of his hat without the crown, but the uncut thatch of hair which hung over it had not kept the sun from burning his face a blackish bronze. By the late afternoon everyone was gasping with thirst, and we welcomed the cry of the female water-carrier, «aguadora», with its prolonged final syllable, and her alternating call of «quién quiere agua» (who wants water). Scores of arms would be stretched from the windows to seize a glass in return for a *perro chico,* the smallest copper coin. It was not the moment to ponder the probable presence of germs in that salvaging drink.

When twilight approached we had been done to a turn by the fire of heaven, and as we puffed at last into Ronda we felt like Saint Lawrence on the gridiron. This unique city showed remarkable traces of oriental culture left by centuries of commerce and racial fusion. The vagaries of history have divided its site into the old town and the new. The old retained much of its ancient character, notably in its fantastic conglomerate of houses which seemed to cling to the rock-face by magic. Narrow passageways, Moorish arches, stoutly grated windows still gave to daily life something of the romance and mystery that it had had a thousand years earlier.

Between the two towns stretches an immense mountain fissure, a rent of titanic violence opened at some distant geologic age. At the bottom of this narrow rock-strewn chasm, six hundred feet below, flows one of the many torrents which cleave the Sierra in various directions. After issuing from the center of the hills the stream turns into a turbulent mass of foam. The eye can hardly follow its speedy course through a widening gash in the valley which seemed a miniature counterpart of our Grand Canyon as it flowed into the peaceful widening land beyond.

The amazing single span of the «new bridge» which joins the old with the modern site, far from seeming new, might have been a part of that rock structure from the beginning of time. Occasional life was given to the immensity of the picture by large birds of prey that lazily winged their way across our line of vision and cast their elongated shadows on the sheer wall as they passed between it and the slanting sun. As long as one did not have the privilege of such wings, the next best gift to reach those inaccessible ledges and terraces would have been the skill of the mountain goat, that leaped along the vertical surfaces of those plunging sides with ease as it looked down on inferior man.

From Ronda the train carried us to Bobadilla, an artificial village which is one of the peculiar but common phenomena of the Spanish railway system. It is only a junction for the trains from all cardinal points; it consists chiefly of a large station restaurant which caters to the travelers whose trains arrive at more or less the same hour, and then sends them off well fed to their different destinations. This particular restaurant at the center of the spider-web of the rail network lured and caught us in our famished state like wandering flies; but being exceptionally considerate, the proprietor stung us only reasonably for our meal, and let us go revived and ready for the second half of our journey. Having flung ourselves from the train we joined the mobs flowing together from east or west, north or south, from Granada or Seville, from Córdoba or Gibraltar. There were all nationalities and languages, tourists and natives, rich man poor man, perhaps also beggar-man and thief. At the entrance we were funneled into the restaurant and once inside we leaped into the nearest empty chair.

At these accelerated meals experienced transients never tolerated any disguises without creating a row, and no chef ever dared to serve a cat for a hare, *gato por liebre*, as the Spaniard puts it. A reasonable amount of deception, however, might have gone undetected on account of the speed with which we were obliged to devour food. At intervals some announcer would come to the door and shout, «Señores, ten minutes more», or after an interval, «Five minutes more», and the din of eating would be very audibly increased. The most trying moment was the last, when the announcer came right into the room and shouted, «Señores, all aboard.» Then the diners, turned into gobblers, would contemplate their untouched dessert or their unfinished wine or coffee, and crowd the consumption of ten minutes into one.

At Bobadilla I saw for the first time that large individual loaf of Spanish bread which had been put at each plate. It was pure white, fine-grained, with a hard smooth brown crust, equalled by no bread on earth if you liked it. The waiter now brought an omelette two feet in diameter and served it with a skill that made the spectators stretch their eyes. Balancing the immense platter on his left hand he would cut off the exact portion of omelette in mid-air, and land it on each plate in a single sweeping gesture. Then followed the inescapable roast veal which to my personal knowledge was served all over Europe in homes and restaurants, and now in railway stations; it made me wonder how a sufficient number of calves ever grew up to become cows. A small bottle of potable red wine was included gratis. Some may have had two, for they went back to the train without a true sense of direction and took a seat with the befogged premonition that they were in the wrong compartment, and that the baggage up there in the rack was not really theirs.

I paid the waiter with some pesetas that I had received at Gibraltar, but his experienced eye immediately singled out one of the coins, and after biting it savagely he smilingly returned it with the one word *falso*, counterfeit. I told him how and where I had come by it. «Gibraltar,» he said, «is a nest of bandits who flood Spain with bad money. *Mucho ojo*, keep a sharp lookout.» Then he showed me half a dozen defects in my coin, among them the marks of teeth including his own. So I had to pocket the piece of lead and hand out real coin of the realm, having completely forgotten my French garçon and his advice, and realizing how little I had learned since my Parisian days.

We ourselves managed to take the right train headed for Granada. That part of Spain is packed with history which has found an echo in chronicle or tale or unwritten popular song. We came upon colorful towns already well known in the dim past. At a distance they would be invisible, fused with their gray and rugged background. Sometimes, as at Antequera, we would become aware that a city set on a hill cannot be hid; its ancient castle tower stood clear against the blue of the sky.

My first visit to Granada passed like a watch in the night. When we looked over the fertile river valley and saw the walls and towers of the Alhambra rising against a range of snow-capped peaks, we were conscious of approaching the most romantic and unreal spot in Spain. I had a card addressed to an elderly Spaniard of Granada, highly reputed as a specialist in the history and legends connected with the Alhambra. He lived in one of its rooms and after some inquiry we were directed to a certain door and knocked. It was opened by a tall, very thin personage with fine aquiline features, impressive black eyes and a fringe of gray hair extending from ear to ear and running in a circle just above his neck. I gave him my card and was apologizing for our intrusion when he immediately overflowed with courtesy and offered us his room, his services and the entire Alhambra. Best of all he invited us to return in the evening when the tourists would be gone and silence would have returned to the courts and galleries. It turned out to be a rare privilege, for spurred by our extraordinarily informed guide our imagination could readily bring back reality to the Alhambra. He filled the empty halls with people, he told us about their customs, and he could even sing Moorish songs. There was something eery about his thin form and we wondered now and then whether there were any legs at all in his ample trousers and whether he was not some specter of the Moorish past haunting the spot which he had loved best.

But the unsurpassed views that we had from tower windows had to come to an end; as we walked back through the gardens with a half moon lighting up the scene, the last thing which our guide pointed out was the capricious pattern of shadows which lay across the deserted halls. Washington Irving had had the privilege of living in the Alhambra, and his room is still shown there next to that occupied by our guide.

The practical aims of my summer called me back to reality. The companions of my journey stayed behind at Granada and I hastened on to Madrid. A brief stay in Seville gave me a respite from the baking sun. The casual visitor does not have to stretch his imagination to reconstruct that ancient harbor emporium on the Guadalquivir. Although a hundred miles from the sea, Seville was during the middle ages and the subsequent years of the conquest of America an internationally important shipping center. Wandering along the banks I could readily visualize the great sails that came and went up and down the river. Seville is at its best in late Autumn or early Spring before the sun drives human beings into hiding in any dark or cool spot available. Only the coming of the night and the lengthening shadows bring the needed relief. Then you venture forth once more and join the revived crowds which surge through the streets and fill the squares with animation.

When an unattached man is marooned in a strange town he is justified in his search for another unattached congenial soul. In the darkness of the hotel lobby, I detected a solitary black figure; it turned out to be that of a priest likewise imprisoned by the heat. At first we mopped our foreheads at each other in silence and sighed alternately over the rising temperature. When the concierge finally opened the doors and pronounced the enemy in retreat we decided to hire a cab together, requesting the driver to provide whatever drafts of fresh air the evening might offer. We were willing to be carried anywhere far into the night. We passed by the river bank where dozens of couples were dancing, we strolled along the noted Sierpes Street and looked into shops, we had a cooling drink and ate a very late dinner as was the custom of the land. And over our wine I heard about the Spanish church and its relation to the people from a friendly liberal churchman who could be both entertaining and wise, and contributed signally to my Spanish education.

On the following day I betook myself and my limited hand-baggage to a night train which seemed rather hesitatingly bound for Madrid. In my crowded third class compartment I had to sit up and be satisfied with mere snatches of sleep. The sun had evidently been beating on the benches of the car during the entire day, so I hardly ventured to sit down at first to escape the blistering effect of the hot seats.

My arrival at Madrid in the very early morning was an unforgettable experience. In summer the madrileño wakes up nearer noon than dawn. So I learned what a metropolis still asleep in the bright sunlight can be like. Such inhabitants as were up must have gathered about the train. We had no sooner come to a final stop in the great smoky glass-covered station, than I heard an infernal din of mingled shouts raised by scores of porters and cab-drivers. You can scarcely get in or out of crowded Spanish trains except at the point of a bayonet. Your first problem after that is to salvage your baggage from the grasp of a dozen porters and your person from that of some cab-driver who insists on conveying you bodily to his cab, ostensibly to protect you from the clutches of his competitors. Then the excise-tax pops up again, and you go through your routine explanations of how you never carry wine or tobacco. A porter dragged me through a large hall and a narrow passage leading to the outside, shouting gangway at other travelers, at the ticket-collector, at everyone in our way. The various policemen as well as all the officials standing about looked as though they had been peacefully reposing on the station benches when they were aroused by the approach of our early train.

My porter like all his peers carried in the off corner of his mouth the flapping end of a cigarette which he never once removed in the process of shouldering my bag, of shouting and pushing and landing me in the cab. The only incentive which awakened and kept going for a brief time these indispensable public servants was the prospect of exchanging a fee for coffee and for tobacco; this they rolled into cigarettes and let hang from their mouths from the first to the last puff. They all wore brimless caps or *gorras,* trousers which were held up by a wide cloth or *faja,* and rope-soled shoes which permitted them to sneak up on you unnoticed.

Once in the cab I resorted to my usual appeal to the Virgin and we started from the station yard with a loud crack of the driver's whip. Not a soul was on the sidewalks at that early hour and I could almost hear the great metropolis snore. Most of the streets of Madrid, notably the steeper ones, are paved with round boulders or square granite blocks. The cab consequently pursued a swaying rattling course making a clatter fit to arouse the town, and it took the driver only the briefest time to carry me to my lodging. The street door had just been opened by the house porter who is supposed to keep a watchful eye on every stranger. Madrid concierges and their families generally live in a purposely designed dark nook immediately behind the front portal. Here they sleep, cook, mind the children and, if in a hospitable mood, they may direct your steps to the proper floor in the building.

My boarding house on la Montera was near the very heart of Madrid, the Puerta del Sol. It was a fourth-story institution of long standing and occupied an entire rambling floor with high ceilings. Back in the eighteenth century the house must have been inhabited by well-to-do families, before strange partitions had sprung up here and there, dividing the old mansion into a set of rooms difficult to find in the dark. During the many years in which I enjoyed its hospitality I discovered how down at the heels the whole edifice really was. The original floor-tiles had been worn thin, and many a gilded plaster ornament of the walls and ceilings might have disappeared in the previous century, concealed in the knapsacks of Napoleon's soldiery when they were ousted from Madrid. The passageways leading from corridors to bedrooms formed a labyrinth subdivided by doors with funny latches which I could never find, to say nothing of open, in the dark.

When I arrived the landlord was the only person up. He proved a taciturn, slow-moving Castilian and seemed quite disposed to admit another boarder. The mention of friends who had been former guests paved the way to pleasant relations, and I occupied in successive years the same room assigned to me on that auspicious first morning. The host, whom all the guests called Santiago, first clapped his hands and shouted «Pilar, Maria, Narcisa» through the corridors without any response. Presently a girl aroused from some corner behind the kitchen, where she slept with the wood and the coal, put in an appearance. She piloted me through various passages to a large apartment combining sitting-room and alcove, and opening on the busy Montera. Stepping out on the balcony I could look down on a small square where several main streets crossed; at the lower end of la Montera the Puerta del Sol was just visible. The rhythm of the awakening city was becoming audible, and I had had no breakfast; so when Santiago came in to look after my welfare, I made the necessary signs and uttered sundry Spanish sounds to indicate my immediate need of food. Before giving the proper orders he discreetly closed first the outer shutters, then the casement and last some inner shutters, leaving a narrow chink in all three. This appeared to be the customary way of keeping out the heat while letting in a current of air. In consequence I lived all day in a kind of Rembrandtian half-light.

The arrival of a guest at the pension always caused an upheaval resembling the spring cleanings in our American homes. First a maid entered and undid all the precaution of the landlord by throwing open every shutter in the place. Then another flooded the tiles, mopping up just enough of the water to leave me for the rest of the day in a thick vapor which rose from the drying floor. Another servant then brought in bedding and fresh linen and straightened out the room. I could now sit down and acquaint myself with my new surroundings. The sofas and chairs had done service for uncounted decades and were to remain my intimates for many years to come. Many of their springs were gone or no longer supported the human frame. I had to learn to sit or lie in the depressions, thereby avoiding the surviving springs which protruded at queer angles into my anatomy.

In those days only the most modern homes had, with some hesitation, incorporated a bathtub in their domestic life. My abode loyally continued the tradition of the hand-basin and water jug in every bedroom. For a bit of hot water I pulled a cord hanging by a wall, which started a distant bell. This might or might not be heard by a servant. According to the movies Queen Victoria called her flunkies by the same system. The water which I used in my morning ablution ran over the floor and saved the servant time and trouble in her daily task of mopping up the tiles.

Madrid furnished public baths for a small fee by the occasional use of which I managed to get some less perfunctory cleansing. The superficial efforts made in the privacy of my room could be improved on at the bath-house according to my choice of a first or second class bath; this entailed paying a first or second class tip to the attendant. The chief difference lay in the amount and the size of the towelling supplied by that functionary. Everywhere in Europe these public baths included a cloth resembling the sheet of a large double bed. The shock of these rare immersions was supposed to be effectively met only by wrapping yourself without delay in yards of linen. A lot of healthy exercise was also involved in the wrappings and rubbings, and when I had added the final touches to my toilet the attendant dismissed me with a *buen provecho*, a courteous wish that I might reap much benefit from the ordeal.

The Spanish system of taking in nourishment differed in every respect from ours. In boardinghouses, restaurants and homes alike, the nightly meal was a late affair, taken at ten o'clock or after. The dining room always had to have a thorough overhauling and scrubbing the next morning, a circumstance which made them entirely impassable. In restaurants the place would be roped off, and the chairs would be piled on the tables. The waiters, converted into servants, would then bring in buckets of water and proceed to throw it about as if they were having some game, and finally mop it up, in part. This method, pursued also in my lodgings, made it imperative for me to eat breakfast in my bedroom. So I would apply my arm once more to the cord on the wall, and the servant would bring me some coffee with a little milk, or some milk with a little coffee, or possibly some Spanish chocolate.

The coffee bean received peculiar treatment in Madrid. According to an old statute the inhabitants could roast coffee on a specific day of the week which many did on the sidewalk. On such occasions the city would be filled with an invigorating perfume, and pedestrians would straighten up and sniff the air as they approached a coffee brazier. But there was something strange in this business too. In the first place, there was an admitted difference between roasted coffee, *café tostado*, and burned coffee, *café quemado,* and I must have had only the latter for breakfast. On the sidewalk it looked like charcoal, and when served in the restaurants I hardly dared to do more than sip it, as there was a chemical potency to a large cupful sufficient to bring on insomnia for several days.

Spanish chocolate contains a lot of cinnamon; it is served in cups the size of a small black, and thick enough to permit one to dip it out with a roll or a ladyfinger. No one ever used a spoon. As for tea, that was taken in Spain only for a cough.

The boardinghouse was itself an education in the custom of the country. At table there were several permanent boarders and all kinds of transients. Santiago and his wife hovered over us solicitously and waited on us, assisted by the servants and a niece drafted on busy days. The table was a cross-section of Spanish manners and of political, social and religious opinions. After my hesitancy to air my embryo Spanish had worn off due to the encouragement of sympathetic or amused boarders, I managed to keep my head above water in the continuous waves of conversation flowing about me. The compassionate niece, who occasionally wished to throw me a life-belt, got the notion that by coming close and shouting in my ear I would understand the conversation better, until the long-suffering patriarchal boarder seated at the head of the table brought his authority to bear and protested, «Por Dios, stop shrieking, girl; is the man deaf?» This same worthy, a bachelor-misogynist, then mollified me by muttering his secret opinion that all females were woefully deficient in the upper story.

My first practical step had been to look for a teacher of the language and I found one among the students at the University. Presently he appeared and I was confronted with a diminutive person who might have qualified as Falstaff's page. The difficulty lay entirely in his legs, for when he sat opposite me at my study table the upper part of his frame took on several inches which his extremities immediately subtracted the moment he stood up. He had a completely round face with two prominent black eyes in which fright alternated with hopefulness as the lessons proceeded. I heard with incredulity that he was already married and saw with distress that he was underfed. His fees turned out so moderate that I gladly threw occasional refreshments or meals into the hopper of our educational mill. These supplements not only benefitted my mentor, but increased my vocabularly also in the whole range of food and drink of the Spanish people.

We also read novels and plays, and in the early evening we strolled through the streets and boulevards in the receding heat. Owing to my companions's sawed-off size we might have been taken for father and son. As he constantly carried a cane to establish his adult state, I was on occasion apprehensive of being stopped and asked why I let my little boy carry a cane instead of carrying one myself.

By these methods I laid the first practical row of stones in a modest Spanish edifice, playing the part of a mason's novice under the pleasant directions of the least domineering boss imaginable. On Sundays I sometimes went with him to the Prado galleries to become acquainted with the paintings of Velázquez and Goya who are reputed to have learned their art directly from God. At least I became relatively indifferent to a thousand other pictures and always returned to those chosen two.

One morning at the entrance of the museum I unexpectedly ran into a friend from Munich, an actor named Herr Stury. He had just managed to live through his first view of the finest and largest collection of pictures in the world. Before greeting him I let him wipe his perspiring face and recover from an apparent daze. His first words showed his need of an immediate restorative. «Did you ever see such miles of canvas how did they do it take me at once where I can get a drink.» I promptly gave him the benefit of such experience as I had with Madrid cafés; it was neither wide nor deep, but it served. After slaking his thirst in the dusky interior of a cool beer hall, Herr Stury quickly revived and his speechless look seemed to ask how I had come to know such an appropriate place. I told him that to understand a people thoroughly you have to follow them into their favorite drinking haunts which are unknown to ignorant transients. It was by this time evident that we required more substantial sustenance, so I led the way to *la Casa de Botín*. This was a small unspoiled restaurant concealed on a side street. It had preserved an ancient tradition, together with the old kitchen, in its time-worn precincts, for the place is mentioned in seventeenth century comedies. At the very front door we passed an immense charcoal fire and over its glowing coals we could watch the roasting of a fowl or a leg of mutton or crackling young pig.

After a strenuous effort at Botíns to sustain the body we required a little diversion for the mind. So we looked for some Midsummer Night's entertainment. The Theatre consisted only of one-act farces called *tandas,* performed with or without music and lasting about an hour. They were at their best when given in restaurant gardens, or in the open night air of the Retiro Park. The cheaper theaters were stuffy smoke-filled hothouses and furnished at best a mediocre pastime. Not too much was to be expected of the players or singers: the noted actors of the companies were always absent during the summer. Those who remained did their best for a modest entrance-fee, and the cool night air compensated us for the dreadful notes which often escaped from human throats or from a makeshift orchestra. However inadequate the acting, the plays always contained something typical of Spanish life; the language was rich in the native idiom and in the songs characteristic of the people.

In time I learned much from Spanish friends who were more intimate with quaint wine shops and eating houses than with the learned contents of their libraries, since Madrid was their favorite book. Spaniards will amaze you by the ease with which they can cut short routine occupations to join you in some casually suggested entertainment. I had to get used to spending the nights around a table in conversations which might be broken off long after midnight, when the waiters would begin to yawn and take catnaps in the hope that their lingering guests would stop talking and go home to bed.

In this way my first acquaintance with Spain was more happily and profitably used than in purely scholastic endeavor. I also concluded that if I had to stew in the summer season it was just as well to simmer traveling as sitting still in the chiaro-oscuro of my room.

My tutor had an aunt who lived in Toledo. This fact led him to suggest a trip to the famous city where his relative might give us our meals and lodging for a night or two. The nature of the compensation had to be left to a later inspiration since money does not constitute a fitting reward for this kind of friendly Spanish hospitality.

The earliest train for Toledo left when the summer heat was already sending the thermometer up. Before noon the temperature on the Castilian upland plateau would hard-boil an egg in a few minutes. A popular expression to describe the intensity of the heat was that it made birds drop from the trees roasted to a crisp. The train dawdled over the two hours' run across the baked waterless land which only sparingly produces wheat or vegetables, fruit or wine. Here too the very landscape helped to explain the toughness of the native race. Only such a hardy stock could do without the variety of products yielded in abundance by the rainy provinces of the north. The Castilian peasant has accepted as a matter of course his diet of bread and cheese, his stews of lean meat with the staple chickpea or occasionally some greens. Of course there is always the local wine, apt to have a resinous taste from the wineskins in which it is stored.

In its astounding manner of piling up layers or relics of history Toledo has no rival among ancient cities. The various nations which have moved across Spain have built their individual walls around a great rock in the belief that their might would resist all destructive agencies. But here too time disregarded such futile schemes. A new city presently arose over the old, and the victor always built on top of the vanquished.

In the station which lies at some distance below the city we had the choice of various rickety vehicles drawn by gaunt creatures; they matched the contraptions to which they were loosely hitched. Flapping canvasses intended to keep out the sun were no protection against the clouds of dust that rose from the unpaved road as we started amid the cracking of whips and the drivers' rivalling yells to their poor roused animals. The opening breakneck speed gave way to a snail's pace as we began to climb into the city so fantastically situated on its rocky eminence. The shining thread of the Tagus river was the only water visible for miles. Its winding banks were lined with green bands of orchard and vinyard. How did its water ever get into the city? The present age with the power-driven pump has solved the difficulty easily enough. In earlier centuries, however, lads played the role of water-carriers. Amid quarrelings and the brawling of competition they filled their barrels at the river's brink, loaded them on that indispensable vehicle, the back of an ass, and distributed the water throughout the town.

We arrived at our destination parched and hardly recognizable under our layer of dust. The coach dropped us in the old square, called Zocodover, surrounded by yellowish timeless façades which hung over the sidewalks and their darkened shops. We went into alleys too narrow for vehicles where a donkey laden with wine or vegetables could stop all progress. We mounted an obscure flight of narrow stone steps that might have been hewn out of the rock before the house was built around it. The house was one of Toledo's typical human dovecots with little rooms inserted wherever the stonemason could get them in; and that must have been long ago.

We were met under the housetop by an elderly woman, spare, very neat, with her hair smoothed back and her sleeves rolled up like one who never found time to sit. She welcomed her nephew with his «yankee» friend (North Americans are yankees) and took us to our room all stone and tiles and darkened by a piece of burlap. There was a handmade stand with basin and water jug, a solitary chair and, occupying a good part of the room, a bed. It was an irregularly shaped bulk with which I was to become acquainted that night. The straw mattress has been mentioned in centuries of literature without the added detail that it might contain also a few cornstalks or twigs of trees. From a small window I could see only the discolored tiles of roofs inclined at all angles with stubby chimneys, and here and there family linen spread out to bleach and dry. A small barefooted boy with prehensile feet was the one to negotiate the steep roof; he alone could spread out and recover the freshly washed laundry without rolling into some yawning patio.

Among these country folk there is almost always a very aged member who does not know the date of his birth, who connects the family with an epoch long past and keeps up its unbroken ties with the enduring Spanish earth, their first mother. These elderly persons were always worth knowing for they were likely to remember the times of Napoleon and Godoy, or some guerrilla warrior who had overturned governments and run the country. The patriarch on this occasion was a grandfather, alert and dignified, with an unimpaired appetite worthy of earlier decades. His years were engraved on his face which was as furrowed as a physical school map. He knew every monument in Toledo and had taken part in every event worth while farther back than anyone else could remember.

When we were seated at the table all the members of the family crossed themselves first; we were then served the typical meal which hardly varied from day to day or from year to year. We had the usual *puchero* or stew based on the chickpea which has gone into the making of every Spaniard, a small individual loaf that you broke and dipped into your stew, and the local dark pitchy wine. There was also some fruit and a hard cheese in the eating of which you might forfeit a tooth. This trait of simplicity and moderation was typical of the Spanish people in town and village where the food has always been primitive and the bed hard and rude. Their pleasures were derived chiefly from casual meetings and walks in the customary streets, or from dances in the dusty squares during Church fiestas.

The speech of these Toledans has always been considered a model of purity. It contains many fine old turns of phrase, quaint greetings and courtesies, homely good wishes and blessings. These put you under the protection of God or one of His Saints, and make you feel a bit safer when facing the risks of picking your way up and down Toledo's steep and ill paved alleyways.

Our first impression of Toledo took us through a maze of ancient streets, and we had to develop an unusual sense of direction to reach the object of our search. Success at first was a triumph in the explorer's art. All barefooted boys are guides, so it was no trick at all for one of them to lead us to the cathedral, although it is tucked away in the midst of jumbled buildings which irreverently lean right up against it. On burning summer afternoons it makes a cool haven for anyone wishing to escape suffocation at home. Boys and dogs also seek the vast interior of the edifice, where they disport themselves until a ferocious official called dog-beater pounces out of the dark and evicts them with shouts and threats. This warfare has supposedly been going on since the beginnings of the cathedral. Being ignorant of this internecine antagonism I was taken aback when, on entering the north door, its protecting canvas was violently thrust aside and I collided head on with two boys who were attempting a quick getaway. Behind them came the dog-beater, waving a stick and yelling: «Devils, have you no regard for the temple of God?» And then more to himself than to me: «That is the third time today, the next time, por Dios, I shall kill them.»

Owing to the huddle of houses and roofs all about the cathedral only the façade can be seen from a small open square. In the quiet grandeur of the interior we were amply recompensed for everything we missed on the outside. Nothing equalled the glory of the sunset which illuminated the stained glass windows and sent through the vast gloom long fiery rays of light. Images of saints and images of famous men who were not saints were side by side, but a worthier artistic effort had been devoted to commemorate the unsaintly and made us turn with relief from a holy effigy to the reclining figure on some tomb.

It was a wrench to leave behind the amazing pageant that is Toledo. Back again in Madrid there remained a few typical Spanish sights which the traveler coached by the guide-book dare not miss. Toward the end of my stay a young bull-fighter stopped at the boardinghouse. He was not a day over eighteen and still belonged to the novice class who fight only in the off season of summer and with young bulls as much novices as he. He was physically perfect and paraded his iron muscles with pride. He was sunburned and like most of his profession he was erect, dignified and laconic. I went to his performance but of its details he talked very little, accepting my praise with proud reserve. I am far from being a Hemingway and the noblest corridas never stirred me to any enthusiasm over the fine points of that ancient national pastime. I called my friends a bloodthirsty bunch whenever they returned from a fight emotionally satisfied, and they called me something else because I couldn't take it.

No life anywhere with our fellowmen could ever be compared with life in a Spanish boarding house. I slowly became immune to the cries and noises of every variety which pierced my ear. It was not only the roar coming from the street; from the enclosed patio there constantly arose the clatter of dishes of a dozen kitchens, and the servant girls would at the same time proclaim their personal feelings by shrieking in their open voices some tragic ballad within earshot of agonized listeners. The meals themselves were often battles in which vociferous debates seemed fraught with possible violence and plates seemed about to be hurled. But when the soup was brought on it would be

contentedly inhaled amid peace and quiet. In this round of distur-
bances I thought of the stillness of the Toledan nights broken only by
the voice of the *sereno*, or night watchman, as he musically proclaimed the weather and the hour, and banged his pike on the pave-
ment to assure the sleepers of his unslackened vigilance.

These miscellaneous impressions of my first summer in Spain
were fitly capped by a concentrated picture of significant phases of the
national history. This picture was supplied by the Escorial where I
made a brief stop on my way north. It is the gigantic mausoleum of
Philip II who lies buried there among all his descendants, the mon-
archs who reigned over the declining land. His solitary personality and
his tragic reign are of vital importance to the comprehension of the
people whom he attempted to govern amid a succession of failures and
catastrophes. The Escorial was conceived by Philip in all its gloomy
grandeur, and has become the symbolic tomb of the Empire which he
struggled so futilely to hold together.

Names which have a poetic ring, Segovia, Valladolid, Burgos
were likewise historical landmarks which spoke of epochs long gone.
But the present was marked predominantly by poverty, stoical indifference and inefficiency. From the French frontier the Spanish
panorama presented to the mind's eye a confusing picture of extremes
and opposites. The Spanish dailies, so frank in self-criticism after the
defeat of 1898, attempted, in spite of discordant political biases, to
bring out the various causes of Spain's sorry role in the international
political arena. But nothing particular was ever achieved by them
unless it was that governments rose and fell more frequently.

But I learned to love this people with whose general history I
myself have in a vague sense become involved. The chief vagaries of
my career and its unimportant results date from the days just reviewed. An early conviction also took root more deeply that travel
alternating with work forms the most acceptable solution of life. The
work must not be excessive lest it unfit one for the pleasures of travel;
it might also fill the mind with merely bookish ideas, whereas travel is
apt to be most helpful in getting rid of ideas that one has, in exchange
for better ones that abound on the open road.

RETURN TO YALE

My admission to the teaching staff of Yale was a divided act. As a kind of acrobatic feat it was a run and jump repeated in two successive years. With the first hand I landed in the Sheffield School as instructor in German, with the second, in the following year, I landed in Yale College as instructor in French and Spanish. The possibility of changing over to the latter field, an event to which I had looked forward eagerly, was assured after another brief but helpful interlude spent in France and Spain in the summer of 1901.

Teaching at «Sheff» was exacting but pleasant. In the first place, there were no women as in my previous co-educational classes, which permitted me to concentrate my skill on the men. Then there was the old jest of «Publicans and Sheff men», originated of course in rival Yale College, which made me wonder what I would be up against. The study of languages imposed on men who were planning a purely scientific curriculum might turn out an unpopular ordeal for the students and an unhappy job for the teacher. But things went smoothly enough, even if my assignments occasionally brought forth a whistle or two, with mutterings here and there, not loud but deep. I labored harder than the director of an orchestra at a rehearsal, and probably agonized more than my classes to achieve the regulation minimum required by Sheff for the B.S. Finally, what started as a routine task ended in glory, since practically all of my students passed their final tests.

The few hours of useful toil which I had to spend in the classroom had their reward in the pleasure of being again with my old friends, and of making new ones. The room assigned to me for a lodging was in the attic of Sheffield hall, an ancient brick building originally designed for class-rooms and storage. The quarters in which I was stored had two small windows under the eaves. As the ceiling was a high one and as the windows were five feet or more above my line of vision, the only thing required to turn the space into a satisfactory cage for a giraffe would have been a manger and a bale of hay. When I stood on my own feet I could look up into the crowns of neighboring elms; but by standing on the shoulders of friends who lived in other giraffes' cages on the same floor I could look down into one of the oldest churchyards in New England. When I was «at home» these conditions did not lend themselves to ease and comfort; in fact all of those who occupied the attic would seldom be found there except around bedtime.

We turned out congenial floor-mates, I think, because I told them that I was not interested in languages, but in science. Among them were Herbert Gregory, a geologist, to become later head of the Peabody Museum in New Haven and of the Bishop Museum in Honolulu, and Robert Hall, a many-sided biologist, subsequently a professor at Lehigh. Their idle habit of being «in the field» most of the time, on the pretense of examining rocks and marine life or the like, was catching and I took to the field with them. Bob Hall was invariably attracted by stagnant pools or any old horse-trough which still contained the fetid water of past seasons. He would eagerly bend over it goggle-eyed for a glimpse of infinitesimal wriggling things while his nose almost touched the surface. On such occasions it was impossible to resist the temptation of breaking his trance by pushing his face into the liquid. After experiences of this nature he would first look around to see that we were at a safe distance before pursuing his scientific bent.

Our attic lodgings combined entertainment with education. There was a large lecture room on the ground floor with circular rows of seats rising precipitously from the central platform. Here during the winter months the prosaic surroundings were enlivened by chamber music and song recitals patronized especially by the New Haven public. We also heard many lectures given by eminent members of the faculty. There were distinguished men among the teachers of the Scientific School. Among them had been the great geologist James Dwight Dana, recently deceased, who might have been present at the Creator's right hand when it set the hills in order and gave the earth her frame. There was the mineralogist George J. Brush, the internationally known English scholar Thomas R. Lounsbury and the unique William H. Brewer, omnivorous devourer of facts in every field. According to the printed page Brewer was Professor of Agriculture, but he might well have been professor of a dozen miscellaneous subjects. He had a tall awkward frame on which his clothes hung loosely, a most impressive forehead and an irregular beard. His solid neck rose above a thin black ribbon tie. He was never without a certain quizzical look as he gazed at you through thick glasses and retailed a long string of natural phenomena without ever boring himself. It was a fascinating experience to see him function in his study. The room was filled with books and notes scattered over all available space, and some of the shelves looked as though the janitor had emptied his paper-baskets there. A rare feature was Brewer's substitute for a filing cabinet. If you happened to look at the ceiling you would have seen suspended there a number of baskets manipulated by pulleys and cords fastened to hooks on a side wall. They were filled with thousands of jottings, scientific records, fragments of diaries and the like. There were mystic symbols attached to each basket, that might have been the alphabet; but the chief agency which generally exhumed the right note had to be the memory of the writer. In the midst of a lively discussion or harangue on any subject which was engrossing his tentacular mind, Brewer would pause and gaze skyward. After scrutinizing all the swinging cages with a hand in his beard, he would rise and go to the wall, and, having unfastened the corresponding cable he would let down a basket and seize a handful of its heterogeneous contents. It was not always of major importance to him to lay hold of the desired item, for if the chase turned out futile, Brewer's fabulous memory would furnish the desired information. If, however, his eye had been caught by some unrelated stray jotting which happened to stir an ancient interest you were sunk.

His public lectures resembled the contents of one of his baskets, the announcement of a definite subject being to him one of those meaningless customs to which a lecturer did not have to feel bound. I have among my collection of notable handwritings a specimen of Professor Brewer's. His words were scrawled across the page, not more than four or five to the line and resembled thin rubber bands released and coiled into ideas. He would bring to a stereopticon lecture a thick bunch of manuscript sheets. After a brief preliminary scrutiny of a few pages, he would cast the rest to the wind. Then with the aid of his arms and a pointer he would launch himself into a rehearsal of anything suggested to him by the pictures on the screen. There was one lecture the general character of which I well remember. It dealt with geysers, volcanos and other natural forces; it contained references to the formation of river deltas and explained the tendency of water to hold indefinitely the debris suspended in it. The lecturer would throw in details about the development of trotting horses and the introduction of merino sheep into the United States. Brewer would also refer to his own boyhood passed in central New York State in the thirties when the railroad first came upon the scene, and he would tell the public with glee how his father had assured him that the railroad would never compete successfully with the Erie Canal. At such moments his youthful enthusiasm would get the better of him and raise the pitch of his voice already characterized by a muffled raucous note. On these moving occasions we would look at the speaker and entirely forget the pictures.

Some of the noted men on the Sheffield faculty were especially congenial friends. Late at night you might have come upon two of them in earnest conversation walking slowly through the New Haven streets. Their talks were apparently so absorbing that neither would remember who was walking home with whom. When they reached the proper door-step the one residing there, having just begun another topic, would offer to accompany his companion to his door. By the time they had arrived, the man residing there would have just got his second wind and promptly offer to accompany his friend to the first door. This procedure might have continued longer if there had not arisen the need of explaining behind home doors and with convincing reasons what had kept the men out of their beds at so late an hour.

New Haven was always favored by much good music. Before Woolsey hall was built, visiting orchestras played in the Hyperion theatre, but luckily for us Sheffield Hall remained the usual place for the performance of all intimate forms of music. We had only to run down three flights of stairs to hear a song recital or a pianist or a chamber quartet. In those years the Kneisel quartet appeared frequently. Of its artistic ensemble I recall most vividly the cellist Alvin Schroeder, whose playing was often unsurpassable in its purity of tone, its colorful and poetic interpretations.

A number of noted singers came also, among them the very popular pair Max Heinrich and his wife who had a wide range of songs and duets in various languages. Some of the youngest faculty members would now and then be detailed to take charge of these musical lights, to gather them up at the station, see that they were properly bestowed, or even fed at the appropriate hour. The latter procedure often depended on the whim of a temperamental guest who nourished his body at unpredictable hours, or on the hospitality of some New Haven resident with a flair for handling artists. When a foreigner arrived who was not at home in our vernacular he would be put at his ease by the most cultured members of the university, the young language instructors who served as interpreters and guides.

Max Heinrich and his wife were among those whom we led about town with every precaution, so that they would fulfill their social as well as their professional engagements promptly. Our chief care thereafter was to insure the guests' earliest safe departure. Heinrich had a fine baritone and sang with great artistry. When he sang in his native German he felt freest, but when he had to contend with French or English, he would pay especial, almost painful, attention to his enunciation. He had prominent features and little black eyes and when he tackled an English song he would look coyly at the audience nodding his head as an added interpretation of «se leetle baird sang at se vindow» or «my luff is a rose». His accompaniment added much to the vivacity of his performances, and his linguistic peculiarities did not lessen the applause accorded him and his wife at the end of the performance.

Singers would, as a rule, come to their concerts without previous nourishment. By ten-thirty no vow of abstinence would have sufficed to make them disregard the call of the flesh. All aesthetic considerations would be cast to the winds at the sight of succulent viands and alcoholic restoratives. Many a New Haven host would come to the rescue by setting forth a late table with a variety of cold meats and relishes, and adorned with a generously calculated number of bottles of beer. Under such happy conditions these fasting artists would readily forget every song ever composed.

Some of us younger instructors were members of a singing society called the Choral Union and by unappreciative listeners, the Chloral Onion. It drew its members from both town and gown. We sang operas and oratorios with equal effrontery and indifferent artistic success. The great enjoyment which we derived from rehearsals and performances alike gave us the persistence to continue in the face of all doubts and apprehensions unceasingly expressed by our patient and amusing drillmaster, called maestro Agramonte. He was every inch an Italian; he had a generous build with massive features, in spite of which he was exceedingly mobile in frame and in the varying expressions of his face, the chief one generally being one of despair. He had a minimum of hair on the top of his skull and on his upper lip, which added to the roundness of his large head.

I contributed my effort to the tenors who always turn out the weakest section of every chorus and who in our case were feebleness personified. Agramonte would wave his arms, sing our part for us, tear his bald head and finally rap his stand with his baton as he wailed at our group: «Where are the tenors? If I had a sousand ears I would hear nossing, niente niente.» Then the few of us would proceed to yell until we were on the verge of bursting a blood-vessel and Agramonte would wipe his head at the close of the performance with a huge handkerchief and look like a stricken man. One concert which almost proved fatal to him was Lohengrin. The tenors were eager to make up for lack of volume by their style and finish. As there are several bad spots in the opera's score, where the different voices have to come in together or else..., we were a bit nervous when the ordeal arrived. We had reached the place where we were to shout «This is sheer wonder, See the Swan!» In our desire to see the bird we pointed it out a whole bar too soon, and in consequence, struggled for the right of way with the basses several minutes before we got back on an even keel.

Gala performances were given in connection with the Yale orchestra under the direction of Horatio Parker. He had troubles of his own with his musicians some of whom happily never heard by what epithet he described them backstage. There his desire to commit murder found relief in some muttered caustic remark. On one occasion when the orchestra had struck a new low in his disfavor, I heard him give vent to his opinion in a telling German epithet, *Hornviecher,* which struck twice, since it could mean either *cattle*, in general, or the duffers who play the horns or brasses, in particular.

The days moved with incredible speed as the end of my Sheffield year approached. Another summer abroad loomed ahead, with further study dictated by the prospect of entering the department of romance languages in Yale College in the fall. The day of the last faculty meeting came, always convincing proof that the end of the term had arrived. At these final assemblies there was always much discussion of the difficult cases of the graduating class, and much haggling took place over the marks of the delinquent students. I recall one case which puzzled Director Chittenden. Turning to a teacher of chemistry known for his freaks of humor the Director asked how it came that the name under discussion had against it a final mark in chemistry of .005. That must be, of course, an error of the recorder. «Oh, no,» answered the teacher, «I looked over his paper very carefully and couldn't find a single thing in it that was correct, except the spelling of his name, so I gave him credit for that.»

I had planned only to attend the summer school at Grenoble, in France's picturesque Dauphiné, but was enabled to stretch my trip to three months, and so managed to get in a month at Madrid also. My year in Paris had mingled purposeful academic pursuits with a round of urban activities. I had never found it possible to be free of the presence of Paris or of the thousand compelling voices of that most fascinating of all cities. On the other hand, at Grenoble, study might turn out a matter of minor importance; but, at all events, there would be no distracting metropolis. Compared with the lure of Grenoble's mountain scenery, books and classes were bound to become insignificant.

Grenoble turned out properly remote from civilization, typically provincial, delightfully unhurried and suggesting no pressure of accumulated obligations. My boarding house offered ample opportunities to speak French and to capture the spirit of a people who were in no sense Parisian. The house was a spacious one with many rooms. It had a garden supplied with tables and chairs where we could read and converse whenever intermittant mountain showers stopped and the sun came up over the peaks. Two elderly sisters, Mesdames Balmes and Barral, assisted by Jeanne, the daughter and niece, conducted the pension. Mme. Balmes was the dominating spirit, short in stature, intelligent, well-read and active in directing our doings. Her sister unobtrusively attended to the household and gave orders to the servants; with characteristic thrift, she kept a watchful eye on the food at table so that a reasonable balance would be maintained between her supply and our demand.

We were a miscellaneous lot of boarders and represented many nationalities, the largest number being a group of German school teachers. Both by training and character or natural cussedness, they knew everything; at least, they knew everything better. Of the two hostesses, one sat at the head and one at the foot of our long table and I often had occasion to admire the dexterity with which they handled the difficult task of steering the conversation and keeping us out of rough waters. Their skill and understanding were, no doubt, based on years of experience. At table the boarder who had a hostess to himself always reaped the greatest benefit by listening to her flawless French. The kind of French which most of us spoke could not have been described by any complimentary word. One drawback was the difficulty of listening to the gentle native speech at either end of the table without having it drowned out by the ruder attempt which came from the throats beyond the Rhine.

To round out my international acquaintances, I made friends with a young Swede (who was constantly shadowing a girl from Finland), an Austrian student, a girl from Brittany and a Scotchman who introduced a burr into his French which defied phonetic transcription. There was also a fellow American in this special group of ours who could never explain to anyone's satisfaction why he wanted to learn French. No one ever had less language sense. By clever maneuvering, we constituted ourselves into an inner circle which laid claim to all the leisure time of our hostesses. Our most profitable conversations reviewed the day's gossip, and we learned a great deal of French talking about our German table companions. On those occasions I would turn to Mme. Balmes the ear which, according to the procedure of one of Molière's characters, should be reserved entirely for foreign languages, and she would confide into it her opinion that certain guests of hers were but half civilized. Some of the Germans proved to be well educated and learned, but there were also some over-serious, syntax-laden and grammar-conscious ones, who made their presence felt, especially at table or during our excursions. I recall one young man from Leipzig, with close-cropped hair and spectacles, with the name of Obermeyer. Whenever he entered the room he would bend at the hip with the stiffness of the two arms of a compass, in a kind of general salutation meant for everybody. At table he would listen to all conversations at once, turn his head in this or that direction, and keep track of every subject. Since many of our topics dealt with French and how to say certain things, he was always ready with his «She fous le dirai». His information was always right and his pronunciation always wrong and moreover highly detrimental to the rest of us.

One day my American friend and I were in a little hallway off the kitchen, scraping mud off our boots, a thing we always had to do after hiking in the rain. «This business reminds me,» he said, «that I tried to tell a story about Lincoln in French the other day and I got stuck in the middle.» The story which he told was that one day the President was polishing his boots when his rather snobbish Secretary of State caught him in the act and remarked: «What, Mr. President, you polish your own boots?» To which Lincoln replied: «Well, Mr. Secretary, whose boots do you suppose I am polishing?» «I couldn't translate the main point,» my friend went on, «you know how rotten my French is. When I got to 'whose boots do you suppose', my French gave out.» At this moment we heard another pair of heavy boots behind us and the familiar «she fous le dirai». «First,» the American answered in a mixture which he often employed, «je vous dirai something. You sit here and think hard of something you don't know.» Then he pushed the blinking German into a seat and said, «Pas bouger until you can tell us.» As we went out, he added, rather irrelevantly, «And remember the Maine».

Organized excursions into the mountains were the unique feature of the Grenoble summer school. It was, of course, impossible to attempt these hikes ill shod, so my first step was to order a stout pair of hobnail mountain boots. They proved a godsend on many a rough path, and, as evidence of my prowess, they were religiously preserved for several years. But, to retain their suppleness, they required an occasional thick coat of tallow, which they never got, and so they soon turned into cast-iron. For the third time in my life, I also bought a second-hand bicycle.

Our excursions were arranged with due consideration for the tenderfoot novice. We began with easy climbs and many intermissions which permitted us to lie down on the grassy slopes and enjoy the distant prospects of the Isère Valley. We were guided through pine forests and across upland meadows sprinkled with a choice combination of bluebells and poppies. The occasions were made gay with prearranged meals under the open sky at some mountain inn. The tables would be set out with bread and wine already in place on our arrival. We would be encouraged to make impromptu speeches and to sing popular French songs, the carrying power of which would be much increased by the excellent contents of the bottles. After each one had been called upon to exercise his gift of oratory in a foreign tongue, we would take the good will for the terrible deed and applaud the worst efforts the most generously.

Our teachers at the summer session would accompany us on these outings in a body, and they turned out excellent companions, being entertainers and hosts in one. In the open air of the mountains, they seemed even more at ease than in the classroom. Sometimes we would be only a small group and walk to the Chateau de Beauregard or we would follow the picturesque road to St. Nizier or climb to the top of la Moucherotte with its savage rocky immensity. To sail through the air, I took my bicycle to Uriage; whatever work I had in going up was repaid by an effortless descent of several miles.

A bit of venerable history was rudely ended soon after that memorable summer. It concerned the story of the Grande Chartreuse, which, with other religious congregations, was suppressed by the French government early in the century. This mother-house of the Carthusian communities had supposedly been founded by Saint Bruno who lived some nine hundred years ago. Its rambling buildings clung to sloping hills, high above Grenoble, and we made their inspection the objective of one of our excursions. My recollections associate the Grande Chartreuse mainly with profits of the spirit, contained in their famous liqueur. By distilling the green and yellow chartreuse exported to all parts of the world, the monks had combined their pious mediaeval existence with a productive commercialism which they carried on in their vast domain on the mountain side. The monastery, with its many cells, was an extraordinary human bee hive. There was a huge kitchen with refectory, and the monks could also enjoy the benefits of a library with the daily associations of chapter house and church. But many nameless lives had passed in their routine course: the guides always terminated the visitors' round at the cemetery where countless rows of crosses marked the last resting places of the pious processions which had come and gone.

At the distillery of the monastery each of us was given a beautiful pint bottle of chartreuse. The monk who bestowed the gift suggested that we divide the consumption of its contents into three solemn occasions: the first to commemorate marriage, the second the birth of a son, the third when we are about to die. As I implicitly follow such suggestions I still have enough of the precious liquor to ease my final transit to a land where there should be more chartreuse.

The summer session classes gave us an opportunity to attend a number of excellent courses. Since so many worthy names disappear into the night of oblivion which likes especially to engulf university professors, it is a satisfaction for me to rehearse the names of professors Paul Morillot, an authority in French literature, Joseph de Crozals, Dean of the faculty of letters and historian, and Marcel Raymond who made archeology a living subject. Not far from Grenoble are the ruins of the chateau de Bayard, «the chevalier without fear and without stain.» It was, therefore, appropriate that professor de Crozals should review for us the story of that soldier, as set down in the unique biography written by his anonymous «loyal servant». The book is notable for its moving record of individual prowess and for being one of the latest tales of ideal and honorable knighthood. But Bayard himself was not only a type of warrior whom Plutarch might have placed among his illustrious lives, he was a fusion of antiquity and Christianity, resplendant in his valor and in patriotic service. He was killed in battle in middle life and died in the arms of his loyal servant. Even Francis the First mourned his loss and, after his defeat and capture by the Spaniards at Pavia, he is reported to have cried out that, if the incomparable Bayard had been spared, this disaster could not have befallen him.

In connection with various courses, I managed to do some reading, whenever inclement weather deferred our excursions, or when exhaustion, brought on by carrying my heavy shoes up mountainsides, made rest imperative. At Morillot's suggestion, I read Fénelon's *Adventures of Telemachus*. The famous work seemed to me a novel way of turning a tract for teachers into a story of adventure. As a system for training boys, it was more than a bit on the dull side, but, as an ideal, diversified education, it made my own cut a sorry figure. I also read Ernest Renan with appreciation for the first time and got a clearer insight into the history of Christianity and the philosophy of religion. It was a special treat to get hold of Renan's moving personal story, «Recollections of my infancy and youth».

Finally I went through *Don Quixote* in the original for the second time.

With these varied activities, the summer sojourn at Grenoble came to an end. The nearness of the Spanish border was an inescapable lure. There were four weeks left which I could again spend in the land of the hidalgo. So I used my bicycle for one last run down the valley of the Rhone as far as Montpellier, from where I could go on to Madrid by train. At the town of Montélimar I fell in with a local fête which filled the old streets with merrymakers. As there was no bed to be found in the whole town, I sat up in the hotel parlour, consoling myself with a small bottle and a bag of nougat, or almond candy, supposed to go exceedingly well with wine since each nullifies the possible harm of the other. At Avignon I had to seek shelter from the mistral, that unflinching wind which permanently bends the trees, and modifies the aspect of the landscape as well as the temper of the people of the Midi.

This time I entered Spain from the north-east and had a glimpse of those lands of historical turmoil, Catalonia and Aragon. In France, the summer sun had not betrayed the ageing effect which it seemed to have in Spain. On the uplands which stretched from Aragon into Castille the earth looked baked and shrunken, the very houses seemed to crack in the merciless heat and glare. The problem which Spanish towns had had to face throughout Castille is the scarcity of rain. I would like to write a story of the Spanish people in which the villain would be the scorching sun. It would then be easy to show how lack of water is the cause of all the calamities which have befallen human society.

Among all Spanish cities, so different one from the other, Madrid at once became my favorite. As a community, it combined all the qualities which seemed most genuinely Spanish. It was in Madrid, too, where friendly associations and the open doors of public and private libraries created my happiest working center.

I am reaching the home stretch of this particular stage of my travels and shall record only a few more of the significant events of my Spanish journey. At Madrid I returned to the same *casa de huéspedes* which was, for many successive years, to be my lodging. The *patrón* of the house and my former table companions had not changed an iota. When I again entered the dining room, they had their knives poised over the familiar dish of lentils or chick peas or *bacalao* (cod fish); the talk concerning their government, in dire need of immediate reorganization, or the climate was continued exactly as of old. After seeing them, I felt inclined to accept the story told of a Salamancan professor who, having spent some years in the dungeons of the inquisition, resumed his classes after his release with the words, «as we were saying yesterday.»

For such inhabitants of Madrid as were tied during the day to routine duties, their pleasures and leisures were entirely affairs of the night. At all seasons of the year the Madrileños have had the habit of flooding the streets at the approach of twilight. This procedure always began gradually, and, by nightfall, it reached high tide in the main squares, and the arterial streets became well nigh impassable. But Madrid was especially attractive on mild spring or autumn nights; at those seasons it was not necessary to contend either with the enervating effects of the scorching summer sun or with the dangerous wintry blasts that would swoop down on unprotected strollers from the Guadarrama mountains.

Having been admitted at more doors, I made the acquaintance of various writers and scholars who, like their lesser town-fellows, would remain in hiding during the day to prowl at night in search of refreshment and convivial company. On occasion I met a group of men who forgathered by unwritten custom and who welcomed me to their meetings. We came together most frequently at a café which has long since disappeared. It occupied the basement of the old *Bolsa,* or stock-exchange, which stood behind the famous monument commemorating the patriotic explosion against Napoleon on the second of May, 1808. In the summer, its tables and chairs were set out on a gravel-strewn esplanade in front of the building. The first man to arrive would always choose the table which offered the most desirable advantages; it had to be in the directest line of the night breeze, and its position was to permit us to watch the day idlers who passed without cessation along the spacious *Salón del Prado*. The spirit of cameraderie at our table included the waiter, who was on friendly terms with everyone. He would respond to the call of José or Manuel, instead of the usual *oiga* (listen), and, in a fair exchange, we gave him a cigarette for his political or social opinions. It was a good example of the noted Spanish democracy which has never countenanced kowtowing and has been, since time immemorial, a common meeting ground for the upper and lower classes.

The participants of the gathering would bring to the common table information which ranged more comprehensively over every field than the newspapers; they would indulge in vivacious discussions which had more meat to them than a critical essay. Owing to my feeling of insecurity in the speech, it cost me many qualms before I ventured to take part in the discussions and «carry my candle in the funeral procession» as a popular phrase has it. Unknown names in politics and literature became familiar to me, uncounted beers with *bocadillos*, the toothsome Spanish sandwich, crossed the table. A gust of night wind might whirl a cloud of dust through the nearby Retiro, the passing crowd might diminish and the waiters begin to stack chairs and tables, the tobacco scavengers who haunted the restaurants for discarded cigarette butts might arrive to gather their harvest; still our talk would continue unabated. Sometimes when a tower bell struck two, its suggestive clang might at last break up the session. Then some would definitely bid good night, while others exchanged the hard chairs they had occupied three or four hours for a supplementary stroll out to the broad aristocratic Castellana boulevard, perhaps for a final enjoyment of the night air, but more likely because no Spaniard has ever willingly relinquished the greatest pleasure that he knows, an animated conversation with his friends.

A source of constant wonder in my associations with Spaniards was the many-sided nature of their activities and gifts. There were some who, by profession, were lawyers or doctors, but they were also novelists, poets, critics or journalists, by avocation. They would drop one profession for another like a suit of old clothes; they might relinquish the law for a chair in literature, or give up a doctor's career for the insecure future of novelist. An incredibly large number of Spaniards have always kept body and soul together as well as the family, by holding a small government job, but it was never allowed to become too exacting, lest it interfere with the composition of a book of verse.

Bees from every part of Spain incessantly arrived for a share of the intellectual honey which the Capital alone could provide. Indeed they would come to Madrid from foreign parts also and I met there for the first time French, English, and even American scholars. This very summer, a happy chance had brought to Spain welcome companions, the rotund Benjamin Bourland from Western Reserve University, the Dutchman, Fonger De Haan, and Carroll Marden, then at Johns Hopkins. The high priest of hispanic studies, Foulché-Delbosc, founder of the Revue Hispanique, the formost Spanish journal, had also arrived. He was an impressive, rather awesome figure, considerably more than six feet tall. He always stood very straight, in an almost stiff attitude, which brought out his long fine beard and gave him a resemblance to the more histrionic, also well-bearded novelist, Valle Inclán. At casual gatherings, De Haan would dominate the conversation, not only because of his superior erudition, but because of his caustic and generally unflattering remarks. Even Foulché seldom offered any opinion which might contradict De Haan's, in apprehension of coming in for a share of the latter's colorful epithets of *burro* and *asno* which he always felt free to dispense at those friendly meetings. My closest friend, Adolfo Bonilla, presently joined our group and became its particular shining light.

Many Spaniards of established renown whom I had the privilege of meeting, passed from the scene in those first years of my life in Spain. Their going, one by one, and the appearance on the horizon of a younger generation in which I formed numerous friendships, gave me a sense of participation in the progress and change of the nation's life.

An adequate portrait gallery of those famous older men who were so soon to disappear would add significance to this record, but I must regretfully limit it here to a few recollections. The first, whom I wish to introduce and segregate from the picture of those brief summers, is Santiago Pérez Triana. He was a striking example of the universally gifted Spanish type, by birth a Columbian but of pure Spanish ancestry. He had become a refugee in his youth, having made himself an obstreperous political figure unusually early; he was, as he designated himself, a born rebel against tyranny. He had fled his country in search of liberty and a battle-ground on which no kind of rebelliousness would be suppressed. He was of a heavy, medium-sized build, he had a round face and a short mustache, very weak eyes with thick glasses and a great shock of black hair, like some athlete's. In manner, he was a quiescent volcano, for he could burst into a torrent of eloquence at the least provocation. In Europe the fugitive had developed into a diplomat in various capital cities, as well as an effective orator in international assemblies. He spoke English and French without a trace of accent, and German pretty well with the exception of the cursed case-forms and genders which have brought down many a man. At his home in Madrid or London, he received a long string of friends, and he loved to line his dinner table with fascinated listeners. He could recount serious or entertaining adventures which might or might not have befallen him during his flight down the Magdalena River. He took delight in reciting a great variety of Spanish poetry, and when Americans were present, he would throw in Poe's *Raven,* which he knew equally well in the original and in a Spanish version. His spontaneous histrionic performances would have made him a welcome autocrat at any breakfast table.

Through Pérez Triana, I was able to meet the poet Núñez de Arce. In reply to my letter to him asking for an interview, I received a courteous invitation, bidding me, in the usual form, to come to «your house». So on a late afternoon, I found myself in a huge parlour lugubriously furnished with great ebony tables and chairs. It was also cluttered up with all the keepsakes and tributes which his fame had brought him and which were kept in glass cases standing around the room. When the poet entered I could hardly see him across the obscurity of the room, characteristic of all houses in the summertime. When he had seated himself he seemed a frail little man completely buried in the bric-a-brac which surrounded us. With modesty, and hesitatingly, he told me of his poetry and of himself, with such details as might interest me. He pointed out autiobiographical portions of his verse and gave me reminiscences of his youth spent in Medina del Campo. I was happy to use them later in an edition of one of his plays. His manner made it difficult to believe that this unaggressive personality could have composed the superb dynamic volume of poems called «Battle cries» (*Gritos del combate*).

I was planning, in those days, a class edition of one of Juan Valera's novels. Again through Pérez Triana, I had met Pedro de la Gala, secretary of the great writer now grown blind and living in retirement in Madrid. Gala was an Andalusian from Cabra, Valera's birthplace. He looked like a small, very black Moor and spoke a thick provincial dialect, often so incomprehensible to me that I had to guess his meaning. Gala manifested to me that Valera's home was noted for the readiness with which he received all young aspirants in the world of letters. In consequence, his doors were opened to me also. When we were sitting in his study the curtains parted and Juan Valera stood in the door, guiding his steps with a cane. He was unhappily only the shadow of his former tall, distinguished self, and his conversation rarely showed flashes of the great social and political personality which once dominated all drawing-rooms. We went to meet him and led him to his favorite chair. Among his various diplomatic posts, he had been ambassador at Washington, and I had been told that he was much embittered over the part our country played in the Spanish-American War. He tactfully relieved my apprehension by not mentioning the subject and presently he asked me to read to him something which he had dictated a little while previously. As I read, he would repeat or change some words which I had incorrectly stressed, and I poignantly realized how dependent he had become on others to keep him in touch with a world grown dark. As I left, he said, «Messages cheer me, send me a *fe de vida,* a mere word, and let me hear what you are doing with my novel; above all, see to it that we both get handsome royalties from it.»

These and similar recollections were among the high-water marks of my first summers in Spain. On my way home to America, I tried to survey my rich harvest, and felt more assured that I was gradually taking root in Spanish soil. Plans for later studies were also maturing under the stimulating influence of increasing familiarity with my field of work.

On my return to Yale College, I took a room in South Middle Hall, the only remaining and most venerable of all the brick buildings, to be later remodeled and renamed Connecticut Hall. I lived there for several years. The room bore marked signs of structural collapse. To get from my sleeping-alcove to the front window, I had to walk uphill, the inner wall having sunk a number of inches lower than the outer one. The ceiling was low, even for a short man, and my tall friends would leave scarcely an inch or two between it and their heads. The prize of my antiques was an old student lamp which emitted a dim spiritual ray and reeked with oil, but served my purpose in the absence of electricity. On occasion it would flicker and threaten to go out for lack of «headlight», and long after midnight, I would have to rush downstairs to get the mother oil can and make good my neglect. The use of basin and a water jug was familiar from Spanish days, but I did not have to go forth to a public bath, as that progressive age had left its mark also on the Yale campus, by finding room for make shift showers in the dark cellar of my aged edifice.

From my windows, I could see the statue of Nathan Hall, who symbolized both Yale and country, and as I was only a short distance from my classrooms, I could feel that I was in every sense residing in the very heart of Yale University. Thus far, my story represents only a pause in a long journey. But we have the habit, in our great country, of considering the early twenties as high time to put an end to «education», and a mother will say of her son: «Jim has at last finished at Oberlin and is going into business». So we may all be imagined in the act of running out on our education at the universally accepted age of twenty-two, in order to become useful citizens, and to get all our subsequent information, as did the beloved Will Rogers, from the newspapers.

Having completed my record approximately in accordance with the accepted closing date of the educational process, I hope that I have justified my connection thus far with the academic scene, without blaming more than was fair those who are responsible for my misguided life and impractical career. Some day I may disregard all advice to the contrary and go on with a story packed with further unexciting experiences; they would, like the rest, take in only a bit of the history of our world in my time, and show how, out of its capricious course, I managed to salvage memories of an entertaining educational adventure.

* * *

Rudolph and Isabel in 1940

EPILOGUE

Rudolph Schevill's recorded journey into the past ends here. His continued story would have taken him through his distinguished teaching career at the University of California at Berkeley (1910-1942) and his growing recognition within the scholarly world as a leading authority on Cervantes. He would certainly have included fascinating portraits of distinguished friends: artists and writers such as Pablo Casals, Miguel de Unamuno, José Ortega y Gasset, Erico Verissimo and others. A chapter on the Spanish Civil War of 1936-39 would have revealed his sensitivity to human suffering, his concern for the poor, for the underprivileged, for the victims of any political regime that denies human rights to an individual because of race, religion, sex, social or economic position.

His love and appreciation of music was largely due to the influence and close friendship of the renowned cellist, Pablo Casals. During his sabbaticals, Rudolph frequently stayed at Casals' home in Barcelona. When I visited Pablo Casals in Prades in 1957 during his then self imposed exile, he greeted me with tears in his eyes and we talked an entire afternoon about my husband whom Casals called «mi hermano del alma» (my soul brother).

One of the great writers of modern times is the Spanish philosopher Don Miguel de Unamuno (1864-1936). An intellectual, spiritual and even political affinity was inevitable between Rudolph Schevill and this distinguished Spaniard — a supreme individualist who taught at and became Rector of the University of Salamanca. Unamuno was exiled during the Spanish Civil War of 1936-39 because he dared to question the political and religious ethics that governed Spain during the first part of the twentieth century.

Rudolph met this remarkable poet-philosopher when he visited Salamanca in 1906. On his return to Yale University, he began a correspondence with Unamuno which extended over a number of years. In his letters, he frequently urged the Spanish philosopher to come to Yale — and later, to the University of California at Berkeley— to lecture on whatever subject he might wish. Their mutual interest in Cervantes created a very special bond. Their correspondence mentions an exchange of books and articles such as Unamuno's *Rosario de sonetos líricos* (Rosary of Lyric Sonnets) and Rudolph Schevill's lengthy treatise on Cervantes' *Persiles y Sigismunda.*

Unamuno expressed a sincere desire to visit both the United States and Argentina, but his dreams were never realized, perhaps because of political or economic reasons, or possibly because he was never able to tear himself away from his «beloved Salamanca.»

Miguel de Unamuno's extraordinary personality and very personal philosophy and style left an indelible imprint on the minds and hearts of many of his literary friends and admirers in this country. Rudolph Schevill was certainly one of them. This is clearly evident in the tone and content of their correspondence.

Adolfo Bonilla y San Martín (1875-1926), a superb Spanish scholar in a number of fields, became Rudolph's co-author in the publication of the complete works of Cervantes. This eighteen volume Schevill-Bonilla edition, financed by and dedicated to Phoebe Apperson Hearst, is considered an outstanding contribution to Spanish scholarship. Although Adolfo Bonilla died some time before the series was completed, Rudolph retained the Spanish scholar's name throughout the eighteen volumes.

In 1919, Rudolph was invited to Spain to give an address as the representative of Spanish scholarship in the United States. The ceremony was to take place in Santander, Spain, and the occasion was the dedication of the Menéndez y Pelayo Library. It was a unique event, attended by many distinguished scholars and writers from Spain and other countries. King Alfonso the XIIIth presided. The Duke of Alba was also a member of this distinguished audience.

According to the official account,* which I had the occasion to read when I visited the Menéndez y Pelayo Library in 1957, the King opened the meeting with a few words, then yielded to the distinguished scholar Adolfo Bonilla y San Martín who began his introduction of Rudolph Schevill with the following words:

> «In order to begin the series of ceremonies that are to take place in memory of a distinguished teacher revered by all Spaniards, the Society Menéndez y Pelayo has fortunately agreed to invite one of the most eminent representatives of the Hispanic culture in the United States—Rudolph Schevill, professor of Spanish language and literature at the University of California, and chairman of the said Department of Romance Languages. This has been an excellent choice, since that University is perhaps the most Spanish of all in North America...»

Dr. Bonilla then proceeded to describe briefly Rudolph's academic career, mentioning his studies in Berlin with the distinguished philologist Tobler, in Paris with Gaston Paris, and in Spain with Menéndez y Pelayo, the renowned Spanish scholar. He then characterized Rudolph Schevill's scholarship as a synthesis of these three influences in addition to those in his own country:

«From the Germanic culture, Rudolph Schevill assimilated intense tenacity and endeavour, the ability for detailed gathering and patient analysis of material needed for serious work and critical judgment. From the French he has acquired the exquisite gift of pleasing form and clarity of thought. Add to these the restraint and wit so characteristic of his native land, and you shall perceive the outstanding traits of this illustrious scholar who will now interpret for us his own ideas and those shared by his colleagues regarding our Spanish culture, especially with reference to our revered teacher (Menéndez y Pelayo) ...»

Mr. Bonilla ended his introductory remarks praising the scholar from the United States who was responsible for the first complete, critical edition of Cervantes. The record then states that Rudolph Schevill «read his beautiful work on *'Menéndez y Pelayo and the Study of Spanish Culture in the United States.'*** At the end of the reading, the applause turned into a 'resounding ovation.'»

Rudolph's devotion to Spain—its people and its culture—was strengthened and greatly increased by his frequent and lengthy visits to that country. Not only did he speak the language like a Spaniard. He also understood their way of life, their customs, their mentality. Spain became his second country and he was accepted as a Spaniard by scholars, by artists, by the common man. His was not only a scholarly affinity. It was also a spiritual and emotional identity with the nation of my maternal parents.

In 1941, the year before his official retirement, the Hispanic Society of America awarded Rudolph Schevill the Medal of Arts and Literature in recognition of his distinguished work as a scholar and as an inspiring teacher.

Because this is Rudolph Schevill's partial autobiography, it seems fitting to complete the picture of the man himself as he was near the end of his life with the words of a well known Brazilian novelist, Erico Verissimo, who describes his two years in the United States in a delightful book entitled *A Volta do Gato Preto* (The Return of the Black Cat).

Erico Verissimo had been invited by the State Department to lecture on Brazilian literature at the University of California in Berkeley. Rudolph had already retired, but the eminent president of Mills College, Dr. Aurelia Henry Reinhardt, who had befriended me as a member of her college for many years and also knew and greatly admired Rudolph, appointed him as Director of the Summer Session's «Casa Panamericana». Rudolph, in turn, recommended Erico Verissimo, and so Erico, his lovely wife Mafalda, and their two charming children, Clara and Luis, joined our Summer Session group at the «Casa». They thus shared with us, on a daily basis, the social, academic and cultural events at Mills College, a highlight being the entire series of the Beethoven String Quartets, performed by the well known Budapest String Quartet.

To Rudolph's and Erico's literary and political affinity was added their deep appreciation of Beethoven's special genius. The following passage, quoted in translation from the original version of Verissimo's book, *A Volta do Gato Preto*,*** is clear evidence of the sincere affection and respect developed between Erico Verissimo and Rudolph Schevill.

«I see the tower of the Empire State Building; towering above the mass of cement, steel and stone of Manhattan, it shines like the point of an enormous needle.

But what I now recall most vividly is another tower of much greater significance for me: the Campanile of the University of California. I recall the day before our departure from Berkeley... I went out for a last stroll across the campus with Rudolph Schevill. We talked about war and peace and Rudolph, who loves Spain, expressed the hope that he might one day see the land of Cervantes free of Franco and Falangism. We recalled with nostalgia a certain evening at Mills College when we listened together to the Beethoven Quartet number 8, Opus 59. Suddenly Rudolph stopped, took my arm and said:

«I wish you and your family could stay with us always!»

His ruddy face, contrasting with his completely white hair, was the only note of color in that greyish morning. Rudolph shook his head slowly and added:

«But I realize that you must return. I am forgetting that Brazil is your country.»

We continued our walk and, feeling more intensely than ever the futility of words, I said:

«We shall return one day...»

Rudolph was silent for a moment and then, without looking at me, he murmured in his soft, husky voice: «Perhaps...you will no longer find me...» I felt a sudden chill, as if those words of death had been blown in by the ashen wind from the sea. On the train, during our entire trip from Berkeley to New York, and even during the twenty six days that we spent in that city of turmoil, the scene that I most frequently recalled as a kind of summation of all our sentimental experiences in this country, was the one in which Rudolph, his soft, white hair fluttering in the wind, kept following our moving train along the station platform, waving to us with tears in his eyes. In that moment, he symbolized everything that is best, that is most noble and most human in the United States. He was *the* Friend. His expression had such a wonderfully beautiful significance that I dare not even try to define it.» ...

The unwritten Second Part of Rudolph Schevill's life is best exemplified, perhaps, by his scholarly works. It is also evident in the love, admiration and devotion he inspired in his colleagues and friends, in those students of his who pursued scholarly careers, in his two distinguished sons by his first marriage —Dr. Karl Schevill, Director of Foreign Language Teacher Training at the University of California in Berkeley from 1952 until his death in 1981, and James Schevill, a talented and well known poet and professor of English at Brown University, and in those of us who were fortunate to have known him, loved him and shared his life. My own life and professional career were determined and guided by Rudolph Schevill.

This partial autobiography, so full of humor and optimism, was written during the last seven years of his life —years of peace and happiness which I shared with him as his wife. He was unable to fulfill his promise of a second part. In February of 1946, at the age of seventy two, Rudolph Schevill suffered a fatal heart attack.

Isabel Magaña Schevill
Professor of Spanish Literature, Emerita
Stanford University

---

* In: *Boletín de la Biblioteca Menéndez y Pelayo*. Julio y agosto, Santander, 1919.

** *Menéndez y Pelayo y el estudio de la cultura española en los Estados Unidos* por el Dr. Rodolfo Schevill. Sociedad de Menéndez y Pelayo, Santander, 1919.

*** A Volta do Gato Preto. Porto Alegre. Livraria do Globo, 1947 (pp. 438-439).

THE SHINING DUST OF SCHOLARSHIP
by
James Schevill
Professor of English
Brown University

THE SHINING DUST OF SCHOLARSHIP
For Rudolph Schevill

(1)

An immense long table for a desk
Piled with books and papers,
Black, yellow-eyed cat
Sleeping on the papers,
Purring metaphysical paperweight—
High-stacked bookcases in the large study,
Books flowering with musty print odors
Like a shining, diseased orchard:
  «I am that man sentenced to study dullness,
  to define historical time, and to discover
  in that process the real masters of imagination.»
A couch more for reading and contemplation
Than for sleeping. Myself entering timidly,
Asking, «Father, what are you doing in there?
Are you playing with ghosts?» Small boy
Searching for a father, not a spectre of books,
Finding a gentle presence, ghostly eyelids
Flickering through historical distance:
  «Beware, son. Ghosts are real beings,
  Books the white speeches that they make.»

(2)

What is the unseen, I learned, but that realm
Where ghosts gather in time for sorting,
Where white speech measures fame,
    And the scholar translates white speech.

A boy suspects the triumphant knowledge of ghosts,
He cannot hear their legendary white speech,

Languages of magical, archaic diction,
Ghosts revelling in ancient penmanship.

I stare at your handwriting now, father.
To reach you I cross many continents
Through mysteriously inscribed gates of time,
Embrace finally where ghost-languages unite.

(3)

«*I am that man sentenced to study dullness...*»
Isn't a boy sentenced to search for excitement?
A poet destined to the language of exaltation?
How do we understand the paradoxical unity of opposites?

«*Scholarship is for those with shovels,*» wrote Mark Van Doren
to John Berryman, «*You're a man of the pen, the wind, the flying
horse, the shining angel, the glittering fiend— anything but the
manure where scholars have buried the masterpieces of the world!*»

Here speaks the Double, ironically,
The poet to his scholarly self,
Delighting in the reflected mud of scholarship,
Yet great scholarship flourishes close to creativity—
Coleridge, Arnold, Schiller, Unamuno—
Poets and critics both taking from manure
The illuminated roots of redemption that grow
With fiery traces through terror into light.

(4)

1937, in San Francisco, during the Spanish Civil War:

I wait for my father to speak in a waterfront union hall filled with
huge workers smoking, laughing, drinking, shouting. To my awed
teenage eyes, every foot wears a heavy shoe, every muscled arm can
bend an iron bar or smash a nose. Speaking to these men is like addressing lions— where are the glittering, snapping words?

My father heads the West Coast Committee for the Defense of
the Spanish Republic attacked by Franco's insurrection. With Fernando de los Rios, Spanish Ambassador to the United States, my father is
to speak in defense of the Republic to this rally sponsored by Harry

Bridges's longshoremen's union. To my startled eyes these powerful men are the champion weightlifters of the world.

Suddenly, my father and de los Rios appear trapped in formal tuxedos! I gape in terror. They look like dolls in formal costumes standing before roughly dressed demons. When they speak surely straw will come from their mouths! Restless, the workers listen to passionate appeals for democracy, unions, civil rights. De los Rios condemns Lorca's recent murder by Franco's Civil Guard, the threat of Franco's military dictatorship. Workers stand cheering, passing the hat for donations. Suddenly, to me my father's absurd rented tuxedo becomes Don Quixote's armor attacking the windmills.

Later I learn that the absurd tuxedos are on their way to a formal civic dinner to raise money for ambulances for the Spanish Republic. I begin to understand my father's unique dedication to Cervantes and the cause of Spanish freedom; why my father wrote at the end of his Cervantes biography: «*Spiritual poise and the triumphant heroism that greets the unseen with a cheer...*» My father marking the scholar's stance in his absurd tuxedo; my father to be blacklisted for these efforts by the Un-American Affairs Committee.

«*Clothes are only a costume, son, to create the role you must play in the theatre of life.*»

Running blindly to maturity in sweatshirt and jeans, I could only learn by experience the white speech of ghosts. Now, in dreams, I walk with you, father, through the Prado staring at Goya's Black Paintings, the dark fantasies that rule our destinies. I hear with you the ghostly voice of St. Theresa challenging death: «*muero porque no muero.*»

«*Spanish, my son, is the language of romantic opposites, the balance of cruel death against redemptive death that will not die.*»

My father's romantic, factual stance, five feet four inches tall like his hero, Don Quixote, blending honor with chivalry, where the difficult discovery of sane words shapes the insane battlegrounds of history.

(5)

My father's voice singing through library dust
Summoning us to the visionary scholar's task:
   «*Breaking the seals of dusty boxes,*
   I search darkening, lost pages
   Of unknown poets. So many revisions,
   As if time consists only of rages

For order, violence assaulting peace
To create a complex formal mystery:
The art of learning how to feel
Through the knowledge of how to see.

I sit at my table in time's dust,
Puzzling out the treacherous facts;
Watch, slowly rising, dust's dancing lesson
Trace honor's enduring, defining acts.»

James Schevill

A BIBLIOGRAPHY OF RUDOLPH SCHEVILL'S
PUBLICATIONS
by
Karl Schevill (1915-1981)

Rudolph with Karl and James
1936

A BIBLIOGRAPHY OF RUDOLPH SCHEVILL'S PUBLICATIONS
prepared by
Dr. Karl E. Schevill (1915-1981)

I

CERVANTES' COMPLETE WORKS

Obras completas de Miguel de Cervantes Saavedra, edición publicada por Rodolfo Schevill y Adolfo Bonilla. Vols. 1-8, Madrid, Imprenta de Fernando Rodríguez (1914-1918). Vols. 9-18, Madrid, Gráficas reunidas (1920-1941).

II

BOOKS

Ovid and the Renascence in Spain. Berkeley, *University of California Publications in Modern Philology,* U.C. Press, 1913.

The Dramatic Art of Lope de Vega together with «La Dama Boba.» Berkeley, University of California Press, 1918.

Cervantes: Master Spirits of Spanish Literature. New York, Duffield and Co., 1919.

The Dramatic Works of Luis Vélez de Guevara, in collaboration with Forrest Eugene Spencer. Berkeley, U.C. Press, 1937.

III

EDITED TEXTS

El haz de leña by Nuñez de Arce. New York, Heath, 1903.

El niño de la bola by D. Pedro A. de Alarcón. Amer. Book Co., 1903.
A First Reader in Spanish. Boston, Ginn and Co., 1917.
Cervantes: Selections from his Works. Boston, Ginn and Co., 1928.

IV

ARTICLES

1. «August Wilhelm Schlegel und Das Theater der Franzosen» (Thesis). München (1899).
2. «Persiles y Sigismunda.» *Studies in Cervantes*, 1, in *Modern Philology* 4, 1 (July 1906).
3. «On the influence of Spanish literature upon English in the 17th century.» *Rom. Forsch* 20 (1907).
4. «On the Bibliography of the Spanish 'Comedia'.» *Rom. Forsch* 23 (1907).
5. «Persiles y Sigismunda.» *Studies in Cervantes*, 2, in *Modern Philology* 4, 4 (April 1907).
6. «Persiles y Sigismunda.» *Studies in Cervantes*, 3, in *Publications of Yale University* (May 1908).
7. «Swift's Hoax on Partridge, the Astrologer.» *Transactions of the Connecticut Academy of Arts and Sciences*, 15 (July 1909).
8. «A Note on *El Curioso Impertinente.*» *Extrait de la Revue Hispanique* 23 (1910).
9. «Juan Timoneda, *El Buen Aviso y Portacuentos.*» *Extrait de la Revue Hispanique* 24 (1911).
10. «Theobald's Double Falsehood.» Reprint *Modern Philology* 9, 2 (Oct. 1911).
11. «Some Forms of the Riddle Question and the Exercise of the Wits in Popular Fiction and Formal Literature.» *University of California Publications in Modern Philology* 2, 3 (Nov. 1911).
12. «Three Centuries of *Don Quixote.*» *University of California Chronicle* 15, 2 (1913).
13. «A Plea for some Neglected Standards and Values.» Phi Beta Kappa address. *University of California Chronicle* 15, 3 (1913).
14. «George Borrow: An English Humorist in Spain.» *University of California Chronicle* 18, 1 (1916).
15. «A Four Years' Course in Spanish for Secondary Schools.» Berkeley, U.C. Press (1916).

16. «Cervantes and Spain's Golden Age of Letters.» Faculty research Lecture. University of California (1918).
17. «Menéndez y Pelayo y el estudio de la cultura española en los Estados Unidos.» Santander, *Sociedad de Menéndez y Pelayo* (1919).
18. «Menéndez y Pelayo and the Study of Spanish Civilization in the United States.» *University of California Chronicle* 22, 1 (1920).
19. «Laínez, Figueroa and Cervantes.» In *Homenaje a Menéndez Pidal*. Madrid, Imprenta Sucesores de Hernando (1924).
20. «The Study of Letters and our Modern World.» An address to the Graduate School, University of California, *Hispania* 15, 3 (May 1932).
21. «The Education and Culture of Cervantes.» *Hispanic Review,* 1, 1 (Jan. 1933).
22. «*Virtudes vencen señales* and *La vida es sueño.*» *Hispanic Review* 1,3 (July 1933).
23. «History and the Individual.» Commencement address at Fountain Valley School. *Hispania* 16 (Oct. 1933).
24. «Algunas poesías de Pedro Laínez.» *Revue Hispanique* 81 (1933).
25. «Desiderata in our Histories of the Spanish Language and Literature.» *Modern Language Forum* 19 (Feb. 1934).
26. «Lope de Vega, 1562-1635.» *Modern Language Journal* 19 (Jan. 1935).
27. «Lope de Vega and the Golden Age.» *Hispanic Review* 3 (July 1935).
28. «¿Quién era Alonso Fernández de Avellaneda?» In «*Homenaje a Antoni Rubió i Lluch.*» *Miscelania d'estudis* 3 (1936).
29. «Cervantes and Lope de Vega: A contrast of two master spirits of the Golden Age in Spain.» *Spanish Review* 3 (March 1936).
30. «Spain Today: Whence and Whither?» *Books Abroad* (Spring 1937).
31. «Erasmus and the Fate of a Liberalistic Movement.» *Hispanic Review* 5, 2 (April 1937).
32. «Aspects of Peninsular Civilization.» *Modern Language Forum* (May 1937).
33. «Erasmus and Spain.» *Hispanic Review* 7, 2 (April 1939).
34. «Spain Yesterday and Tomorrow.» *Hispania* 23, 3 (Oct. 1940).
35. «Lope de Vega and the Year 1588.» *Hispanic Review* 9 (1941).
36. «Mass Education and the Individual.» Presidential address for the Modern Language Association of America. PMLA 58 (supplement) (1943).

37. «The Fate of 'Liberty' and the Spanish Empire.» *University Review* 10 (Spring 1944).

*   *   *

APPENDIX

Medal of Arts and Literature Award from the
Hispanic Society of America (1941)

Samples of Correspondence with Miguel de Unamuno
and Pablo Casals

Excerpts from Rudolph Schevill's Publications

156ᵀᴴ STREET WEST OF BROADWAY
NEW YORK, NEW YORK

November 6th, 1941

Dear Sir:

I have the honour to inform you that,
at a meeting of the Board of Trustees of The
Hispanic Society of America held in New York on
November first, nineteen hundred forty-one, you
were awarded the Medal of Arts and Literature of
the Society.

I have the honour to be, Dear Sir,

Yours very truly,

President

Dr. Rudolph Schevill
University of California
Berkeley
California

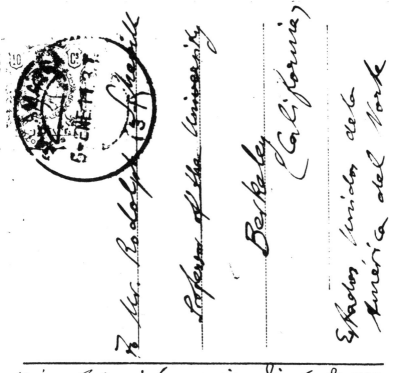

y á usted, mi buen amigo, Dios le depare
un año 1911 de trabajo y de esperanzas. Es to
do lo más que se debe desear á un hombre
sano de espíritu. Este año recibirá usted, de
volente, un nuevo libro mío "Rosario de sone
tos líricos" (más bien trágicos) conteniendo
más de 120 sonetos. Fuera de esto no hago
sino ensayos (essays) discursos y mi contri
bución quincenal á La Nación de Buenos
Aires. Ansío dar una vuelta por esas Repú
blicas. Hasta para mi salud, un poco quebran
tada, me convendría. Adiós. Su amigo y
comp.º Miguel de Unamuno

Salamanca, 5 I 11

· Señas: 2203 Chapel St.
Berkeley
California
EE.UU.

Sr. D. Miguel de Unamuno,
Salamanca,

Muy Señor mío y querido amigo: Aun
le debo mil gracias por el envío de
su Rosario de sonetos líricos. Me gustaron
en sumo grado, y también varios amigos
míos de la Cort los han tributado grandes
alabanzas. ¡Ojalá! ¡ si pudiera verle á ud.
para hablarle largamente todos los
asuntos de España, para cambiar pareceres
sobre los acontecimientos de este mundo
y las locuras, y guerras que hay en todas
partes! Usted en su pacífico hogar me
parece el verdadero "sabio en su retiro"
que lo nota todo, señalando el camino
que deberíamos tomar, el único que lleva
á la salud del espíritu. ¿Cuándo vamos á
verle á ud. por aquí? Ya sabe ud. que
siempre puede contar con su admirador
y buen amigo
Rodolfo Schevill
University of California

Festival de Prades
du 14 Juin au 5 Juillet 1953

Bach
Mozart
Beethoven
Schubert
·
Direction
Pablo Casals

7 Oct. 1953

Mi querido Dr. Schweill, su carta
ha sido una gran sorpresa que nunca
esperaba — Cuanto le agradezco su
consentimiento y proyecto de deferencia escrito
Prades en donde interpretaremos entero
a la (Lourdes) — el 17 o 18 —
Tanto pena de no poder ofrecerle
la capitalización que su Casa ... repuesto —
demasiado por sí mismo ... en capitas
... cuidados estaré aquí consolándose. No
y te sonrío en ellas de recuerdo de
Rodolfo y juntos esperamos la ...
visita de Vd.

Suyo afmo.

Pablo Casals

TRANSLATIONS

(Unamuno to Rudolph Schevill):

And to you, my good friend, may God grant that the year 1911 be one of work and realized hopes. This is the most that one can wish for a man with a healthy mind. This year you will receive, God willing, a new book of mine: a Rosary of Lyric Sonnets (or rather tragic ones), containing more than 120 sonnets. Except for this, I am only writing *ensayos* (essays), speeches and a bi-monthly contribution to *La Nación* of Buenos Aires. I am anxious to take a trip to the Americas. It would be good for me, and especially for my health which is a bit undermined. Good bye. Your friend and comrade,

Miguel de Unamuno
Salamanca, January 5th, 1911

* * * * * * *

(Rudolph to Unamuno):

My dear Sir and dear friend:

I have yet to thank you a thousand times for sending me your *Rosarios de Sonetos líricos*. I liked them immensely, as did also several friends of mine from the (West) coast who have praised them very highly. Oh, how I wish that I could see you so that we might talk at leisure about so many aspects of Spain, (and) exchange opinions regarding the events in this world of ours, and the madness, the wars everywhere! You, in your sheltered home are, in my opinion, the truly «wise man in his retreat» who can see all, pointing out the road that we should take—the only one that leads to spiritual peace. When shall we be able to see you here? You know that you can always count on your admiring and loyal friend,

Rudolph Schevill
Univeristy of California

* * * * * * *

(From Pablo Casals to Isabel Schevill):

Oct. 7, 1953

My dear Mrs. Schevill, your letter has been a great surprise which moved me— How grateful I am to you for your desire and project to come to Prades where I shall certainly be at your arrival — on the 17th or 18th.

I am sorry that I cannot offer you hospitality in my very small home during your stay. Mrs. Capdeoila and my sister-in-law are here with me. They have not forgotten Rodolfo and together we await your ineffable visit.

Affectionately yours,
Pablo Casals

EXCERPTS FROM RUDOLPH SCHEVILL'S PUBLICATIONS

I ON CERVANTES AND DON QUIXOTE

It was an unprepossessing book which three-hundred years ago saw the light with the name on the title-page of Miguel de Cervantes Saavedra. Indeed, it seemed to have been sent into the world scarce half made up, for it had been but meagerly revised and was carelessly printed throughout, and none could have predicted from its superficial shortcomings the enduring fame of the story within its covers. But new editions soon appeared in Spain and Portugal, in the Low Countries and in Italy, and presently translations into all civilized languages were to make the work of Cervantes the common possession of mankind.

In the course of three centuries a notable change has taken place in the esteem in which Don Quixote has been held by the general reading public. Today the romance is prized largely because it satisfies the interest which men have always felt in a sympathetic interpretation of human nature, in a comprehensive picture of the life of man and of society, whatever the age or the nation depicted may be. Such a view, however, is somewhat different from the one held in the Spanish Peninsula during the early part of the seventeenth century. At that time the vast majority of readers looked on the story of the crack-brained knight chiefly as a *libro de entretenimiento,* a simple yarn or book of adventure to be enjoyed much as were the popular rogue-stories of the day. Such an attitude was logical, since the very nearness of the age portrayed hindered contemporaries from getting the true perspective of all the subtle qualities of the novel which in addition to its humor, have endeared it to readers of recent times.

From: «Three Centuries of *Don Quixote*,» pp. 1 and 2.

* * * * * * *

Don Quixote has an advantage over most famous works, in so far as its wit and humor lure the reader at the outset; and, having obtained his good will, they can proceed without further drawback to induce him to discover the fulness and variety of its serious human imagery. It would, therefore, be a mistake to suppose that only the gaiety and laughter of *Don Quixote* give the work its vitality; the book rests also on a very complete and perennially fresh interpretation of life: and such an interpretation requires the normal leavening of pathos, of sorrow, of broken purposes.

. . . .

Wherever we find incidents which terminate in disillusionment or misfortune, we note also the accompanying counsel of stoic patience and courage. This is nowhere more beautifully expressed than on one of the last pages which Cervantes penned:

> We cannot call that hope which may be resisted and overthrown by adversity, for as light shines most in the darkness, even so hope must remain unshaken in the midst of toil; for to despair is the act of cowardly hearts, and there is no greater pusillanimity or baseness than to allow the spirit, no matter how beset by difficulties it may be, to yield to discouragement. *[«Persiles and Sigismunda,» I, 9.]*

Don Quixote, which embodies this sentiment, is thus by the great simplicity of its thought, by the ease with which it may be comprehended, a book for the average person, and so for every man. It voices those qualities from which humanity draws its noblest inspirations, an unclouded faith in God and His world, spiritual poise, and the triumphant heroism that greets the unseen with a cheer.

From: *Cervantes: Master Spirits of Spanish Literature,* pp. 368-371.

* * * * * * *

II ON SPAIN AND THE SPANISH PEOPLE

One of the fine and really attractive qualities of the average Spaniard is his conservatism: he finds certain features of his life as endurable and proper as they were two thousand years ago, perhaps because they were endurable and proper that long ago. Much that is implied in the unpoetic word innovation has remained a sealed book to him. Speed has been contrary to his native dignity, and he has never appreciated the advantage of travelling faster to places to which he does not care to go. Just so his provincial customs, his altar and his hearth have been dear to him. He has developed a homely and sound philosophy in the midst of humble conditions; he has accumulated an inexhaustible fund of humor with which to illustrate this most imperfect scheme of life; he has become convinced that the universal hardships of all existence, intensified by the hot Spanish sun, justify protracted repose and deliberate procedure in daily routine.

. . . .

The intricate characteristics of the Spanish people, their immemorial traditions, their vast literature, their art, the moulding facts of their history are never referred to by Borrow, and unquestionably never interested him. Above all his idea of humor was certainly not that of the Spanish people, nor of the genial Ford... He had come to Spain with a single object, and it aroused his resentment to find himself hampered by an ignorant people in carrying out his ostentatiously philanthropic plans. Borrow was thus the last man in England to understand the Peninsular character on which the sun, Oriental traditions and the Roman Catholic Church—among other un-English influences—had placed a unique stamp.

From: «George Borrow: An English Humorist in Spain,» pp. 5-7.

*   *   *   *   *   *   *

Let me dwell a moment on the Spaniard's sense of realism in aesthetic realms. Spanish literature is at its best an unvarnished study of manners and morals, a *critique de moeurs.* Painting boasts of great realists such as Velázquez and Goya. Sculpture and wood-carving show impressive attempts to produce life-like effects. In many churches are preserved images of Christ and of Saints whose bodily sufferings were brought home to the people by an almost repugnant representation of blood and wounds. Religious festivals, such as the celebration of Corpus Christi, have since time immemorial furnished an opportunity to bring forth these images into the market place; Biblical scenes of pronounced crudeness and realism, intended to represent every phase of anguish and physical pain, were paraded on certain Church holidays. This satisfied the common people's matter-of-fact idea of piety; it expressed their familiar relationship to protecting saints, to the Virgin and her Son in a naïve and tangible form. There are also *autos sacramentales,* festival plays acted in connection with Corpus Christi, in which crass details appear side by side with devotional and sentimental features. Thus even religious material of a symbolistic or abstract nature is shot through with realistic elements.

. . . .

Only the course of time can permit the hope that we shall at some distant day return to the first description of Spain by King Alphonso and find his fair land restored to its rich endowments, and renewing its worthy achievements. A quaint legend tells us that once a king of Spain was walking in his garden when Santiago, the Patron Saint of Spain, appeared to him to grant the king the privilege of three favors. «First, I desire for my country,» said the king, «a beautiful climate, a fertile soil, with all the gifts of earth's products.» «Your wish shall be granted,» said the Saint. «Let Spain be blessed with valiant sons and beautiful daughters,» continued the king. «That also I grant,» said the Saint. «May Spain,» demanded the king as a final plea, «always be favored by good government.» «Never,» cried the Saint, «for if I were to grant you good government in addition to all your other blessings, the angels would descend from heaven to dwell in Spain.»

University of California   Rudolph Schevill

From: «Aspects of Peninsular Civilization,» pp. 113, 117.

* * * * * * *

III   ON IDEALS AND INTELLECTUAL VALUES

Years ago we inherited from German higher educational methods a peculiar scheme of graduate study which took such deep root that it is current among us to this day. I refer to the so-called scholarly process of handling imaginative literature. As an example, I recall a personal experience which can no doubt be duplicated from the schooling of other language specialists throughout the land. Long ago in what seems now the dawn of real history, I was raising the modest edifice of a Ph.D. at Munich. I enrolled in a course given by the foremost Germanic scholar of his time, Hermann Paul, and the subject was the *Niebelungenlied*. A great part of the opening term was devoted to a review of all that had ever been written on the poem in textual criticism and the like. Every day Paul himself staggered into the room with a load of books out of all proportion with his diminutive person. They were intended to illustrate the defective achievements of his predecessors, and we were given detailed evidence that most of the criticism would have to be done over again. This was hardly treating the *Niebelungenlied* as imaginative literature, since weeks elapsed before we had a nodding acquaintance with the poem itself. Paul could be most helpful outside the classroom, but once ensconced behind his books and engrossed in dissecting them, he was completely swamped by «scholarship.» Of the academic runners who had enrolled in that philological race, few continued to the end of its dusty course.

We are keeping up this method with little flexibility, no matter how unlike the native endowments of the seekers of a higher degree may be. If we examine our catalogues covering the last decades, we shall see how little we have deviated from a tradition rooted in a distant past. Not only the future of effective graduate study but the very existence of our Association as an influence is at stake. There is abroad a vocal demand for a system which envisages the creation of genuine teachers to give the liberal colleges, notably the languages and literatures, their rightful place in the education of our people.

From: «Mass Education and the Individual,» p. 1302.

*   *   *   *   *   *   *

It has been said that we are all under sentence of death with a kind of indefinite stay or reprieve. This is less gloomy than it sounds if we disregard the sentence and remember only the privilege of the reprieve—that brief interval given us to make the adventure of living worth while. The confused civilization which we have achieved stands revealed in its many defects; its builders and leaders have been largely dethroned. It has thus become incumbent upon the latest generations to build anew, to use this propitious moment to raise something better than an unsurpassed material structure. Perhaps the resolve may prove timely to cease building chiefly for the benefit of the undifferentiated many, and to begin, rather selfishly, but realistically, to think each of himself and for himself. The achievement of a more abundant life demands that we fill the interval of our reprieve with some definite habit, some persistent devotion. The best habit that occurs to me is that of choice, and, therefore, few companions. The persistent devotion which pays most in the long run is a search for the significant values of life and art. Now you know that the great philosophers have never been explicit on the nature of the human soul. Some have generously granted that each of us possesses one. The more cautious among them have cunningly guessed that not every one can boast that divine attribute. Whatever the truth may be, a choice friendship depends on the happy discovery of a real soul in some person, with whom to argue and quarrel, to discuss your thoughts and your reading, and, best of all, to seek out through mutual incentive those fundamental realities of life, of which no trivial portion may be discovered through a love of letters.

* * * * * * *

The foundation worth pleading for, perhaps forgivably from my point of view, is that derived from an interest, first, in the language or languages which we use, in their history and content; and, second, in selected and preserved humanity, booked and shelved with devotion by the choice of the years.

From: «The Study of Letters and our Modern World,» pp. 199-200.

* * * * * * *

Some men catch their biggest fish in their routine hours of work, others in their moments of play and relaxation. So it is good to find a hobby as well as a hero. As you devote your chief time and energy to rational professional tasks, leave some creative energy for those scattered opportunities which permit the irrational, or subconscious, or artistic expression of yourself. Once Socrates, weary with labor, heard a voice in a dream say, «Go and play the flute.» If you are claimed too much by the work of the world, you may find a recompense and recreation according to that wise suggestion of Voltaire: cultivate your garden. This implies every kind of avocation: the skilled use of your hands in red earth, or in nurturing plants and flowers; knowledge of the craftsman's tools; a lover of the fine arts, of music, of favorite literature.

From: «History and the Individual,» p. 246.

* * * * * * *

This leads me to the conviction that we can never exaggerate this wisdom of possessing a small library of a few, at least, of the world's master spirits. For, after all, there is a great deal of humanity upon our book-shelves, and, unless I am greatly mistaken, it has an evident advantage, for various reasons, over the humanity of daily contact. The humanity selected for our shelves can be of the choicest kind and capable of responding to every mood, whether it be to stimulate or to heal. We need this intercourse with the world's great minds, with those classics of every age, to keep before us standards of thinking, standards of knowledge, and standards of character; we need them to keep unclouded that sense of values which makes us remember that to interpret current events the records of humanity are necessary; we need the thoughts, the selected culture of those choice spirits of the past—in the words of Saint Beuve—«to reconcile us with the world and often with ourselves.»

From: «A Plea for Some Neglected Standards and Values,» pp. 11 and 12.

* * * * * * *

C.V. of RUDOLPH SCHEVILL (1874-1946)

Born June 18th, 1874; son of Ferdinand August Schevill and Johanna Hartmann Schevill. B.A. Yale, 1896; Ph.D. University of Munich, 1898. Studied at the Sorbonne, Paris, College de France, and Universidad Central, Madrid. Married Margaret Erwin, May 22nd, 1912. Children: Erwin (dec.), Karl (dec.) and James. Married Isabel Magaña, June 4th, 1939.

Instructor in French and German, Bucknell University, Lewisburg, Pennsylvania, 1899-1900. Instructor in German, Sheffield Scientific School, Yale, 1900-1901. Instructor in French and Spanish and Assistant Professor of Spanish, Yale, 1901-1910. Professor of Spanish and Chairman of the Department of Spanish and Portuguese from 1910 until his retirement in 1942, at the University of California, Berkeley.

Member of the Hispanic Society of America (New York), Phi Beta Kappa (Yale), Corresponding Member of the Spanish Royal Academy, member of the Academy of History, Academy of Political and Moral Sciences, Academy of Buenas Letras, Barcelona, member of Hispano-American Academy of Cádiz. Fellow of the American Academy of Arts and Sciences, and President of the Modern Language Association of America, 1942-43. Awarded the Medal of Arts and Literature of the Hispanic Society of America (New York), in 1942.